KT-547-744

ACCOUNTING *for* NON ACCOUNTANTS

ACCOUNTING *for* NON ACCOUNTANTS

A Manual For Managers and Students

FOURTH EDITION

Graham Mott

To Valerie

First published in 1984 by Pan Books
Second edition 1988
Third edition published in 1990 by Kogan Page
Fourth edition 1993, reprinted with revisions 1994

Kogan Page Limited Printed by
120 Pentonville Road
London N1 9JN

British Library Cataloguing in Publication Data

A CIP record for this book is available from the British Library.

ISBN 0-7494-0672-0

Typeset by Books Unlimited (Nottm), Sutton-in-Ashfield, NG17 1AL

Printed and bound in Great Britain by Clays Ltd, St Ives plc

Contents

Introduction **7**

Part 1 The annual accounts **11**
1 Financial recording *13*
2 The profit and loss account *24*
3 The balance sheet *35*
4 Accounting for different business organisations *49*
5 Inflation accounting *55*
6 Performance ratios *66*
7 Cash flow and value added statements *76*

Part 2 Management accounting **87**
8 Costing basics *89*
9 Cost-based pricing *103*
10 Marginal costing *111*
11 Standard costing *123*
12 Budgetary control *133*

Part 3 Financial management **145**
13 The cost of capital *147*
14 Capital investment appraisal *156*
15 Managing the working capital *175*
16 Share values *189*
17 Mergers, takeovers, and buy-outs *203*
18 Company taxation *211*
19 Overseas transactions *221*

Appendices **229**
1 Manufacturing, trading, and profit and loss account *229*
2 Balance sheet *230*
3 Glossary of terms *231*
4 Present value of £1 *237*
5 Cumulative present value of £1 per annum *238*
6 Financial Reporting Standards and Statements of Standard Accounting Practice *239*
7 Answers to self-check questions *242*
8 Further questions *254*

Index *263*

Introduction

Accounting and finance have a language of their own with a variety of statements and techniques that can mystify non-accounting colleagues. This new edition, like its predecessors, is written primarily for those non-financial students and managers who need to know about finance and accounting in any organisation. The aim is to cut through as much of the jargon as possible and explain the various statements and techniques in a straightforward manner that requires no prior training.

This fourth edition is being updated at a time of public debate and detailed scrutiny as to the manner in which a firm's financial affairs are reported. A number of company failures and alleged wrongdoings among large companies, such as BCCI, Polly Peck, and the Maxwell empire have posed various questions.

It has been suggested that many well-known companies have been putting the best face on their financial performance by the use of what is now called 'creative accounting'. There has also been debate, and some independent initiatives, relating to putting brand values (arguably part of goodwill) on to the balance sheet.

All this has called into question the reliability and purpose of a company's annual accounts; the role of auditors and to whom they owe a duty of care (resulting from the Caparo case); and financial aspects of corporate governance. The latter is highlighted by the Cadbury Committee report (1992) calling for a 'code of best practice'.

Within the profession, the old Accounting Standards Committee responsible for Statements of Standard Accounting Practice (SSAPs) has been superseded by the Accounting Standards Board and its new

Financial Reporting Standards (FRSs). It will take some time before all contentious areas are covered but a start has already been made with new standards (FRSs) relating to the profit and loss account, the cash flow statement, and accounting for subsidiary undertakings.

There are three parts to this book. The first deals with the types of statement found in the annual report and their interpretation. These include profit and loss account, balance sheet, cash flow, inflation adjustments, and performance ratios. Some chapters have been rewritten to provide a sharper focus on each financial statement and to reflect recent changes in accounting practice. Not only is the purpose of these statements explained but also the principles underlying their preparation and their limitations.

The second section of the book gets down to the nitty-gritty and includes a new chapter on basic costing concepts and terminology. Managers need to know about the costs of products and the running costs of their departments. They are responsible for the cost of resources under their control - people, materials, equipment, vehicles - and must plan for their efficient future use.

We therefore need to look at how firms cost products and services before progressing to the planning and control techniques of standard costing and budgetary control. Many decisions are based on an analysis of costs to determine the best course of action. 'Marginal costing' is the name of the technique we shall use here.

The final part of the book deals with the techniques of financial management, which concentrate on the efficient use of capital. This covers the capital structure of the firm and the manner in which that capital is invested in the assets of the business.

The efficiency with which a company carries out these operations is reflected in the profit and loss account and ultimately in the value of that company. It also has wider ramifications for all companies in their ability to attract new capital and offer employment opportunities to existing and additional personnel.

Most of the book relates to any form of business organisation, large or small, in both public and private sectors. Employees of public bodies will, however, find the chapters on performance ratios, share values, and taxation largely irrelevant, except where they come into contact with the private sector.

I have been very pleased that this book has stood the test of time as an introductory text on finance and accountancy for non-financial students and managers. It is recommended reading on a variety of business and management courses, and technical degree courses, at a number of colleges and universities. I am particularly pleased to see it included as recommended reading for the Certified Diploma in Accounting and Finance.

I hope you enjoy this new fourth edition.

Graham Mott
December 1992

Part 1
The annual accounts

1
Financial recording

Firms disclose financial information to outside parties in their annual report and accounts. If they are a quoted public company, they also publish an interim statement of the first six months' profits, together with the interim dividend announcement. The Cadbury Committee report (1992) on the 'financial aspects of corporate governance' recommended that balance sheet information should also be included in a company's interim report and that auditors should review the whole statement.

There are no upper limits to the amount of information that can be provided to shareholders, employees, suppliers, and others, but minimum disclosure requirements are stipulated by law, by stock exchange listing regulations, and by the profession's own accounting standards.

The relevant law is mainly contained in the Companies Act 1985, which consolidated previous legislation and which gets minor modification each year. There is an obligation to inform employees of the financial results of their organisation but the specific form is not laid down. Many firms use a value added format, in place of a profit and loss account, to communicate such information to their staff.

Way back in 1975 the accountancy profession produced the Corporate Report, setting out high standards of disclosure at which to aim. Not all of them have been achieved. In December 1992 we had the publication of the Cadbury Committee report on corporate governance aimed at improving confidence in financial reporting and making boards of directors more accountable. A key recommendation of Cadbury is that companies state whether they have complied with the 'code of best practice' or not. The statement is mandatory for listed companies if they wish to maintain their Stock Exchange quotation.

In addition to statute, the accountancy profession exercises control over disclosure with its new financial reporting standards (FRSs). Only five FRSs have been issued at the time of writing by the new Accounting Standards Board, but they have left little doubt that tougher rules will be forthcoming to make financial statements more meaningful to their users and less capable of manipulation.

Previously, companies and their accountants/auditors had not necessarily interpreted the old Statements of Standard Accounting Practice (SSAPs) either in the same way as each other, or as intended by the Accounting Standards Committee. Thus some companies sought to put a gloss on their figures while seeming to observe the letter of the law, if not the spirit. In this way 'creative accounting' was born. The new Financial Reporting Review Panel, which can take legal action against companies which refuse to comply with the rules, will add bite to the new standards now appearing.

These internal and external controls provide the framework within which accountants produce the financial statements of profit and loss account, balance sheet, and cash flow. Before we look at these statements in subsequent chapters, we need to be aware of the conventions on which they are based and the way financial transactions are recorded. We will then trace the financial transactions into the financial statements of profit and loss account and the balance sheet.

Accounting conventions

Accounting conventions refers to the basic principles and concepts underlying the preparation of financial statements. The main ones we consider here are:

- separate entity;
- money measurement;
- double entry bookkeeping;
- realisation;
- accrual;
- matching;
- depreciation;
- continuity;
- stability of the value of money.

Every business is regarded as a *separate entity*. If we are to measure the financial performance of any business enterprise, we need to keep its financial transactions separate from those of other businesses and from the personal transactions of its owners.

Accountants can only record transactions that have a *money measurement*. Money is the means of adding transactions together, which is only possible when we can express transactions in money terms. For this reason, internally generated goodwill never appears in a list of assets as its value is unknown until someone wants to take over the business and buy the goodwill. Only if we buy up another company and pay £X for its goodwill will it appear as a financial transaction.

Most people have heard of *double entry bookkeeping* even if they were hard put to define it precisely! It refers to the dual aspects of recording financial transactions. By this is meant that every transaction is recorded twice, recognising its giving and receiving aspects separately, in two different accounts.

With the exception of the retail trade, most business is done on credit rather than for immediate cash settlement. It is therefore important to define when exactly a sale takes place. Is it when goods or services change hands or when the cash is finally received by the supplier? The *realisation* concept adopts the former timing, so we place a sale in the month the goods and services are delivered to the customer, regardless of when the cash is due to be received.

In a similar way, the *accrual* principle takes account of any expenditure that has been incurred even if it is not yet paid for. These two principles of realisation and accrual are crucial to measuring business performance. They enable us to *match* the cost of sales against the value of those same sales in the same time period.

When preparing financial statements, the assumption is made of *continuity*; that the business is a 'going concern'. If a firm ceases to trade, its possessions are sold off to the highest bidder, but it would be very unlikely they would fetch their cost price. Buildings may fetch more, but stocks, work-in-progress, and specialist equipment may fetch much less on a liquidation.

In general terms, accountants ignore inflation and assume the *stability* of money in financial statements. We tend to prefer the certainty of what things cost, but we may amend this approach for certain items, such as land and buildings, and revalue them from time to time.

All of these accounting conventions find their way into the financial statements of profit and loss account and balance sheet. We first need to find out how all the information going into those statements is recorded, and then see how we sort out which information goes into which statement.

Single entry bookkeeping

If you have ever been the treasurer of a small club or society you most probably kept your financial records in a small cash book, entering cash receipts on the left-hand page and cash payments on the right. In both cases the date and a brief description would be given against each item.

A 'receipts and payments' account is a summary of the cash book. It is prepared by small, non-profit-seeking organisations with few, if any, assets and liabilities. The cash balance at the beginning of the accounting year heads the receipts and the cash balance at the year end is the balancing figure between total receipts and total payments. A typical example is shown in Figure 1.1.

Cash receipts	£	*Cash payments*	£
Cash balance at start	257	Hire of hall	50
Add		Hire of costumes	180
Members' subscriptions	50	Refreshments	45
Sale of tickets	385	Printing and stationery	65
		Advertising	120
		Sub-total	460
		Cash balance at end	232
	£692		£692

Figure 1.1 *St Mary's Drama Club receipts and payments account 199X*

Many small businesses use a system of recording similar to that described above for the small club or society. In their case a larger cash book, say with 16 columns each side, is required to analyse the purpose of each receipt and payment. Figure 1.2 gives a simplified example of this approach.

The great advantage of this system of recording is its simplicity. You do not have to be a trained bookkeeper to keep records this way! If the small business comes within the VAT system, some further analysis of sales and purchases will be required. A decision will have to be made whether to treat the VAT tax point as the time the sale or purchase is made, or when the cash settlement is made at a later date.

Receipts					Payments						
Date	*Description*	*Cash sales*	*Credit sales*	*Other receipts*	*Date*	*Description*	*Purchases*	*Wages*	*Office expenses*	*Other payments*
May 10	F. Smith		200		May 11	B. Gas			320	
11	J. Brown		175		11	ABC Co.	510			
11	Cash sale	25			13	XYZ Co.	293			
14	Loan			1,000	14	Payroll		990		

Figure 1.2 *Small company cash book*

The UK Customs and Excise allow small businesses to choose either point, but larger organisations must adopt the former.

There are some disadvantages of this simple way of recording transactions. Most firms buy and sell on credit. When a statement of cash receipts and payments is prepared it will not disclose the amount of money owing to suppliers nor the amount owed by customers. This is the case at both the beginning and the end of the year. Nor is any distinction made between expenditure on running costs that have been used up in the period, as opposed to expenditure on such assets as equipment, which still have value remaining for future use.

We need to take account of all these aspects when preparing statements describing a firm's financial state. It is for this reason that most business organisations use a system of double entry bookkeeping. This system automatically discloses amounts owing and other assets and liabilities so all information is readily available to prepare the financial statements.

Double entry bookkeeping

Most companies employing more than a handful of staff use the system of recording called double entry bookkeeping. This system records both *cash* and *credit* transactions as they occur at their different times. The name 'double entry' derives from the fact that each individual transaction is entered twice, recognising two aspects. These two aspects are referred to by accountants as 'debits' and 'credits'.

In the old days when firms recorded transactions in books or ledgers, the left side was the debit side and the right the credit side. The left side got all expense items and assets of value to the business. The right side got the sources of income and any liabilities to repay money in the future. Cash received went on the left and cash paid out on the right. To summarise so far:

Debit side	*Credit side*
Expenses	Income
Assets (including customer debts)	Liabilities (including owing to suppliers)
Cash received	Cash paid out

Accounts are opened in a ledger for each item of expense, asset, income, and liability. Think of an account as a letter T, with the name of the account on the cross bar and any entries of figures on the left or right side of the vertical bar. Each financial transaction is entered in two separate accounts in a double entry system. One entry will be on the debit (left) side in one account while the other entry will always be on the credit (right) side of the second account involved. Let us look at a few simple examples.

Example
Paid £200 wages on 2 Aug. with money from the bank account.

The two T accounts involved here are the wages account (a/c) and the bank a/c. Wages are an expense so the entry goes on the debit side of the wages a/c. Money paid out for any reason is always a credit entry in the bank a/c as it is shown here. You will notice that the name of the other account involved is always given as a cross reference and as an explanation of what happened, and the date is included to record when it happened. The two entries will now appear as:

Wages a/c		*Bank a/c*	
Aug. 2 Bank 200			Aug. 2 Wages 200

Example
The purchase of £900 goods on credit from A. Supplier on Aug. 5.

The two accounts involved here are the purchases a/c (an expense item) and that of A. Supplier a/c (a liability). Note that every credit customer and every supplier will have their own separate account so we can keep track of all amounts owing to and by the business.

Purchases a/c		*A. Supplier a/c*	
Aug. 5 A. Supplier 900			Aug. 5 Purchases 900

Example
The part payment of £600 to A. Supplier on Aug. 29.

The two accounts now involved are A. Supplier a/c which gets a debit entry to reduce the liability, and the bank a/c which gets a credit entry for cash paid out.

A. Supplier a/c		*Bank a/c*	
Aug. 29 Bank 600			Aug. 29 A. Supplier 600

The trial balance

At the end of an accounting period, say at the end of a month, we need to total up on each account to find out how it stands. If entries are only on one side of the account, as will be the case with wages, we add up the four weekly entries and arrive at the total or 'balance' as it is called.

When an account has entries on both sides, as will the A. Supplier a/c and the bank a/c in the above examples, we need to deduct the items on the smaller side from the larger side to find the balance. In the case of the A. Supplier a/c, this balance will be £300 on the credit side as there is still a remaining liability of £300 to pay some time in the near future. This is illustrated now:

A. Supplier a/c

Aug. 29	Bank	600	Aug. 5	Purchases	900
			Aug. 31	Balance	300

All accounts are balanced off at the end of the month, or other accounting period. All accounts with a balance on them are then listed in what is called a 'trial balance'. In the few accounts that we entered transactions above, the trial balance would come out like this:

Trial balance at 31 August

Debit balances		*Credit balances*	
Purchases a/c	900	Bank a/c	800
Wages a/c	200	A. Supplier a/c	300
	£1,100		£1,100

The trial balance must always balance because we have entered each transaction in two separate accounts, on opposite sides, and in balancing each account have cancelled out a like amount on both sides. This is some proof of numerical accuracy but it does not prove we have entered amounts in the right accounts! It is also possible to enter an identical wrong amount in both accounts!

The T accounts are not seen as such when computers are used to record double entry, but the basic principles of debit and credit are still observed. Accounting packages are available to do all the double entry bookkeeping, extract the trial balance, and go on to produce the profit and loss account and balance sheet statements. As managers, our interest in bookkeeping has not been for its own sake but as an explanation of why a balance sheet balances and where all the information comes from to produce the monthly and annual accounts. This can be shown diagrammatically as in Figure 1.3.

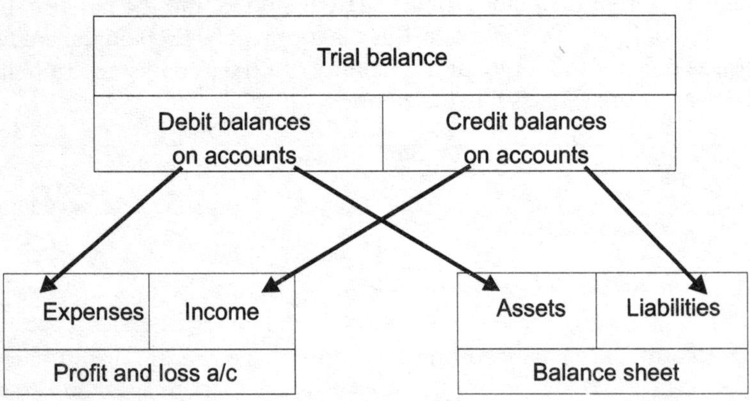

Figure 1.3 *Trial balance leading to final accounts*

Let us now take an example of the trial balance shown in Figure 1.4 relating to a market trader and produce a profit and loss account and balance sheet from it. Profit is the difference between income and expenses, but to keep the double entry principle going, we will show the second entry of profit as an increase in the business owner's capital. This is true if the owner retains all the profit in the business.

Trial balance

Debit balances		*Credit balances*	
Cash a/c	400	Capital a/c	500
Purchases a/c	4,000	A. Supplier a/c (creditor)	200
Wages a/c	1,300	Sales a/c	8,200
Rent a/c	1,000		
Equipment a/c	1,500		
Customer a/c (debtor)	700		
	£8,900		£8,900

Profit and Loss account

Expenses		*Income*	
Purchases	4,000	Sales	8,200
Wages	1,300		
Rent	1,000		
Total expenses	6,300		
Profit (8,200 – 6,300)	1,900		
	£8,200		£8,200

Balance sheet

Assets		*Liabilities*	
Equipment	1,500	Original capital	500
Debtors (A. Customer)	700	Retained profit	1,900
Cash	400	Total capital	2,400
		Creditor (A. Supplier)	200
	£2,600		£2,600

Figure 1.4 *Trial balance*

No matter how large the organisation, these principles still apply, although more detailed descriptions of expenses, assets, and liabilities will result in more complex statements than those in Figure 1.4. The type of business organisation also affects the title and layout of the statements. We look at the details of the profit and loss account and balance sheet in the following chapters.

Further reading

Business Accounting, Book 1, F Wood, Pitman.

Business Accounts, D Cox, Osborne.

Self-check questions

1 List as many as you can of the accounting conventions on which financial recording is based.

2 Identify whether the following are debit or credit account balances:

(a) Expenses.
(b) Liabilities.
(c) Assets.

3 Prepare a receipts and payments account from the following information for Gosforth Gardeners Association, showing the cash balance at the end of the year:

Cash at start of year	£1,270
Bulk purchase of seeds and fertilisers	£2,510
Members' annual subscriptions	£560
Sales of seeds and fertilisers to members	£2,250
Purchase of equipment for hire	£1,500
Hire fees received	£450

4 Prepare T accounts and a trial balance for John Deel, a market trader, who has provided you with the following information relating to his first year in business:

(a) Opened a business bank account with £1,500 of his own capital.
(b) Paid £1,200 for a stall and scales.
(c) During the year he purchased goods worth £17,000 from A. Wholesaler on credit.
(d) Received £28,000 from cash sales to customers during the year.
(e) He hired a van for business use at a cost of £300 per month inclusive of all running costs.
(f) During the year he made drawings of £6,000 cash to live on.
(g) Paid A. Wholesaler a total of £16,000 during the year.
(h) He had no stock left at the year end. Assume there was no depreciation.

5 Prepare a profit and loss account and balance sheet from the following trial balance relating to a baker's shop. Ignore depreciation. Assume there was nil stock at the year end and that any profit is retained in the business.

Trial balance

Fixtures and fittings a/c	6,300	Capital a/c	6,000
Purchases a/c	47,200	Creditors a/c	3,500
Wages a/c	22,700	Sales a/c	86,500
Rent, rates, electricity a/c	7,300		
Sundry expenses a/c	2,700		
Bank balance	9,800		
	£96,000		£96,000

2

The profit and loss account

The annual accounts consist essentially of an income statement and a balance sheet, which are also usually produced each month for internal consumption by management. The most well-known income statement is a profit and loss account but a 'revenue account' or an 'income and expenditure account' are the alternatives used by non-profit-seeking organisations. All three statements compare income with expenses consumed in the same period and broadly follow the same accounting principles.

One difference between the three income statements relates to their sources of income. For example, a local authority will have rates, council tax, and government grants as its main sources of income in its revenue account. Any charges for services provided will be a minor source of income for a local authority, but in a profit-seeking company, will be the main, or only, source of income.

The other main difference between types of income statements is the treatment of the resulting profit or loss. Non-profit-seeking organisations will use the terms surplus or deficit. Profit-seeking enterprises will have to account for tax on the profit, and reward the owners of the business with dividends, if a limited company, or a share of profits if unincorporated. Any remaining profit is left in the company as extra capital. Having highlighted the differences, we are going to concentrate our attention on the profit and loss account relating to companies. The income statements of other business organisations are addressed in Chapter 4.

Profit and loss account

We now need to examine exactly what is meant by a profit or a loss. The layperson's definition of a profit or loss being the difference between what something cost and its sales value is true overall. However, this definition has to be considerably tightened up when accountants come to measure profit or loss during specific time periods; so much so that the layperson may not recognise the original definition!

A profit and loss account is a summary of a firm's trading income from its customers, offset by the cost of the goods or services sold, plus other running expenses for the same period. Therefore:

Income	–	Expenses	=	Profit (or loss)

Income is defined as sales to customers and also includes rent or investment income received. The realisation principle states that we count income when delivery of the goods or services takes place, and not at the time cash is actually received in settlement of credit sales.

For example, if credit sales were £120,000 during a year, while cash received from those same sales amounted to only £110,000 by the year end, it is the former figure of £120,000 which counts as income. Double entry bookkeeping will have recorded all the sales as £120,000 and the cash received as £110,000, while the outstanding balances on various customer accounts will total the other £10,000 and be shown as debtors in the balance sheet.

Expenses are the cost of wages, materials, and overheads used up during the period on the goods and services sold to customers. Accountants refer to these costs as 'revenue expenditure', as opposed to the purchase cost of assets, such as buildings, vehicles, and equipment, which last a number of years and which are termed 'capital expenditure'.

There are two tests as to whether or not an expense goes into the profit and loss account (the alternative being the balance sheet). First, it must relate to the time period covered by the statement irrespective of whether the cash payment has been completed (any bills waiting to be paid are shown as creditors in the liabilities section of the balance sheet).

Second, the expense must relate to goods and services included as sales income in the same statement. Expenses incurred for a later period, or on goods or services not yet sold to customers, go into the balance sheet as assets.

It is a common misconception to think of the profit and loss account as a summary of all cash flowing into and out of the business, and that the excess of cash receipts over payments represents the profit. Such thinking ignores all the cash transactions that affect the balance sheet, for example, when a company receives a bank loan, or when it buys new equipment.

A loan is a cash receipt but it cannot be counted as income in the profit and loss account as it must be repaid at some future time. It is therefore shown as a liability in the balance sheet. When the loan is eventually repaid, such repayment is not an expense in the profit and loss account, but a reduction of the asset cash in the balance sheet.

Before looking at a comprehensive example of a profit and loss account we need to discuss the treatment of stocks and the concept of 'depreciation'.

Stocks

In most businesses, goods purchased or manufactured are rarely all sold in the same accounting period and therefore give rise to stocks at the month or year end. A basic principle of the profit and loss account is that sales must be matched with the cost of goods sold, not with the cost of goods purchased:

In ongoing companies we therefore have two stock figures to contend with – the opening stock at the beginning of the period and the closing stock at the end of that same period. Opening stock is an expense brought forward from a previous period to the present one, while closing stock is an expense to take from this period and carry forward in the balance sheet list of assets to the next period.

Example
A retail firm sold goods for £50,000 one month when purchases cost £30,000. Stock at the beginning of the month was £12,000 and this had increased to £15,000 by the month end.

Figure 2.1 shows the part of a profit and loss account called the 'trading account'. Instead of using the two-sided format based on double entry we will now switch to the more usual vertical format.

	£	£
Sales		50,000
Opening stock	12,000	
Purchases	30,000	
	42,000	
Less Closing stock	15,000	
Cost of goods sold		27,000
Gross profit		£23,000

Figure 2.1 *Trading account showing treatment of stocks*

Depreciation

A business spends cash in one of two ways – either on expenses or on assets. The expenses of labour, materials, and overheads go into the profit and loss account, but not so the cost of fixed assets, such as vehicles or equipment. All may be thought of as necessary expenditure but the crucial difference is that of time.

Labour, material, and overhead expenses are used up almost immediately unless expended on items remaining in stock. Fixed assets usually last for a number of years and it would be unfair to charge their whole acquisition cost against one month's, or even one year's, income. This problem is overcome by the simple expedient of charging a proportion of the cost, called depreciation, in each profit and loss account.

The amount of depreciation to charge each month or each year is based on the expected life of an asset. To take a simple example of a machine costing £10,000 and expected to last five years before being scrapped, this would result in a depreciation charge of £2,000 each year for five years.

The actual life may not turn out to be five years. If shorter, then additional depreciation will be needed in the last year of its life. If longer, then the business gets a free ride after the fifth year. This evens itself out to some extent, taking a swings-and-roundabouts view of things. It is better to be, say, 90% correct than not attempt to calculate depreciation at all, so hitting the profit with the full cost of the asset in the year it is scrapped.

There are two main methods used to calculate depreciation in the UK:

- Straight-line method
- Reducing balance method.

The method described earlier reduced the value of the machine by the same £2,000 each year. This is called the 'straight-line method' because the depreciated value of the asset falls in a linear fashion.

The 'reducing balance method' charges a smaller amount of depreciation as each year goes by. This is because a fixed percentage is applied to the falling value each year. On this basis we never get an asset value down to zero until it is scrapped. These two methods of depreciation can be contrasted in a simple diagram showing how the remaining value of the asset varies, as in Figure 2.2.

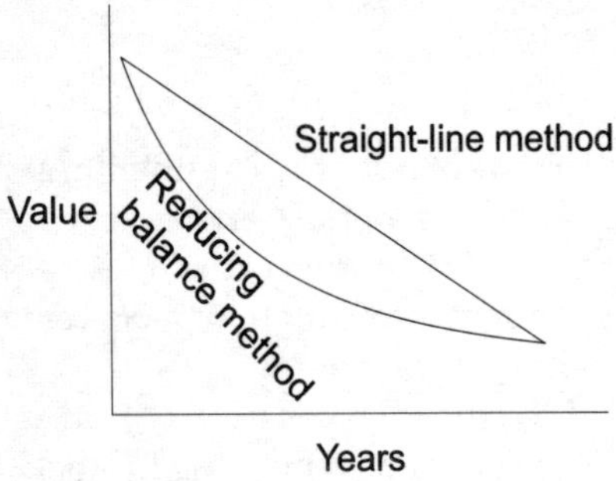

Figure 2.2 *Asset values under different depreciation methods*

If the remaining value varies on the two methods, so must the yearly depreciation charge. Let us apply the two methods to an example, now bringing in a residual value of the asset at the end of its life.

Example

A machine costs £11,000 and has an estimated value of £1,000 at the end of its five-year life.

The straight-line method takes the residual value from the original cost and divides by five, giving a depreciation charge of £2,000 per annum (pa) as follows:

$$\frac{\text{Cost of machine} - \text{resale value}}{\text{Expected life}} = \frac{£10{,}000}{5}$$

$$= £2{,}000 \text{ pa}$$

A variation of this straight-line method is to calculate the life in hours rather than years, so expressing the depreciation charge as £X per hour. This 'machine-hour rate' method is often used in internal costings.

To calculate the reducing balance method of depreciation we need to find what percentage rate which, when applied to the reducing value of the machine each year, will reduce its value to £1,000 by the end of the fifth year. This is found from the formula:

$$r = 100 - \left(\sqrt[n]{\frac{\text{Residual value}}{\text{Original cost}}} \times 100 \right)$$

where *n* equals the estimated life in years and *r* equals the depreciations rate. Using the previous example we can solve the equation:

$$r = 100 - \left(\sqrt[5]{\frac{£1{,}000}{£11{,}000}} \times 100 \right)$$

$$\therefore\ r = 38\%$$

The calculations are now set out side by side in Figure 2.3 for the two methods, both resulting in approximately the same residual value of £1,000 after five years.

	Reducing balance method	*Straight-line method*
	£	£
Original cost	11,000	11,000
First-year depreciation (38%)	4,180	2,000
Balance sheet value – end year 1	6,820	9,000
Second-year depreciation (38%)	2,592	2,000
Balance sheet value – end year 2	4,228	7,000
Third-year depreciation (38%)	1,607	2,000
Balance sheet value – end year 3	2,621	5,000
Fourth-year depreciation (38%)	996	2,000
Balance sheet value – end year 4	1,625	3,000
Fifth-year depreciation (38%)	618	2,000
Balance sheet value – end year 5	1,007	1,000

Figure 2.3 *Calculating depreciation*

Under the reducing balance method, the depreciation charge is greater than under the straight-line method for the first two years. After that the roles are reversed with straight-line depreciation being more in the last three years than under the reducing balance method.

Both methods are acceptable but the reducing balance method is not normally used to depreciate buildings or leases. Either method can be used on plant, equipment, and vehicles but it is on motor cars that the reducing balance method is most commonly seen.

The Inland Revenue ignore a company's own depreciation charge when calculating how much tax is chargeable on the profit made, and substitute their own tax or capital allowances in its place. There are only two rates of tax allowance:

- 4% pa based on the original cost of industrial buildings and calculated on a straight-line basis.
- 25% pa on the reducing balance of plant, equipment, fixtures, furnishings, and vehicles.

In the Chancellor's autumn statement in 1992, these tax allowances were temporarily increased for capital expenditure in the year ended 31 October 1993. These tax allowances, and other aspects of taxation are discussed in Chapter 18.

We can now look at a fuller version of the profit and loss account, suitable for a trading organisation where stocks are relevant. This is shown in Figure 2.4. A service organisation could use a similar format but omitting the stocks items and the reference to gross profit.

Manufacturing companies would need a more detailed statement to take account of the three possible kinds of stock – raw materials, work-in-progress, and finished goods. Appendix 1 illustrates this more complex situation.

	£	£
Sales		50,000
Opening stock	12,000	
Purchases	30,000	
	42,000	
Less Closing stock	15,000	
Cost of goods sold		27,000
Gross profit		23,000
Less Wages and salaries	7,500	
Directors fees	2,500	
NI and pension contributions	2,300	
Rent, business tax	3,500	
Depreciation	1,400	
Electricity, gas, etc.	700	
Stationery, postage, telephone	650	
Vehicle running expenses	2,500	
Auditors fees and other professional fees	200	
Bank interest and charges	360	21,610
Net profit		£1,390

Figure 2.4 *Example of a monthly profit and loss account*

Strictly speaking, what we are calling the profit and loss account comprises four stages, of which companies select those relevant to their business. The four stages are as follows:

- *Stage 1 Manufacturing account.* If appropriate to the business this shows the cost of goods manufactured.
- *Stage 2 Trading account.* This shows the gross profit earned by matching the income against the cost of sales.
- *Stage 3 Profit and loss account.* The overhead expenses of running the business are deducted from gross profit to arrive at net profit.
- *Stage 4 Appropriation account.* This shows how the profit is appropriated in tax provisions, payments to shareholders, and retention in the business.

Published profit and loss accounts never disclose the degree of detail about expenses shown in Figure 2.4, although some individual expense items are shown tucked away in the notes to the accounts to comply with legal requirements.

Very often, expenses are grouped together under a limited number of functional headings, for example: cost of sales; distribution costs; administrative expenses. This is one of four ways of reporting expenses allowed by the Companies Act 1985. Figure 2.5 shows this sample format.

	£000
Sales	15,750
Cost of sales	10,500
Gross profit	5,250
Distribution costs	1,700
Administrative expenses	1,410
Other operating income	20
Operating profit	2,160
Interest payable	160
Profit on ordinary activities before tax	2,000
Tax on profit of ordinary activities	700
Profit for the year	1,300
Dividends paid and proposed	550
Retained profit	750
Earnings per share	12.5p

Figure 2.5 *Published profit and loss account*

The Financial Reporting Standard (FRS No 3) issued in October 1992 and entitled *Reporting Financial Performance* aims to make the profit and loss account statement more reliable an indicator of financial performance and less vulnerable to creative accounting. It specifically requires companies:

- to separate turnover and operating profit between continuing operations, acquisitions, and discontinued operations;
- to disclose profits and losses resulting from restructuring/reorganisation or from the disposal of fixed assets or parts of the business; and
- to disclose extraordinary items (which should now be a rare event) and to calculate earnings per share after taking them into account.

A suitable format for presenting the profit and loss account in FRS 3 style is shown in Figure 2.6.

	£m	£m
Turnover:		
Continuing operations	510	
Acquisitions	100	
	610	
Discontinued operations	90	700
Cost of sales		500
Gross profit		200
Net operating expenses (distribution, admin., etc.)		120
Operating profit		
Continuing operations	90	
Acquisitions	10	
Discontinued operations (loss)	(20)	80
Profit on sale of properties in continuing ops.		8
Loss on disposal of discontinued operations		(15)
Profit on ordinary activities before interest		73
Interest payable		(20)
Profit on ordinary activities before taxation		53
Tax on profit on ordinary activities		(17)
Profit on ordinary activities after taxation		36
Minority interests		(4)
Profit before extraordinary items		32
Extraordinary items		(2)
Profit for the financial year earned for ordy. shareholders		30
Dividends		(18)
Retained profit for the financial year		12
Earnings per share (eps)		17p

(eps is based on profit earned for ordinary shareholders divided by the number of shares in issue.)

Figure 2.6 *Published company profit and loss account*

In addition, the standard requires a note to the profit and loss account statement disclosing what the profit would have been if revaluations of property were excluded, and the amount of any consequent adjustment to depreciation charges. This is to enable comparison to be made with other organisations that have used 'historic cost accounting' throughout their lives. You may wish to refer to Chapter 5 dealing with historic/current cost accounting to follow up this point.

Finally, the standard requires a statement showing the total recognised gains and losses in the period, comprising the profit for the period plus any other movements in balance sheet reserves. The purpose of this requirement is to give a picture of the overall performance, which previously was obscured (as in the case of Polly Peck plc) by items being reported in the separate accounting statements.

Some further illustrations of income statements for different types of business organisations are contained in Chapter 4.

Further reading

Financial Reporting Standard No 3.

Advanced Financial Accounting, R Lewis and D Pendmill, Pitman.

Company Accounts, M Pendlebury and R Groves, Unwin Hyman.

Self-check questions

1 Name three possible kinds of income statement.

2 A profit and loss account is a statement of all monies received during a period less all monies paid out. True or false? Give reasons.

3 Define depreciation.

4 What is the balance sheet value of an asset after three years if its original cost of £16,000 is depreciated at 20 per cent pa on the reducing balance method?

5 On inheriting £9,000, you decided to open a shop and paid three months'rent, in advance on 1 October. The annual rental is £6,000. In the first week you fitted out the shop at a cost of £4,800 and you expect the fittings to last about four years.

You started trading in the second week by buying £3,000 of goods for resale; £1,000 of which you managed to get on credit for settlement by the end of November; the other £2,000 you paid for in cash immediately.

During October you paid out £600 in assistant's wages/NI and £200 on sundry expenses. The previous tenant had paid about £450 this quarter for electricity but you have not had the meter read yet.

By the end of October your sales (all for cash) amounted to £3,600 and you still had half your purchases left in stock for sale the next month. How much profit or loss did you make in October?

3
The balance sheet

When we talk about a set of accounts we are essentially talking about the profit and loss account statement (discussed in the previous chapter) and the balance sheet statement, to which we now turn. This is not to deny the existence of a third statement dealing with cash flow, which also plays an important role in informing managers and other parties and which is discussed in Chapter 7.

Balance sheet

A balance sheet is a snapshot picture at a moment in time. On the one hand it shows the value of assets (possessions) owned by the business and, on the other, it shows who provided the funds with which to finance those assets and to whom the business is ultimately liable. Here we have an example of the dual aspects of recording which explains why a balance sheet must always balance. We can express this in the equation:

Assets = Liabilities

This balance sheet equation can best be understood by showing a few simple examples of transactions that affect either assets or liabilities, or both at the same time.

Example 1
Joe Bloggs starts up a business and pays £1,000 into a newly opened business bank account. The balance sheet now reflects the asset of

£1,000 cash and the liability of the business to the owner who provided the £1,000 capital:

Balance sheet for Joe Bloggs +

Assets	£	*Liabilities*	£
Cash	1,000	Owner's capital	1,000

Example 2

If some of the cash is now spent on stock costing £400 there is no change to the balance sheet totals, but a switch from cash to stocks on the assets side as follows:

Balance sheet for Joe Bloggs +

Assets	£	*Liabilities*	£
Stock	400	Owner's capital	1,000
Cash (1,000 – 400)	600		
	1,000		1,000

Example 3

Further stock costing £200 is now bought on credit. The asset of stock is now increased in value by £200, which is balanced by the new liability of 'creditors' on the other side for the same amount, as follows:

Balance sheet for Joe Bloggs +

Assets	£	*Liabilities*	£
Stock (400 + 200)	600	Owner's capital	1,000
Cash	600	Creditors	200
	1,200		1,200

Example 4

Some stock originally costing £100 is now sold for cash of £150, making a profit of £50. This shows as a switch from one asset to another asset, but also partly shows as an increased liability. Stock reduces by £100 but cash increases by £150. The seeming imbalance of £50 is corrected by showing the owner's capital increasing by £50 to £1,050 on the liabilities side. This is because retained profits in any business belong to the owner(s) who would ultimately get that amount if all the assets were turned back into cash and the liabilities were then paid off. The balance sheet now looks like this:

Balance sheet for Joe Bloggs +

Assets	£	*Liabilities*	£
Stock (600 – 100	500	Owner's capital (1,000 + 50)	1,050
Cash (600 + 150)	750	Creditors	200
	1,250		1,250

Having justified (it is hoped!) why a balance sheet must always balance, let us return to examining this statement in some detail.

Assets are of two main types and are classified under the headings 'fixed assets' or 'current assets'. Fixed assets are the hardware or physical things used by the business itself and which are not for sale to customers. Examples of fixed assets include buildings, plant, machinery, vehicles, furniture, and fittings.

Other assets in the process of eventually being turned into cash from customers are called current assets, and include stocks, work-in-progress, debts owed by customers, and cash itself. Therefore we can say:

Total assets = Fixed assets + Current assets

Assets can only be bought with funds provided by the owners or borrowed from someone else, for example, bankers or creditors. Owners provide funds by directly investing in the business (say, when they buy shares issued by the company) or indirectly as we have seen earlier, by allowing the company to retain some of the profits. Therefore for a limited company:

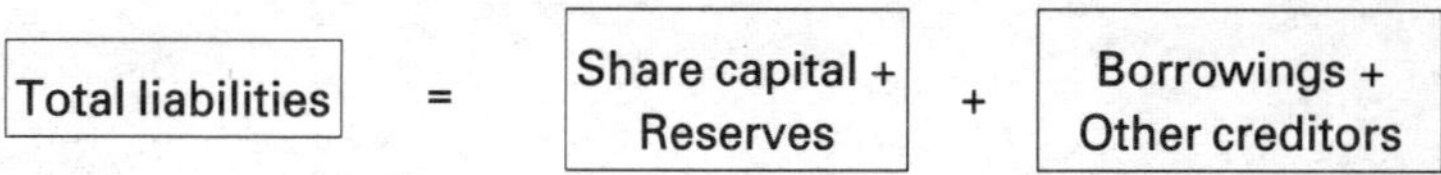

This same identity is also true for non-incorporated businesses when the owner's capital comprises the initial investment plus any retained profits, while further finance is provided by borrowings and, indirectly, by credit from suppliers.

Borrowed capital can take the form of a long-term loan at a fixed rate of interest or a short-term loan, such as a bank overdraft. All short-term debts owed by a business and due for payment within 12 months are referred to as 'creditors falling due within one year' and long-term indebtedness is called 'creditors falling due after one year'.

Having identified all the items in a balance sheet, the total picture can be shown as in Figure 3.1, keeping to the balance sheet equation of assets equal liabilities.

	£000		£000
Capital and reserves	200	Fixed assets	100
Creditors falling due after one year	50	Current assets	250
Creditors falling due within one year	100		
Total liabilities	350	Total assets	350

Figure 3.1 *Balance sheet structure (horizontal format)*

This horizontal presentation is rarely used, certainly in the case of published accounts that have to comply with the relevant standards. A vertical presentation is now the norm and the same balance sheet items shown in Figure 3.1 are now represented vertically in Figure 3.2:

	£000	£000
Fixed assets		100
Current assets	250	
Less		
Creditors falling due within one year	100	
Net current assets (ie working capital)		150
Total assets *less* current liabilities		250
Less Creditors falling due after one year		50
Net assets (wealth owned by shareholders)		200
Capital and reserves		200

Figure 3.2 *Balance sheet structure (vertical format)*

Assets

A firm's possessions or assets are normally divided into two broad categories based on a time distinction – 'fixed' or long-term assets and 'current' or short-term assets. These various categories of asset are normally based on the original cost of the items which is referred to as the 'historic cost convention'. Sometimes a valuable building may be revalued to its current value but this is the exception rather than the rule. 'Current cost accounting', where assets are revalued regularly, is the subject of Chapter 5.

It may come as a surprise but some assets are not disclosed in a balance sheet. Goodwill, including the value of brands that have been developed over many years, rarely appear in a balance sheet, and only then if purchased from outside. The skills of the workforce, probably any firm's most valuable asset, do not appear at all. This is because the firm does not own its employees, who can leave and go to work for someone else.

These two factors – historic asset values and missing assets – are the main reasons why a balance sheet as published has limited economic meaning. It certainly does not purport to show the value of a business or what its shares are worth. It merely records what assets the organisation has spent its money on and who provided that money. With this big proviso in mind, let us now examine the balance sheet in detail.

Fixed assets

These are assets held in the business for use rather than for resale and can be regarded as long-term assets to be used for a number of years. Fixed assets are grouped under three possible headings – tangible assets, intangible assets, and investments.

Tangible assets are likely to appear in every balance sheet. They embrace land and buildings, plant and machinery, motor vehicles, and furniture and fittings. They are normally shown in the balance sheet at their original cost reduced by the amount of depreciation written off to profit and loss accounts over the asset lives.

The main object of depreciation is to spread the original cost of the asset over its expected life so that the profit and loss account for any period bears a fair share of the cost of fixed assets. Consequently, the value of fixed assets in the balance sheet may not reflect their saleable value at that time because of inflation.

This practice of depreciating owned fixed assets is extended to some leased assets. First, a distinction has to be made between 'operating leases' and 'finance leases'. The former would describe the short-term hire of an asset, for example, the renting of a vehicle or piece of equipment for a few weeks or months. These operating lease payments are charged to the profit and loss account when incurred, and no entry is needed in the balance sheet.

Finance leases, however, are seen as conferring all the benefits of outright ownership except that the asset is financed in a somewhat similar way to hire purchase. In this case, the assets being leased are originally shown in the balance sheet at their full cost together with the capital amount outstanding on the finance agreement. The asset value is then depreciated each year by the amount of capital repayments that have been made in that year.

It is a mammoth task in large organisations to keep records of all fixed assets showing their cost and depreciation amounts over time.

Maintaining an asset register is a very suitable task for computers, and accounting packages dedicated to this specific purpose are available.

Intangible assets

This category embraces goodwill, brands, patents, trade marks, licences, etc. Such items will only appear on a balance sheet if they are separately identifiable and money is spent on their acquisition.

Goodwill and brands are very contentious items at the present time. After a company is acquired, any goodwill paid for is written off against reserves as a matter of accounting policy. This puts acquired goodwill on the same footing as internally generated goodwill: a cost that, of course, cannot be identified and never appears in the balance sheet.

The alternative accounting treatment is to put acquired goodwill in the balance sheet as an intangible asset but then depreciate it in the profit and loss account each year, so reducing reported profits with a possible effect on the share price.

Some firms have jumped the gun and, anticipating a change in the relevant accounting standards, have put brands back into their balance sheets based on some valuation of future profits from sales of the products concerned. It is too early to say what the new Accounting Standards Board will recommend.

Investments

This category only appears under the umbrella of fixed assets if the investments are long term in nature and represent stakes in subsidiaries, joint ventures, and related companies. Sometimes the part ownership refers to a supplier, competitor, or customer and the stake is held for strategic reasons and, possibly, eventual takeover.

Current assets

These are short-term assets which are already cash or which are intended to be turned back into cash in the course of normal trading activity. There are three main types of current assets, namely, stocks, debtors, and cash itself, so we shall examine each in turn.

Stocks

It is possible to have up to three types of stock, depending on the nature of the business. The three categories are raw materials, work-in-progress, and finished goods. A manufacturing firm will have all three kinds whereas a retail outlet will only have finished goods for resale. Service industries may also carry stocks. For example, an architect has considerable work-in-progress, being labour and overhead charges of the drawings not yet charged out to clients.

Stocks are valued on the basis of their cost, or realisable value if lower. Realisable value means their value to the trade not their sale value to a customer. This rule can be important for firms holding stocks of commodities, for example, tin, lead, cocoa whose prices can be volatile at times. Valuing these stocks at the year end may result in a loss if market value happens to be lower than cost at that particular moment. Engineering firms and confectionery manufacturers can see their profits affected either way by sharp changes in commodity prices.

The valuation of work-in-progress and finished goods may also not be quite so straightforward as 'valuing at cost' would suggest. In this context it is debatable what constitutes cost.

Obviously, the direct costs of labour and materials which went into making the product are part of the cost. So too is a share of some overhead costs of running the firm. It can be argued that all production and administrative overheads should be charged to all products whether part or wholly finished. Selling and distribution overheads, however, should only apply to the goods sold and not by definition to the goods in stock. Fortunately, some rules have been formulated by the accountancy bodies and these are found in SSAP 9.

The value of stocks held in store is also influenced by the stores pricing policy. A few alternative systems of pricing stores issues are available, all of which affect the value of items not yet issued. This is discussed in Chapter 8 on costing basics.

Debtors

Debtors arise only when firms sell on credit, but as credit sales are normal for all industries except some retailing, it means debtors are found in most balance sheets. Also included under this heading are payments made in advance of the goods or services being received when, say, rates were already paid for a further period after the balance sheet date.

The basis for valuing trade debtors is to take the value of the customer invoices outstanding at the date of the balance sheet. A small adjustment to this value is then made to reflect past experience that all invoices never get settled in full. Usually this is because some dispute about the goods or services delivered can arise at a later date, or some customers go out of business and cannot pay their debts.

For these reasons, firms make a small provision, based on past experience, of the amount which they should classify as doubtful debts. This provision for bad debts is charged as an expense in the profit and loss account and the global value of the debtors reduced accordingly in the balance sheet. Depending on the actual bad debts occurring within the year, the provision is topped up to a suitable level again at the next year end.

Investments

It is not uncommon to see investments in the list of current assets. This relates to short-term investments of monies that are not immediately required and have been placed to get a good return in the money markets or elsewhere. If the investments are quoted securities, such as shares or gilts, then their current market value must be disclosed.

Cash and bank balances

Included in this heading are cash floats, petty-cash balances, and any takings not yet banked. Businesses always have a bank current account (which will be a liability if overdrawn!) and may also have a deposit account. All these cash and bank balances pose no valuation problems.

Balance sheet sequence

The foregoing groups of assets are normally listed in order of permanence. Fixed assets are therefore listed before current assets and within each group the same practice is recognised. This results in the sequence land and buildings, plant and equipment, motor vehicles, fixtures and fittings for fixed assets. The sequence for current assets becomes stocks of raw materials, work-in-progress, finished goods, debtors, investments, ending with the least permanent assets of cash and bank balances.

Sources of funds

We now turn our attention to a business's sources of funds – where the money comes from with which the assets are bought. The two main sources are shareholders (or owners) and borrowings from financial institutions. Each of these sources can be further divided as we shall see.

In addition, a source of finance is usually found in trade credit. This occurs when a firm buys goods or services from other firms but is allowed a number of weeks to pay. These trade creditors reduce the amount of working capital needed to be provided from shareholder and borrowed sources. It is for this reason that 'creditors falling due within a year' are deducted from the total current assets to show the amount of working capital. We now look at each source of finance in turn.

Share capital

Ordinary shares form the bulk of the shares issued by most companies and are the shares which carry the ordinary risks associated with being in business – indeed, they are often referred to as the risk capital or 'equity'. All the profits of the business, including past retained profits, belong to the ordinary shareholders once any preference share dividends have been deducted. Ordinary shares have no fixed rate of dividend but companies hope to increase their size in good years in line with the growth of company profits.

Preference shares get their name for two reasons. First, they receive their fixed rate of dividend before ordinary shareholders can receive any. Second, in the event of a winding up of the company, any funds remaining go to repay preference share capital before any ordinary share capital is repaid.

A company does not have to issue all its share capital at once; the total amount it is authorised to issue must be shown somewhere in the accounts. Although shares can be partly paid this is a rare occurrence. Partly paid shares on privatisation of a publicly owned organisation are a different thing, as any outstanding monies are owed to the government and not to the company concerned.

Reserves

This is probably the most misleading term in all accounting! In general terms it means profits of various kinds that have been retained in the company as extra capital. Also important is what the term 'reserves' does not mean. It does not mean actual money held back in reserve in bank accounts or elsewhere. Reserves come from retained profits over many years but by now are probably reinvested in buildings, equipment, stocks, or company debts, just like any other source of capital.

The main categories of reserves are as follows:

- *Profit and loss account*, ie retained profits from ordinary trading activities carried forward each year.
- *Revaluation reserve*, ie the paper profit that can arise if certain assets are revalued to current price levels without the assets concerned being sold.
- *Share premium account*, ie the excess over the original par value of a share when new shares are offered for sale at an enhanced price. Only the original value is ever shown as issued share capital.

Creditors falling due after one year

These fall into two main categories – borrowed capital and provisions or charges. Borrowing is attractive to a company if it thinks it can earn a greater return on the money by using it in its business than it costs to service the interest payments. When the government throws in tax relief on the interest payments it becomes irresistible, although excessive borrowing gets risky if pushed too far.

Firms sometimes also make provisions against future events, say, a restructuring or reorganisation and redundancy programme. A provision is made by charging an estimated future cost as an expense in the profit and loss account now. The money has not yet been spent as this is anticipating a future event. Meanwhile, both the cash and the potential liability are shown in their respective places in the balance sheet reflecting the dual aspects of recording.

Creditors falling due within one year

Apart from bank overdrafts or other short-term borrowings, these creditors are liabilities incurred in the normal course of trading. Examples are amounts owing to suppliers (trade creditors), employer's National Insurance (NI) contributions and payroll deductions of NI and PAYE not yet paid over, corporation tax and VAT not yet due for payment, dividends declared but not yet paid.

As already indicated, it is the normal practice now for these current liabilities (as they are also called) to be regarded as a negative current asset in the working capital cycle. This shows them as a deduction from current assets which they help to finance rather than as a separate source of funds in their own right. This working capital cycle is explored more in Chapter 15.

Other sources of funds

There are various hybrid types of finance that are neither pure share nor pure borrowing. A convertible loan or a convertible preference share are cases in point. In both cases the original security is convertible into ordinary shares at some future date(s) on predetermined terms.

There can also be various types of borrowing, some being secured on assets of the business, some not. Loans, debentures, mortgages are all kinds of borrowing with different rights and obligations for the parties concerned. Mezzanine finance provided by venture capitalists is a loan subordinated to major finance and is common in management buy-outs or buy-ins.

It is possible to raise finance by the special use of existing assets. Occasionally one hears of a company selling off its valuable premises to a financial institution, but continuing to occupy them on a long-term lease. This is known as 'sale and leaseback'. Capital previously tied up in the premises is now released for investment in other fixed assets or in more working capital. Future profits earned in this way will be partly offset by the rent charges hitting the profit and loss account.

Another asset which can be turned into cash is trade debtors. This is done by selling the invoices to a specialist finance house who collect the money from the customer later. 'Factoring', as it is called, is discussed in Chapter 15.

Mention has already been made of leasing or hire purchase. By this means a business can acquire the use of fixed assets immediately but pay for them by instalments (plus interest) over a number of years.

When deciding which sources of funds to use, companies have to consider such factors as availability, cost, risk, repayment burden if appropriate, and so on.

We can now look at the complete balance sheet in Figure 3.3, incorporating all the items we have discussed.

	£000	£000
Fixed assets		100
Tangible assets:		
Buildings		
Plant and machinery		
Motor vehicles		
Fixtures and fittings		
Intangible assets:		
Patents, licences		
Investments		
Current assets	250	
Stocks and work-in-progress		
Debtors (customers' debts)		
Short-term investments		
Cash and bank balances		
Less		
Creditors falling due within one year	100	
Trade creditors		
Bank overdraft		
Net current assets (ie working capital)		150
Total assets *less* Current liabilities		250
Less		
Creditors falling due after one year		50
Borrowings		
Provisions and charges		
Net assets (wealth owed to shareholders)		200
Capital and reserves		200
Issued share capital		
Retained profits (accumulated P & L a/cs)		

Figure 3.3 *Balance sheet structure (vertical format)*

In the next chapter we go on to examine the form in which business organisations, other than companies, present their annual income statements and balance sheets. In Chapters 6 and 15 we will return to the interpretation of company balance sheets and profit and loss accounts by the use of accounting ratios.

Audit

Limited companies must submit their annual accounts to audit by an independent, qualified accountant. The trend is towards minimising the cost and procedures for small unquoted companies but their larger brethren face big fees for audit services.

The audit report in a company's annual accounts is usually a very brief but important statement. In it, an independent report is made to the shareholders about whether the accounts give a 'true and fair view' of the company's state of affairs. This means that adequate records have been kept and that the accounting statements comply with the Companies Act 1985 and the professional standards laid down in SSAPs and FRSs.

A qualified report draws some irregularity to the attention of the shareholders for them to pursue at the annual general meeting or elsewhere. If it relates to a technicality that is not significant to the company's financial health, it will not attract much attention. A qualification on a serious matter, such as keeping inadequate records, overvaluation of stock, or using creative accounting to misinform shareholders, would lead to repercussions on the share price initially, followed by pressure on the directors to take immediate action or resign.

Concern has been voiced about the reality of an auditor's independence. The directors of a company are usually empowered to fix the auditor's remuneration; they can recommend a change in auditor to the members; they also negotiate with the auditors about the presentation of the accounts. These factors may seem to leave auditors susceptible to pressure from directors.

Hitherto, interim accounts for the first half year were usually unaudited. The Cadbury Report (1992) requires auditors to review half-yearly figures and the company to produce a balance sheet if it is to comply with the code of best practice. Previously half-year statements were unaudited and few companies published a balance sheet with their profit and loss account at the mid-point.

External auditors have the legal responsibility for audit but many large organisations, not just companies, also employ internal audit staff on complementary work. The external auditor is reporting on the accuracy of the financial statements and any supporting systems and should bear the work of internal auditors in mind in performing this role. Internal auditors will have a much wider brief, taking them into issues of stewardship, costing, and computerised systems to name but a few.

Further reading

Advanced Financial Accounting, R Lewis and D Pendrill, Pitman.
Company Accounts, M Pendlebury and R Groves, Unwin Hyman.
Brand Valuation, edited by John Murphy, Business Books.

Self-check questions

1 Why must a balance sheet always balance?
2 What are the main two groups of assets called?
3 What are the main two sources of long-term capital for a company?
4 Why is the goodwill of a company, built up over many years, not shown as an asset in its balance sheet?
5 Distinguish between 'operating leases' and 'finance leases'.
6 Name the three main types of stocks.
7 Why will there be a difference between the total value of customers' invoices outstanding and the amount shown as debtors in a company's balance sheet?
8 Differentiate between ordinary shares and preference shares.

4
Accounting for different business organisations

For most practical purposes, the layouts of the profit and loss account for sole traders, partnerships, limited companies (and even public authorities) are identical. The exception comes at the very end of the statement which shows the disposition of the profit (or surplus) in taxation, rewards to the owners, and profit retained in the business. The layouts of the balance sheet are also nearly identical except for the section showing the owner's funds invested in the business. Assets owned by any type of business are capable of analysis into the now familiar fixed or current asset categories.

Let us take as an example identical basic information for the year ended 31 December 199X and see how it is treated in the different types of business organisation. The data is:

	£
Capital originally introduced	30,000
Profit retained up to 1 January 199X	18,000
Net profit before tax for the year ended 31 December 199X	24,000
Tax due on profits	9,000
Personal drawings or dividends	10,000
Profit retained in the business	5,000

Self-employed

The sole trader or self-employed situation is the simplest. All the profit belongs to the one person and it is usual to show the profit before any personal drawings are charged. This accords with the profit which the Inland Revenue use to levy income tax as, otherwise, drawings would not be taxed. In the balance sheet the original capital and retained profit are merged into a combined 'capital account' which is reduced by any personal drawings of the proprietor. As income tax is levied on the owner rather than on the business it is not usually shown in the accounts but treated as drawings when actually paid.

	£
End of profit and loss account	
Net profit for the year	24,000
Balance sheet	
Capital account	
Balance at 1 January 199X	48,000 (30,000 + 18,000)
Add Net profit for the year	24,000
	72,000
Less Personal drawings	10,000
Balance at 31 December 199X	62,000

Note The apparent increase in the owner's capital account will be reduced by further drawings at a later date when the £9,000 tax is paid leaving capital of £53,000 – an increase of £5,000.

Figure 4.1

Partnership

The partnership agreement or, in its absence, the Partnership Act 1890, may allow for interest on the original capital, for the payment of salaries to partners, and state the proportions in which remaining profits are to be shared. Interest and salaries paid to partners are still regarded as shares of the profit for tax purposes. It is necessary to show these items in an appropriation section at the end of the profit and loss account together with the agreed division of remaining profit. Tax is dealt with in the same way as in sole trader's accounts. If interest is paid only on the original capital and not on profits retained in the business then it is necessary to have separate capital and current accounts for each partner in the balance sheet. In the following illustration it is assumed that the two partners A and B each receive salaries of £6,000 and £4,000 respectively; that 10% interest is allowed on their capital accounts; and that any balance of profit is shared equally between them.

		£	£
End of profit and loss account			
Net profit for the year			24,000
Interest on capital accounts	A	1,000	
	B	2,000	
Salaries	A	6,000	
	B	4,000	
Balance divisible equally	A	5,500	
	B	5,500	24,000
Balance sheet			£
Capital accounts	A	10,000	
	B	20,000	30,000
Current accounts	*A*	*B*	
Balance as at 1 January 199X	5,700	12,300	
Add Interest on capital	1,000	2,000	
Salary	6,000	4,000	
Share on profit	5,500	5,500	
	18,200	23,800	
Less Personal drawings	4,600	5,400	
Balance as at 31 December 199X	13,600	18,400	32,000

Note The same principle applies here as in the note on self-employed, ie the apparent increase in the partners' current accounts will be reduced by further drawings of £9,000 when they make their personal tax payments. The increase in current account balances will then be £5,000 more than the figure at the start of the year.

Figure 4.2

Limited company

A company is a separate entity from its individual owners or shareholders so that corporation tax payable by the company is shown as an appropriation of profit together with the dividends paid and proposed for the year. Any balance of profit remaining, after tax and dividend have been provided, is not added to the original share capital but is shown as a 'revenue reserve'. Companies are legally obliged to show the issued share capital and reserves separately in their balance sheets, although together they form the total shareholders' funds invested in the business. Tax owing and dividends declared, but unpaid at the year end, appear as current liabilities. If the tax is not due within the next 12 months it is shown as a long-term creditor.

	£	£
End of profit and loss account		
Net profit for the year		24,000
Corporation tax payable on year's profit		9,000
Profit after tax		15,000
Dividends on ordinary shares		10,000
Retained profit added to revenue reserves		5,000
Balance sheet		
Authorised and issued share capital		£
30,000 ordinary shares of £1 each fully paid		30,000
Revenue reserves (retained profits)		23,000
Current liabilities		
Corporation tax payable	9,000	
Proposed dividend	10,000	19,000

Notes The revenue reserve of £23,000 comprises £18,000 + £5,000. Corporation tax could be a long-term liability dependent on the due date for payment and whether it is deferred. If an interim dividend has been paid during the year only the proposed final dividend appears as a current liability.

Figure 4.3

Public authorities

The income statement of a local authority or nationalised industry is prepared on the same principles and conventions as a company profit and loss account. Their format, however, must take account of the different way each is financed and the treatment of surpluses/deficits or profits/losses respectively.

To take nationalised industries first, these are fast becoming a threatened species because of privatisation. Those remaining will report their financial performance in the form of a profit and loss account. Capital allowances apply as in the private sector and, if profit-making, corporation tax will be levied.

A local authority will publish a 'revenue account' as its income statement. The format of this statement is aimed to inform readers of the cost of providing various services and how expenditure on them was financed. The precise format is laid down by statute and guidelines from the relevant professional bodies.

Local authorities use a system of 'fund accounting' for reporting on their activities. Typical funds will include the general rate fund, the housing account, the loans fund, the insurance fund, and the capital fund. When all funds are aggregated, a consolidated revenue account and consolidated balance sheet emerges for the authority.

Of the various funds, the general rate fund embraces many of the functions traditionally associated with local authorities, so an illustration of this is shown in Figure 4.4.

Revenue account for the year		
Income (not specific to any expenditure)	*£m*	*£m*
Rates		50,300
Block grant		49,000
		99,300
Expenditure (net of specific fees, charges, and grants)		
Cultural and leisure activities	7,400	
Education	58,300	
Environmental health	5,600	
Finance	4,100	
Housing	200	
Social services	14,400	
Planning	8,900	
		98,900
Surplus transferred to balance sheet (revenue balances)		400
Balance sheet at year end		
Fixed assets		110,000
Current assets	53,400	
Creditors due within one year	(23,700)	
		29,700
		139,700
Financed by:		
Long-term borrowing		127,000
Provisions for liabilities and charges		900
Revenue balances (including 400 for this year)		11,800
		139,700

Figure 4.4 *Local authority – general rate fund*

Company consolidated or group accounts

Shareholders of limited companies are not necessarily individuals. As a company is a separate legal entity it follows that it can be a shareholder in another company. When the shareholding exceeds 50% of the voting capital then that other company is called a subsidiary of the parent or holding company. This is very commonplace in the UK, where many public and private companies wholly, or partly, own other (subsidiary) companies. Each individual company must produce and distribute to its shareholder(s) a set of annual accounts.

However, the various companies in a group are parts of one single undertaking. Consolidated accounts are the means of informing only the parent company's shareholders of the financial position and performance of all the companies which it controls. These take the form of a consolidated profit and loss account, a parent company balance sheet, and a consolidated balance sheet. The precise requirements are complex and are contained in FRS No 2, entitled *Accounting for Subsidiary Undertakings*, but the basic elements of consolidation are described below.

Consolidated profit and loss account

This statement combines all the separate profit and loss accounts of the parent and subsidiary companies. Where the subsidiary companies are wholly owned, then sales, trading profit, interest, tax, etc., are aggregated item by item. Sales to other group companies which have not been resold to third parties must be eliminated, as must any profits on such sales or interest on inter-group loans. The logic here is that a company cannot sell to, or profit from, itself.

In the case where all subsidiary companies are not wholly owned then all of the profit does not belong to the parent company. The proportion of the profit after tax belonging to the outside shareholders is deducted to arrive at the profit attributable to the parent company's shareholders. These outside or minority shareholders in subsidiary companies are called minority interests. An abbreviated

	£
Sales	10,000,000
Operating costs	9,533,000
Trading profit	467,000
Interest payable	53,000
Profit on ordinary activities before tax	414,000
Tax on profit on ordinary activities	140,000
Profit on ordinary activities after tax	274,000
Minority interests	15,000
Profit attributable to parent company	259,000
Dividends to parent company shareholders	57,000
Retained profit of parent company	202,000

Figure 4.5 *Example of a consolidated profit and loss account*

example of a consolidated profit and loss account showing a share of profits going to such minority interests is illustrated in Figure 4.5.

Sometimes companies own shareholdings in other companies or joint ventures, over which they can exert significant influence but which are less than 50% of the voting capital, so that they are not classified as subsidiary companies. In this case the company in question is called an 'associated company'. When producing a consolidated profit and loss account, the holding company must disclose its proportionate share in associated company profits and losses, irrespective of whether or not it receives such profits as dividends.

Parent company balance sheet

This has all the appearance of a normal balance sheet except that included in the assets will be the cost of shares owned in subsidiary (and related) companies plus any amounts owed by them. Conversely, if the parent company has borrowed money from a subsidiary company this indebtedness will also be disclosed.

Consolidated balance sheet

A consolidated balance sheet is prepared by adding together the individual balance sheets of the parent company and its subsidiaries. This is achieved as follows:

1. All fixed and current assets and external liabilities are amalgamated item by item.
2. Inter-company indebtedness is eliminated.
3. The cost of the investment in subsidiary companies cancels out the proportion of the shareholders' funds acquired in those companies.
4. If there is an excess purchase cost over the value of shareholders' funds acquired, this is called goodwill. Conversely, a capital reserve occurs when the purchase cost is less than the value of shareholders' funds acquired.
5. The amount of shareholders' funds in subsidiary companies owned by outside shareholders is shown separately as 'minority interests'.

Example

The simplest situation is where a parent company (P Ltd) sets up a wholly owned subsidiary (S 100% Ltd) from the beginning. In this case there are no minority interests and no goodwill to concern us. The relevant balance sheets are set out in Figure 4.6 together with the resultant consolidated balance sheet.

P Ltd balance sheet

	£000		£000
Issued share capital	22,000	Fixed assets	11,000
Reserves	1,300	Investment in S 100% Ltd	10,000*
	23,300	Loan to S 100% Ltd	2,000†
Current liabilities	1,200	Current assets	1,500
	£24,500		£24,500

S 100% Ltd balance sheet

	£000		£000
Issued share capital	10,000*	Fixed assets	17,300
Reserves	15,400	Current assets	21,100
	25,400		
Loan from P Ltd	2,000†		
Current liabilities	11,000		
	£38,400		£38,400

P Ltd consolidated balance sheet

	£000	£000		£000	£000
Issued share capital		22,000	Fixed assets	11,000	
Reserves	1,300			17,300	28,300
	15,400	16,700			
Current liabilites	1,200		Current assets	1,500	
	11,000	12,200		21,100	22,600
		£50,900			£50,900

Note The items cross-referenced with symbols † and * cancel each other out in the consolidated balance sheet.

Figure 4.6

When a subsidiary company is only partly owned, then all the assets (less debts) are not owned by the parent company even though they are all shown in the consolidated balance sheet. Therefore the value of these assets, which equals the value of shareholders' funds owned by outsiders in the subsidiary company, is shown as a liability on consolidation. A further example is now taken of a parent company (P Ltd) owning 80% of a subsidiary company (S 80% Ltd) which was set up in conjunction with another company who provided the other 20% of the share capital. The relevant balance sheets are now set out in Figure 4.7.

If the subsidiary was bought at a later stage then the cost of the investment must be matched against the value of shareholders' funds

P Ltd balance sheet

	£000		£000
Issued share capital	30,000	Fixed assets	22,000
Reserves	15,000	Investments in S 80% Ltd	20,000*
	45,000	Loan to S 80% Ltd	5,000†
Current liabilities	5,000	Current assets	3,000
	£50,000		£50,000

S 80% Ltd balance sheet

	£000		£000
Issued share capital	25,000*	Fixed assets	35,000
Reserves	10,000		
	35,000		
Loan from P Ltd	5,000†		
Current liabilities	20,000	Current assets	25,000
	£60,000		£60,000

P Ltd consolidated balance sheet

	£000	£000		£000	£000
Issued share capital		30,000	Fixed assets	22,000	
	15,000			35,000	57,000
Reserves (80%)	8,000	23,000			
		53,000			
Minority interests (20% × 35,000)		7,000			
Current liabilities	5,000		Current assets	3,000	
	20,000	25,000		25,000	28,000
		£85,000			£85,000

Note The inter-company loan cross-referenced † cancels itself out. The investment in the subsidiary of £20,000 cancels out 80% of the issued share capital of the subsidiary; the other 20% being part of minority interests.

Figure 4.7

acquired, including the pre-acquisition profits held in reserves. This comparison determines whether goodwill or a capital reserve arises on consolidation at the year end. Only post-acquisition profits in the subsidiary are included in the consolidated reserves. The distinction of profits of the subsidiaries into 'pre-' and 'post-acquisition' is also important for dividend purposes. The parent company must not pay dividends to its shareholders from pre-acquisition profits of subsidiaries. These matters are more complex than the purpose of this book allows us to pursue, so interested readers should follow them up elsewhere.

In this chapter we have examined the final accounts for differing types of organisation and shown how the statements are usually presented in a modern format. We have also looked at the principle of consolidation because most published accounts of quoted companies represent the activities of a group rather than a single company.

Further reading

Advanced Financial Accounting, R Lewis and D Pendrill, Pitman.
Public Sector Accounting, R Jones and M Pendlebury, Pitman.
The Meaning of Company Accounts, W Reid and D R Myddelton, Gower.
Business Accounts, D Cox, Osborne.

Self-check questions

1 Why does a self-employed person not normally show drawings in his or her profit and loss account list of expenses?
2 Subject to any partnership agreement, in what ways may partners share out the profit between themselves?
3 Is the 'retained profit' for the year for a limited company the profit before or after charging tax and dividends?
4 Why are consolidated accounts prepared for a group of companies?
5 What are 'minority interests'?

5
Inflation accounting

Unfortunately inflation is like the poor – always with us. Economic historians can point to times past when the value of money actually increased but these have been short lived. In the present inflationary era we need to be able to distinguish between the *apparent* profit of a business and its *real* profit after allowing for inflation.

This chapter explains the problems caused by inflation before explaining how accountants can deal with them in accounting statements.

The problem of inflation

Inflation has been present in the UK, as in the world economy, throughout the whole postwar period. When the rate of inflation is at a mild rate of less than 5% pa, accountants along with others largely ignore its existence when preparing the annual accounting statements of profit and loss account and balance sheet. This is not the case when accountants consider the effects of inflation on pricing and other management decisions. Over a number of years, however, even a modest rate of inflation like 5% pa has a dramatic effect on the value of the assets of a firm. Even more important is the effect on the replacement cost of such assets when they eventually wear out and have to be renewed.

For example, a firm buys fixed assets costing £2 million and charges depreciation on their historic cost at £400,000 pa for five years. Profits are fully distributed to shareholders each year so that no additional capital is retained from this source. Assuming inflation at 10% pa the replacement cost of the fixed assets is £3,222,000 at the end of five years, but only £2 million depreciation has been accumulated. Therefore £1,222,000 new capital may have to be raised just to continue in business.

A number of basic problems are presented by inflation when preparing the annual accounting statements of profit and loss account and balance sheet. Profits are overstated when the costs of depreciation and stock consumed during the year are based on their original acquisition cost and not on their current replacement cost. The values of fixed assets and stock shown in the balance sheet are understated when based on their original cost. In turn this undervalues the capital employed in the company. The combination of these factors means that the return on capital is considerably overstated, as the following example illustrates:

£10m historic cost profit (charging depreciation and stocks at original cost) £40m capital employed (basing asset values on original cost *less* depreciation)	= 25% return on capital
£9m current cost profit (charging depreciation and stocks at replacement cost) £45m capital employed (basing asset values on replacement cost *less* depreciation)	= 20% return on capital

Another problem caused by inflation is that assets held in the form of money lose some of their value over time. Debtors and cash itself are cases in point. Conversely, firms gain by borrowing money and owing creditors for supplies because no allowance for inflation is made at the time repayment takes place. These gains and losses are excluded from the conventional profit and loss account.

If *real* profits are not measured there is the danger that firms will be too generous with wage increases, dividend payments, and other benefits to the detriment of reinvestment. Many companies are paying dividends they have not really earned because they have not allowed for the extra costs of inflation in their profit and loss accounts. If inflation is ignored in the day-to-day running of the business, there is also the danger that selling prices may not reflect the up-to-date costs of stock and asset replacements. Hence insufficient cash will be generated to maintain the same trading level without recourse to more and more borrowing.

In the 1970s when the rate of inflation in the UK rose into double figures, and by the mid-1970s threatened to turn us into a banana republic, the professional accountancy bodies were involved in a long debate about how best to show the effects of inflation in accounting statements. One contentious point was whether to use general or specific price indices when revaluing stock or fixed assets. Another issue was whether to show the whole effects of inflation as falling on the firms' owners or whether to apportion it to different providers of capital. Some members of the profession preferred to ignore inflation and advocated continuing to provide statements based on the original value of transactions, ie historic cost accounting.

Current cost accounting

In March 1980 the accountancy profession published its Statement of Standard Accountancy Practice No 16, entitled *Current Cost Accounting*. This SSAP required listed companies and larger private companies to clarify the effects of inflation on both the profit earned in the year and on the value of assets held at the year end. This was achieved by the company producing supplementary statements to the historic cost profit and loss account and balance sheet. Although this SSAP is now not mandatory for reasons explained later, it is useful to examine the processes involved to gain a better insight into the effects of inflation.

Current cost profit and loss account

The supplementary profit and loss account statement contains four adjustments to the 'historic cost' profit to arrive at the 'current cost' profit attributable to the owners as Figure 5.1 illustrates. It is important to realise that the thrust of the statement is to show the effects of inflation on the profit earned for the shareholders.

The historic cost profit of £1,000,000 is shown as being overstated when compared to the current cost operating profit of £400,000, which allows for the inflated costs of replacing fixed assets and stocks and giving more credit to customers. Some of these additional costs are offset by not having to recompense lenders of capital for the effects of inflation, so that the current cost profit earned for the owners comes out at £640,000.

The way the first three adjustments are calculated largely makes use of index numbers supplied by the Central Statistical Office in a monthly publication called *Price Index Numbers for Current Cost Accounting*. In it the price movements of various assets and materials are recorded in detail for a variety of industries. In the event of a suitable index not being published a firm can construct its own in-house index.

		£000	£000
Profit as in 'historic cost' profit and loss account			1,000
Deduct	1 Depreciation adjustment being the extra cost of depreciation calculated on the replacement cost of assets instead of their original cost	200	
	2 Cost of sales adjustment, being the extra cash needed to replace stocks at prices ruling at the time of sale	300	
	3 Monetary working capital adjustment being the additional cash needed to give credit to customers for the value of goods which have cost more to produce	100	600
	= current cost operating profit		400
Add back	4 Gearing adjustment, being the proportion of the above adjustments (1), (2), and (3) not required to be borne by the owners if part of the firm's capital is borrowed (assumed 40% in this example)		240
	= current cost profit earned for owners		640

Figure 5.1 *Example of a current cost profit and loss account*

To illustrate the basic approach the depreciation adjustment is calculated from the following information. A firm bought some fixed assets during 1989 at a cost of £2 million and expected them to have a five-year life. Depreciation on a straight-line basis amounts to £400,000 pa. The average price index for this type of asset was 120 in 1989 and 180 in 1993. The depreciation adjustment for 1993 gives the additional depreciation required to supplement the original £400,000 depreciation charged in the historic cost profit and loss account. In this example the extra depreciation amounts to £200,000 for 1993 and this figure appears in the supplementary current cost profit and loss account. The calculations are:

Total depreciation charge based on current cost £400,000 × $\frac{180}{120}$	= £600,000
Depreciation already provided in historic cost profit and loss account	£400,000
Depreciation adjustment for 1993	£200,000

Current cost balance sheet

The supplementary balance sheet values all assets at their current replacement cost at the balance sheet date. When inflation increases the value of an asset in money terms, it might appear that the balance sheet will no longer balance. This is remedied by creating a special reserve called a 'current cost reserve', which is part of the shareholders' funds and effectively updates the value of the shareholders' investment in the business. If, for example, the value of fixed assets rose by £1 million by the year end then this reserve will also be increased by £1 million. This keeps intact the balance sheet equation that assets must always equal liabilities.

Let us take the example of a firm owning £1 million assets financed totally by share capital. The financial position can be set out:

Balance sheet

Share capital £1,000,000 = Assets £1,000,000

Assume that because of inflation the assets increase in value by £50,000. The position now is:

	Balance sheet	
Share capital	£1,000,000	= Assets £1,050,000
Current cost reserve	£50,000	
	£1,050,000	

The differences between a current cost balance sheet and an historic cost one are limited to the valuation of assets and the current cost reserve. All assets are revalued to their replacement cost at the balance sheet date while debtors and cash remain unaffected. All liabilities are unaffected by inflation except for the current cost reserve, which accumulates the asset revaluations and the four profit adjustments.

Reactions

SSAP 16 was introduced for a trial period of three years to be reviewed in 1983. Its use was extended until 1985 when it ceased to be mandatory due to lack of support from within and without the profession. Accountants found it an expensive and time-consuming task to produce the required data in another form. They also found a mixed response from intended users of the additional information either on the grounds of its complexity or disagreement with the rationale, and it is now applied by few firms. British Gas plc is one of those few companies publishing current cost accounts.

There was hope that the Inland Revenue would accept the current cost procedures outlined in SSAP 16 as a basis for taxing real profits. They appear to have rejected this on the grounds of the subjectivity allowed to individual companies when choosing relevant price indices and asset lives.

It is doubtful if company managers, investors, employees, and possibly even accountants understood all the ramifications of the current cost adjustments. The effects of inflation on pricing policy, working capital requirements, corporation tax assessments, dividend policy, and the cost of capital and wage claims are complex and not easily understood. The tendency was for companies, unions, and the financial press to concentrate on the well-known but misleading figures and ignore the more accurate supplementary information.

In 1980 a leading firm of stockbrokers estimated that 40% of UK companies were paying dividends not covered by 'current cost earnings', ie excessive dividends were eroding the real capital base of these companies. With inflation down to below 5% by the early 1990s, this is no longer the case, especially as many companies pay less than half their profit out as dividends.

This chapter has concentrated on the effects of inflation on information contained in the annual accounting statements of the profit and loss account and balance sheet. It demonstrates how, if inflation is ignored, profits are overstated and assets are understated in terms of the current value of money.

Accountancy procedures used in the early 1980s to correct this, by producing supplementary statements, have been explained. These allow a more correct assessment of the return on capital, of the profits available for distribution as dividends, and of the book value of company shares.

Inflation has other effects on company finances. Questions as to what values to use when pricing, budgeting, setting standards, and appraising investments are left until the relevant chapters containing these techniques. Even if inflation adjustments are not shown in their published annual accounts, organisations will consider the effects of inflation when making these policy decisions.

Further reading

Advanced Financial Accounting, R Lewis and D Pendrill, Pitman.

The Meaning of Company Accounts, W Reid and D R Myddelton, Gower.

Accounting Under Inflationary Conditions, P R A Kirkman, Allen & Unwin.

Statement of Standard Accounting Practice No 16: *Current Cost Accounting.*

Self-check questions

1 What is the difference between an historic cost profit and a current cost profit?

2 What happens if a firm distributes all of its historic cost profit as dividends at a time of high inflation?

3 Name the four adjustments to historic cost profit that appear in a current cost profit and loss account.

4 If an asset is revalued how does a balance sheet still balance?

6
Performance ratios

Previous chapters have examined the two most important financial statements of profit and loss account and balance sheet. The trading performance of a company for a period of time is measured in the profit and loss account by deducting running costs from sales income. A balance sheet sets out the financial position of the company at a particular point in time, namely, the end of the accounting period. It lists the assets still owned by the company at that date matched by an equal list of the sources of finance.

A person experienced in reading company accounts can get some insight into a company's affairs by examining these financial statements. Changes in some of the key figures are apparent from the adjacent figure for the previous year, but such an approach can be misleading. Consider a company whose profit increased by 10% over the previous year. This might appear to be a good performance until one considers either a 15% rate of inflation or the extra 20% of capital employed to earn that extra profit. Experienced and inexperienced readers of accounts will benefit from a more methodical analysis of the figures.

The main analytical approach is to examine the relationship of pairs of figures extracted from the accounts. A pair may be taken from the same statement or one figure from each of the profit and loss account and balance sheet. When brought together the two figures are called ratios, although this term is not always used in the normal sense of the word. Some of the ratios are meaningful in themselves but their value mainly lies in their comparison with the equivalent ratio last year, a target ratio, or a competitor's ratio.

All too frequently one sees television or newspaper reporting that some leading company made £X million profit last year. As a sum of money the figures sound very large and more naïve audiences might be tempted to think of excessive prices being charged. Such reporting is almost meaningless without reference to last year's figure, the size of the company's sales, or amount of capital employed. In other words, the absolute value of profit is not as meaningful as the 'return on capital' or 'profit margin' on sales.

Profitability

Most of the main ratios are concerned with aspects of profitability and, like any investment, the key ratio is the return on the investment. We calculate this by expressing profit as a percentage of capital. This is influenced by two further ratios comprising the profit margin (profit as a percentage of sales) and the rate of asset turnover (sales dividend by capital). Using sample figures when profit is £1 million, sales are £10 million, and capital is £5 million, then:

$$\frac{\text{Profit £1m}}{\text{Capital (assets) £5m}}\% = \frac{\text{Profit £1m}}{\text{Sales £10m}}\% \times \frac{\text{Sales £10m}}{\text{Capital (assets) £5m}}$$

$$\underset{\text{Return on capital}}{20\%} = \underset{\text{Profit margin}}{10\%} \times \underset{\text{Rate of asset turnover}}{2 \text{ times}}$$

The return on capital may vary from one industry to another but wider variations may be found in their profit margin and rates of asset turnover. Figure 6.1 shows various ways in which, say, a 20% return on capital could be achieved in different industries.

Industry	*Return on capital*	=	*Profit margin*	×	*Rate of asset turnover*
Construction	20%	=	4%	×	5 times
Food retailing	20%	=	2%	×	10 times
Heavy engineering	20%	=	10%	×	2 times

Figure 6.1 *Sample performance ratios*

Profit margins in food retailing may be only 2–3% but this is offset by a very high rate of asset turnover. In more capital-intensive industries with a long production cycle the low rate of asset turnover is compensated for by a high profit margin.

These three key ratios are only the starting point from which a number of subsidiary ratios can be calculated relating running costs or assets to sales. Figure 6.2 shows this approach in diagrammatic

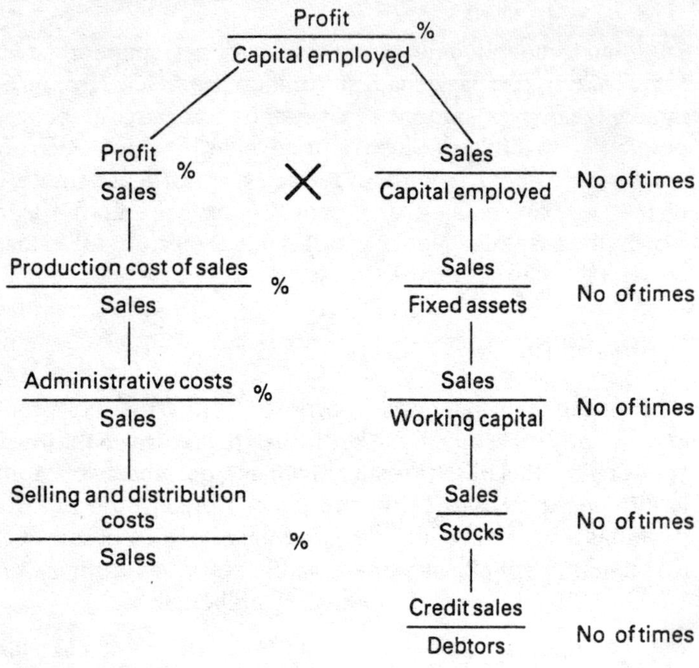

Figure 6.2 *Key performance ratios*

form. The precise definition and meaning of the most important ratios are now given.

Profit/capital

This ratio is usually expressed as a percentage in the way we might think of the return on any financial investment. Both profit and capital may be defined in different ways, the choice of which depends on the use to which the ratio is put. Looked at from the owners' viewpoint, their concern is with the profit earned for them relative to the amount of funds they have invested in the business. The relevant profit here is after interest, tax, and preference dividends have been deducted. This is expressed as a percentage of ordinary shareholders' funds comprising both share capital and reserves:

$$\text{Return on shareholders' funds} = \frac{\text{Profit after tax, interest, and pref. divds}}{\text{Ordinary shareholders' funds}} \%$$

The above ratio will be influenced not only by the trading performance but also by the size of tax allowances and the mix of owners' and borrowed capital used by that particular company. A wider view of company performance can be taken by expressing profit before interest, tax, and preference dividends as a percentage of the total capital employed, irrespective of whether the capital is borrowed or provided by the owners. This states:

$$\text{Return on capital} = \frac{\text{Profit before tax, interest, and dividends}}{\text{Total capital employed}}\ \%$$

Capital employed is defined as 'total assets *less* current liabilities', which amount is described as such in the balance sheet. Where, say, a bank overdraft is included in current liabilities and this varies considerably from year to year, a more reliable ratio to use may be return on total assets. This will facilitate the year-by-year comparison of this ratio and show a more reliable trend.

Profit/sales

In effect this ratio measures the net profit margin as a percentage but it is common practice in many industries to scrutinise the 'gross margin' in addition:

$$\text{Profit margin} = \frac{\text{Net profit before tax, interest, and dividends}}{\text{Sales}}\ \%$$

It is usual to take the profit before tax, interest, and dividends as all three are subject to variations which have nothing to do with the basic trading performance. We are really saying that profit margins are determined by operating costs and selling prices rather than the capital mix or effective tax rate at any point of time. An extension of this ratio is to express every profit and loss item as a percentage of sales. Here is an example with hypothetical figures:

	%
Direct labour/sales	23
Direct material/sales	25
Production overheads/sales	14
Administration overheads/sales	15
Selling and distribution overheads/sales	13
Profit/sales	10
	100

As previously stated, the absolute value of these ratios has little meaning. Ratios are like fingerprints in detective work. They point us in a direction that appears to merit further investigation when they compare adversely with previous experience, targets, or competitors' ratios.

Sales/capital(or assets)

This ratio is usually expressed as a rate of turnover. For example, if capital is £2 million when sales are £4 million, we say capital employed was turned over twice during the year. Another way of expressing this would be to say £0.50 assets were needed per £1 of sales:

$$\text{Turnover of capital} = \frac{\text{Sales £4m}}{\text{Capital employed £2m}} = 2 \text{ times}$$

Capital employed is the total amount of permanent and long-term capital excluding current liabilities. Subsidiary ratios may relate groups of assets, or any individual asset, to sales. If, say, sales are £4 million and fixed assets £0.8 million then:

$$\text{Rate of fixed asset turnover} = \frac{\text{Sales £4m}}{\text{Fixed assets £0.8m}} = 5 \text{ times}$$

An alternative way of expressing this is to say £1 of fixed assets generated £5 of sales in the year. A similar calculation could be performed on working capital to identify the velocity of circulation of the same money being used over and over again.

To illustrate if sales are £4 million and working capital is £1.2 million, then the rate of turnover of working capital is:

$$\text{Rate of turnover of working capital} = \frac{\text{Sales £4m}}{\text{Working capital £1.2m}} = 3.3 \text{ times}$$

When individual current assets are related to sales, however, it is common practice to invert the ratio and multiply by 52 weeks. Applied to debtors the ratio 'debtors/sales × 52' tells us the number of weeks' credit being taken by customers. Ignoring seasonal fluctuations in sales, when annual sales are £4 million and debtors are £0.5 million then:

$$\text{Credit period taken} = \frac{\text{Debtors £0.5m}}{\text{Sales £4m}} \times 52 \text{ weeks} = 6\tfrac{1}{2} \text{ weeks}$$

Similarly the ratio 'stock/cost of sales × 52' tells us the number of weeks' stock being carried and the ratio 'creditors/purchases × 52' denotes the period of credit taken from suppliers. Debtors, creditors, and stock ratios are discussed again in Chapter 15 in relation to the management of working capital.

Liquidity

Previous ratios have examined the performance of a company from the viewpoint of efficiency, both in the control of costs and in the use of its assets. In order to survive, companies must also watch their liquidity position, by which is meant keeping enough short-term assets to pay short-term debts. Companies go out of business compulsorily when they fail to pay money due to employees, bankers, or suppliers. There are two main ratios used to examine the liquidity position of a company, namely, the liquidity ratio and the current ratio.

Liquidity ratio (acid test)

This is sometimes called the 'acid test' or 'quick' ratio because it is the one that really matters. It takes the form of liquid assets:current liabilities, where a 1:1 ratio means a company has sufficient cash or near cash to pay its immediate debts. Liquid assets are defined here as all the current assets excluding stocks, which cannot quickly be converted into cash. In effect liquid assets are debtors, cash, and any short-term investments, such as bank deposits or government securities. Using the figures in Appendix 2, the liquidity ratio can be calculated as follows, showing ample liquid resources at that moment in time:

$$\text{Liquidity ratio} = \frac{\text{Liquid assets £38,000}}{\text{Current liabilities £30,000}} = 1.3:1$$

A company can survive with a liquidity ratio of less than 1:1 if it has unused bank overdraft facilities. Any existing bank overdraft is classified as a current liability but if not called in, it should not really count as a short-term debt. Funding an overdraft with a longer-term loan would also transform an adverse liquidity ratio.

In some industries it is not unusual for stocks and work-in-progress to be turned into cash before all creditors are due for payment. Building construction and food retailing are cases in point where seemingly adverse liquidity ratios pose no threat to the company.

Current ratio

The other test of a company's liquidity includes stocks and work-in-progress on the grounds that stocks eventually turn into debtors and then into cash itself. It is calculated by relating all current assets to current liabilities. A norm of 2:1 is regarded as satisfactory in most industries but this is a somewhat arbitrary figure and it may be a better guide to look at the norm for each particular industry. The above points about bank overdrafts also apply as do the ability of some firms to turn stocks into cash more quickly than most.

Again using the figures in Appendix 2 the current ratio is

$$\text{Current ratio} = \frac{\text{Current assets} \quad £73{,}000}{\text{Current liabilities } £30{,}000} = 2.4{:}1$$

indicating this company has more than sufficient short-term assets to meet its short-term debts.

Debt capacity

The distinguishing features of borrowed capital as opposed to owners' capital are that borrowings must be serviced by interest payments and repaid either in instalments or at the end of a period of years. There is no such legal obligation to pay dividends to owners, nor is share capital repayable. From a liquidity point of view too much debt is risky, as the higher the proportion of capital raised by loans the higher the proportion of profit going as interest. A judicious amount of borrowed capital can be beneficial to the owners and this aspect is measured below and discussed in Chapter 13 under the heading of 'capital gearing'. For the moment let us examine the ratios concerned with measuring the amount of debt a company can assume.

Debt ratio

The proportion of debt to total assets expressed as a percentage is used to quantify the amount of debt owed by a firm. In effect, this ratio measures the proportion of assets owned by a company which is owed to creditors of various kinds. In this context, debt includes all loans, overdrafts, trade creditors, tax, and other liabilities. The higher the percentage, the less willing creditors will be to extend further credit.

Gearing ratio

This measures the proportion of total borrowing, including long-term loans and bank overdrafts, to either total capital employed or shareholders' funds. For example, when total borrowings are £4 million and shareholders' funds are £16 million, then total capital employed equals £20 million. Borrowings therefore represent 25% of shareholders' funds or 20% of total capital employed. This level of borrowing would not be regarded as excessive but the volatility of profits in the past must be considered before making a final judgement.

Income gearing

A measure of the proportion of profit taken up by interest payments can be gained by expressing the annual interest payment as a percentage of the annual profit before interest, tax, and dividend payments. The smaller the percentage then the less vulnerable the company will be to any setback in profits or rise in interest rates on variable loans. The larger the percentage then the more risk that level of borrowing represents to the company. For example, when annual interest is £70,000 and profit £100,000, then

$$\text{Income gearing} = \frac{\text{Interest £70,000}}{\text{Profit £100,000}} = 70\%$$

which figure leaves the company very vulnerable to any profits setback.

Income cover

An alternative way of calculating this risk would be to calculate the 'income cover', being profit divided by interest, which equals 1.4 times in this example. One must also look for peculiarities in any one industry. Property development is heavily dependent on borrowed capital and any dramatic change in market conditions for letting can pose severe problems for the companies concerned. Memories of the property boom and collapse which triggered off the secondary banking crisis of the 1970s were hardly forgotten before the next property slump hit us in 1990, causing many company collapses.

Predicting failure

It is possible to use a combination of a number of ratios to assess the financial health of a company and its likely success or failure. A number of researchers have tried various combinations, and weightings, of ratios to produce a single measure. Altman was the author of the 'Z score', which combined the following five ratios:

Net current assets/Total assets.
Retained earnings/Total assets.
Profit/Total assets.
Market value of equity/Book value of total debt.
Sales/Total assets.

Interfirm comparisons

Mention was made earlier that ratios can be used to compare aspects of one company's performance with competitors. It is possible to conduct such an exercise by using the information in the published annual accounts of similar firms. This information can be requested from the company or more usually extracted from a data base like Extel or Fame, which are found in many large libraries. Alternatively, a search can be instigated at Companies House but this may prove expensive when a number of companies are involved.

Some firms use an organisation called the Centre for Interfirm Comparisons and participate in a study of their industry. Financial information, including detailed costs, is submitted in confidence and comparative ratios produced. Data must be adjusted to a common basis for all firms so that, for instance, a firm which leased all its assets adjusts its costs and assets to align with other firms who own their assets. Proposed studies are advertised from time to time for interested parties to join in.

Public sector

Most of the above ratios have little meaning or application for public-sector organisations which are not profit orientated, nor have owners seeking a return on investment. Ratios that have a role to play in measuring performance in this sector are referred to as the '3 Es' – economy, efficiency, and effectiveness. They relate to various measurements of inputs and outputs and play an important role in the auditing of public-sector activities. (See Further reading, Jones and Pendlebury, for a detailed account.)

Limitations

It should not be thought that performance ratios are a panacea for all ills. They are a relatively crude diagnostic tool which can help managers and investors identify the strengths and weaknesses of a company. They identify the areas to examine in more depth but suffer from the limitations of the financial statements from which they are prepared. In particular, care must be taken when deciding whether to use inflation-adjusted data to calculate ratios.

Further reading

Management Accounting for Decision Makers, G Mott, Pitman.

The Meaning of Company Accounts, W Reid and D R Myddelton, Gower.

How to Use Management Ratios, C A Westwick, Gower.

Public Sector Accounting, R Jones and M Pendlebury, Pitman.

'Uses and abuses of corporate prediction models', J Robertson and R Mills, *Management Accounting*, October 1991.

Corporate Financial Distress and Bankruptcy, 2nd edition, E I Altman, John Wiley.

Self-check questions

1 What is an accounting ratio?

2 Complete the following equation:

$$\text{Return on capital} = \text{profit margin} \times \ldots$$

3 Is there an ideal value for each ratio? If not, how are ratios used?

4 Which ratio would you use to examine whether a company was short of cash if you knew it could not borrow any more money?

5 Which company is more vulnerable? Company A, which pays annual interest of £50,000 and makes a profit of £100,000, or Company B, which pays £150,000 interest and makes £500,000 profit?

6 What ratios are used to measure performance in public-sector services?

7
Cash flow and value added statements

Readers of annual reports need some training to understand profit and loss accounts and balance sheets. They may be heartened by these further two statements whose titles accurately describe their contents.

The cash flow statement is quite literally a statement of the amounts of cash flowing in and out of the company during the period, analysed by the reason and purpose of the flow. This statement is the third member of the trio of statements found in company published accounts (the others being the profit and loss account and balance sheet) and is mandatory for all but small companies.

The value added statement, however, is not mandatory and rarely finds its way into published annual accounts. It is a statement both of the wealth created by a firm during a period of time and also to which parties that wealth has been distributed. A major role of a value added statement is to communicate financial results to employees in a more easily understood manner than a profit and loss account. We shall see an example of this later in the chapter, but first we turn our attention to cash flow.

Cash flow statement

A cash flow statement summarises exactly where cash came from and how it was spent during the year. Because there is a time lag on many cash transactions, for example, tax and dividend payments, the statement is a mixture of some previous year and some current year transactions; the remaining current year transactions go into the following year's cash flow statement during which the cash actually changes hands.

For this reason it is not possible to look at just this year's profit and loss account and balance sheet to find all the cash flows without reference to the previous year's accounts.

Compiling a cash flow statement is quite a technical job and some training plus inside information is needed to complete the task. Nevertheless, the bulk of the items can be identified from an examination of the other two accounting statements. However, managers are interested in how to read the statement, not how to compile one, so we shall concentrate on its interpretation.

The cash flow statement in Figure 7.1 gives an illustration of what it looks like in summary, omitting all the detailed items which would normally be included under each heading. Cash outflows are bracketed; cash inflows are not. We then examine exactly what is contained under each of the headings.

	£000
Operating activities	1,400
Returns on investment and servicing of finance	(350)
Taxation paid	(400)
Investing activities	(870)
Net cash outflow before financing	(220)
Financing activities	300
Increase in cash and cash equivalents	£80

Figure 7.1 *Cash flow statement for the year ended 31 May 199X*

- *Operating activities.* This shows cash generated or paid out on the following: operating profit, depreciation and changes in stocks, debtors and creditors during the period. A prime source of cash for any company should be the sale of goods and services for more than their cost, thus leading to a cash inflow from profit. When depreciation is charged as an expense in the profit and loss account, it lowers profit but does not lead to any cash outflow, unlike all other expenses. For this reason depreciation must be added back to profit to find the cash inflow from trading operations.

  Other operating activities that lead to inflows or outflows of cash are changes in the levels of stocks, debtors, and creditors by the period end. For example, a decrease in stocks allows a company to generate cash from sales without having to incur any cash outflow on purchases. This stock decrease is therefore a cash inflow.

To take another example, any decrease in creditors can only be achieved by paying off creditors – an outflow of cash.

- *Returns on investment and servicing of finance.* This refers to the payment of interest on any loans, overdrafts, or finance leases and all interest received. The section also includes all dividends received and paid out.
- *Taxation.* The tax referred to here is the tax on company profits – corporation tax in the UK or similar taxes overseas on profits earned abroad. Such home and overseas tax cash flows will normally be payments, but tax recovered in certain circumstances could result in a cash inflow.
- *Investing activities.* This refers to the purchase and sale of assets, businesses, or trade investments during the period.
- *Net cash flow before financing.* This discloses the total of all the four previous sections relating to cash flowing in or out, before any new capital is raised or any existing capital is repaid.

	£000	*£000*
Operating activities		
Operating profit	1,340	
Depreciation charges	280	
Increase in stocks	(170)	
Increase in debtors	(120)	
Increase in creditors	70	
Net cash inflow from operating activities		1,400
Returns on investment and servicing of finance		
Interest received	25	
Interest paid	(95)	
Dividends paid	(280)	
Net cash outflow from returns on investment and servicing of finance		(350)
Taxation		
Corporation tax paid		(400)
Investing activities		
Payments to acquire tangible fixed assets	(990)	
Sale of tangible fixed assets	120	
Net cash outflow on investing activities		(870)
Net cash outflow before financing		(220)
Financing activities		
Issue of ordinary shares	450	
Repayment of loan	(150)	
Net cash inflow from financing		300
Increase in cash and cash equivalents		£80

Figure 7.2 *Cash flow statement for the year ended 31 May 199X*

- *Financing.* The issue or repayment of share capital, loans, and finance leases during the period.
- *Change in cash and cash equivalents.* The final result of all the above cash inflows and outflows reflected in the cash and bank balances of the company at the end of the period.

Figure 7.2 now shows a typical cash flow statement including the detailed items discussed above. This uses what is described later as the 'indirect method' when disclosing the cash flow from operating activities.

Interpretation of the statement

The example shown in Figure 7.2 discloses near the end that the company had a net cash outflow before financing of £220,000. An issue of £450,000 new share capital was undertaken, partly to finance this deficit and partly to repay an old loan of £150,000. The remaining £80,000 went to swell the cash and bank balances. Looking higher up the statement, we now want to find reasons why the net cash outflow of £220,000 occurred.

The first calls on operating profit are interest charges, taxation, and dividends – in that order. Payments for all three combined amount to £775,000 – little over half of the £1.34 million earned. The remaining profit plus depreciation provisions are available for new investment in working capital (stocks, debtors, etc.) and new fixed assets. It would appear to be the high level of investment in tangible fixed assets, amounting to £990,000, that has resulted in the company not being totally self-financing in the period and having to resort to new financing.

If the new investment in working capital and fixed assets reflects growth in the scale of operations, this new financing may be quite justified, provided an adequate return is earned on those assets. If, however, the new investment was merely the replacement of old assets at today's prices, then the company may have been guilty of distributing too much profit in the past by way of dividends. The level of dividend payment shown at £280,000 does not seem high relative to profit after tax payments so this possibility seems unlikely.

Direct and indirect methods

The new standard FRS 1, dealing with the presentation of cash flow statements, allows two alternative ways to disclose the net cash flow from operating activities. These are referred to as the direct and indirect methods. It is early days yet, but the indirect method (illustrated in Figure 7.2) seems to be more common. This may be because when the direct method is used a reconciling note to the indirect method is also required.

The indirect method derives the cash flow from operating activities by taking the operating profit plus depreciation and the changes in working capital items. These figures are all easily traceable from the last profit and loss account and the last two balance sheets.

The direct method expresses the cash flow from operating activities in gross cash flow terms, not differentiating between current year's profit and working capital changes. An example of these two approaches is compared in Figure 7.3, both leading to the identical net cash inflow from operating activities.

Direct method:	*£000*
Cash received from customers	9,900
Cash payments to suppliers	(5,200)
Cash paid to and on behalf of employees	(2,700)
Other cash payments	(600)
Net cash inflow from operating activities	£1,400
Indirect method:	
Operating profit	1,340
Depreciation charges	280
Increase in stocks	(170)
Increase in debtors	(120)
Increase in creditors	70
Net cash inflow from operating activities	£1,400

Figure 7.3 *Comparison of direct and indirect methods*

We now turn our attention to the other financial statement in this chapter dealing with the concept of value added.

Value added

The gross domestic product (GDP) of any country is the value of the wealth created in that country during a period of time, usually measured over a year.

This wealth is the value of the goods and services produced by measurable economic activity – in other words, the money value of the output of firms of all sizes in all industries. There are some problems posed for the government statisticians when they tackle this exercise. The most obvious one is how to avoid double counting the same output when it is passed from one firm to another and one industry to another.

The answer lies in calculating the size of output on a value added basis. Take for example the coal industry. Coal is used to generate electricity, which is used to produce steel, which in turn is used to manufacture cars. If we take the total value of coal, electricity, steel, and cars produced in the UK in a year we would be counting the value of some coal four times and not just once. But if we deduct the value of all the bought-in goods and services from the sales of each industry we are left with the value added by that industry alone. This avoids all double counting. Therefore:

Value added = Sales − Bought-in goods and services

Just as we can measure the wealth created by a country or an industry so we can for one company. The wealth created by any business is the value of its sales less the cost of all the bought-in goods and services (which is wealth created by other firms). All firms are creators of wealth. They buy in raw materials and services, which they then convert or process into a product or service, which in turn they sell to their own customers. The difference between the final sales value and the original bought-in materials and services is the value added by that firm. It is this wealth a company has available for distribution to the four interested parties - employees, government, providers of capital, and the company itself.

We can think of a firm as a kind of partnership between these four parties. Employees bring their various skills while the government provides the environment in which firms and employees more easily prosper from the various services provided. Shareholders and loan providers allow their capital to be used to finance the production process while the firm brings together all the assets needed to carry out its economic function. It is these four partners who always share in the wealth created by themselves, although the shares are by no means equal. A typical value added statement for a firm appears in Figure 7.4 but it should be remembered that the four-way split differs from firm to firm and industry to industry.

The principles on which a value added statement is prepared are the same as for a profit and loss account. The conventions of realisation and accrual are followed, as is the concept of matching 'cost of sales' with sales in the same accounting period. Therefore, any

		£000
Sales		230
Less Bought-in goods and services		130
Value added		100
This was distributed as follows:		
To employees – as wages, salaries, pension, and National Insurance contributions	70	
To government – as taxes on profits	8	
To providers of capital – as interest on loans and dividends to shareholders	10	
To reinvestment – as depreciation and retained profits to finance replacement assets	12	100

Figure 7.4 *Typical value added statement*

increase in stocks of work-in-progress and finished goods is not counted as part of wealth created in this period because the sale has not yet taken place. Conversely, a decrease in such stocks counts as wealth created in this period. Government statisticians, however, do take these stock changes into account when calculating the total value of national output. Companies likewise would also have to take these stock changes into account when basing incentive payments on value added.

Value added statements and profit and loss accounts are both prepared from the same financial data. Their difference lies in the presentation and orientation of the contents. A profit and loss account gives a narrow 'shareholder-centred' view of company performance, unashamedly so, because this is the design concept. The very word 'profit' does have an emotive and political undertone when viewed by parties other than shareholders. A value added statement, however, concentrates on wealth creation rather than profit and shows its distribution to all four parties, not just one, who have contributed. In addition to the absolute values, the percentage share of value added going to each of the four parties is shown. We can see both the similarities and the differences if we examine the two statements, both of which are prepared from the same basic data as in Figure 7.5.

Very few companies are producing value added statements as an integral part of their annual report, although the Corporate Report (1975) recommended that practice.

There are no fixed percentage shares of value added applicable to all companies. In a capital-intensive industry, the share of wealth going to labour should be smaller to allow for the servicing of large amounts of capital and a high level of reinvestment to replace worn-

Part(i) Profit and loss account for year 199X

	£000	£000
Sales		1,000
Less Materials used *	300	
Services purchased *	130	
Wages and salaries	350	
Depreciation	90	
Interest on loan	50	920
Profit before tax		80
Corporation tax on profit		30
Profit after tax		50
Dividends		30
Retained profit		20

Part(ii) Value added statement for 199X

	%		£000
Sales			1,000
Less Bought-in materials and services *			430
Value added			570
This was distributed as follows:	%		
To employees – wages, salaries, pensions, and NI	61.4	350	
To government – corporation tax on profit	5.3	30	
To providers of capital – dividends and interest	14.0	80	
To reinvestment – depreciation and retained profits ploughed back	19.3	110	
	100.0	570	

Figure 7.5 *Comparison of profit and loss account with value added statement*

out plant. Conversely, in a labour- or material-intensive industry, the proportion of value added going to labour will be higher because the amount of capital to be serviced and the replacement investment are not so large.

It can be argued that in some firms the proportion of wealth going to one party has been too large resulting in too small a distribution elsewhere. The classic trade-off is between labour and capital reinvestment. Some financial experts have commented that, in many of our declining industries, the level of reinvestment has been much too low to keep us competitive internationally. Others have pointed to our poor productivity which results in low value added, low reinvestment, and an apparently high distribution of wealth to labour. This debate lies at the heart of how we are to improve our economic performance as a nation, particularly on the manufacturing front. Some improvement in productivity and reinvestment levels was evident in the 1980s, sometimes aided by Japanese capital and changed methods of manufacturing!

Uses of value added

There are two main uses to which value added statements can be put. Shareholders reading the statement can note the trend of distributions to themselves, to the labour force, and to reinvestment for growth. Any tendency to an increased labour share at the expense of reinvestment may lead them to reconsider their continued shareholding. Trade-union officials and employees will find the value added statement more helpful to financially untrained minds than the profit and loss account. The size of value added puts an absolute maximum on employee remuneration even if one could ignore the legal claims for interest and tax. Employees are shown to be the recipients of the lion's share of wealth in many companies and the debate on conflicting claims is more easily conducted using the value added statement. Perhaps more emphasis can be placed on increasing the size of the cake (value added) than on squabbling about the size of the four slices which in reality boils down to three or even only two.

The other main use of the value added concept is in measuring performance. Chapter 6 introduced the idea of using ratios to measure aspects of cost control and asset utilisation aimed at improving the return on capital. In a similar way we can examine the trend of value added per worker, or £ wages per £ value added to monitor labour productivity. Likewise, we can appraise capital productivity via the ratio £ value added per £ capital employed. Comparisons of these ratios between similar firms can only stimulate a more informed debate on efficiency and productivity.

Consideration should also be given as to whether the value added statement is produced on an historic or current cost basis. The latter would seem more appropriate because only after allowing for the cost of sales, depreciation, and monetary working capital adjustments can we talk about the real wealth created at today's prices.

Employee reports

This topic is introduced here because of its affinity to the value added statement, which is often used to communicate basic financial information to employees in place of the profit and loss account. Most employees (and many shareholders for that matter) find the annual accounts totally confusing and, increasingly, firms prepare a short salient financial report just for their employees' consumption. The cornerstone of this report is usually a value added approach, describing the wealth created in the year and how it has been distributed.

Sometimes an abbreviated profit and loss account is given but it is perhaps confusing to present both. Balance sheets are rarely given except in a highly summarised manner. The whole purpose of employee reporting is to communicate a few key facts on company performance which can be readily understood, rather than a morass of accounting detail which can thoroughly confuse the untrained reader.

Further reading

Financial Reporting Standard, No 1.
Financial Analysis, B Rees, Prentice Hall.

Self-check questions

1 Why do companies prepare a cash flow statement in addition to a profit and loss account and balance sheet?
2 Define value added.
3 A value added statement is based on the same concepts, and uses the same information, as which statement?
4 How might a firm use the value added to measure changes in productivity and efficiency?
5 Name the four parties to whom value added is distributed.
6 Even when firms do not include a value added statement in their annual reports, they may distribute one to which party?

Part 2
Management accounting

The financial statements found in the annual accounts are used by top management and external parties interested in the performance and financial position of the global enterprise. Functional managers within the firm will not find these financial statements of much help in the day-to-day running and management of resources under their control. Their need is for much more detailed information to allow them to price realistically and to plan and control future activities. Very many decisions which managers take are based on financial information. Knowing what information to ask for and how to use it is an essential requirement for any business person. The second part of this book is concerned with just these techniques, which assist managers in their jobs.

8

Costing basics

Cost is a word used to describe the money spent on a particular thing. In our private lives we talk about the cost of running a car or the cost of heating our home. In a business context we can talk about the cost of labour or the cost of running a department or the cost of a particular product or service sold to customers.

Every business organisation incurs costs. Whether we are self-employed, or work for local government, or are employed in a profit-seeking organisation, all these organisations incur costs.

Costs are incurred on the resources consumed by the organisation when carrying out its business objective of satisfying customers. The resources that are consumed are materials, people effort, bought-in services, the use of equipment, and even money itself, which has an interest cost.

These running or operating costs are referred to by accountants as 'revenue expenditure' to distinguish them from the initial cost of new physical assets, such as buildings, equipment, and vehicles. The acquisition costs of these fixed assets is referred to as 'capital expenditure'. This chapter is primarily concerned with the former, ie revenue expenditure incurred on the day-to-day running costs of the organisation when doing work for its customers and clients.

Costing is the analysis of costs so that they can be allocated to products/services, activities, departments, and specific time periods. This objective analysis of costs is typified when they are charged to the end product or department consuming such costs. There is also a need for a subjective analysis of costs. This looks at the nature and type of cost and describes them in various ways – for which we later need to learn a little jargon. Costing is therefore an in-house accountancy service to provide relevant information to managers in a timely and cost-effective way. We shall start our study of costing by considering where cost information comes from and how accountants deal with it.

Sources of cost data

Accountants receive information about costs from the managers and supervisors in their organisation. It is these managers and supervisors who consume resources and incur costs. They notify their financial colleagues about costs by forwarding documents describing the cost concerned. Typical document names are timesheets, invoices, goods received notes, and stores issue notes.

If accountants receive thousands of these documents each week, how are they to cope with such masses of data? There are two likely answers. First, the information on any document is condensed by using a kind of shorthand known as a cost code. Second, computers are used to sort, store, process, and retrieve the information in a more meaningful form. Let us examine these two solutions in turn.

Cost codes

A cost code is a numbering device that turns a written description of costs into a series of numbers, or into numbers and letters combined in an alpha/numeric code. An example of a cost code outline is shown in Figure 8.1.

01	182	5002
Originating dept, cost centre, or location number	Number describing the type of expense, the work done, or source of income	Job, contract, batch, product, service, or project number

Figure 8.1 *Typical cost code structure*

Cost code numbers tell us:

- what department the cost came from;
- what resource has been consumed and why; and
- to which end product or service the cost is to be charged.

The size and complexity of the cost code depends very much on the size and complexity of the organisation and its products. No two organisations' cost code systems will be the same unless they deliberately use a uniform system. What is suitable for ICI plc, for example, would be way over the top for a small family firm of electrical contractors.

Apart from having cost codes for costs and income, accountants need further codes to describe all assets and liabilities. The term often used to describe the whole accounting code system is the 'chart of accounts'.

Example
Using this electrical contractor as an illustration, the following structure and sample codes would be appropriate:

Cost centre no	Description no	*Customer Job No*
01 Installation	121 Wages – Electricians	5001 ABC Ltd
02 Stores	122 Wages – Storekeepers	5002 DCE Ltd
03 Administration	123 Wages – Cleaners	5003 XYZ Ltd
04 Purchasing	124 Wages – Clerks	etc.
05 Accounts	181 Materials – Cable	
06 Estimating etc.	182 Materials – Boxes	
	183 Materials – Conduit	
	184 Materials – Cleaning	
	201 Rent	
	202 Rates	
	203 Electricity etc.	

Use of computers

Costing documents are passed to the accounting department at regular intervals. Some code numbers are entered by the senders but others are added later by the accountant's staff. This is often the case with numbers of a repetitive nature, as with, say, the departmental code number.

The value of each transaction is entered into the computer along with the relevant codes to say which department it came from, what the cost is about, and the job/product to which it should be charged. Most overhead costs cannot be charged to an end product directly. However, knowledge of the source department and the nature of the overhead cost from the first two series of codes will allow the sharing out of overheads to different products at a later stage. The wider use of computers to process financial data is shown in Figure 8.2.

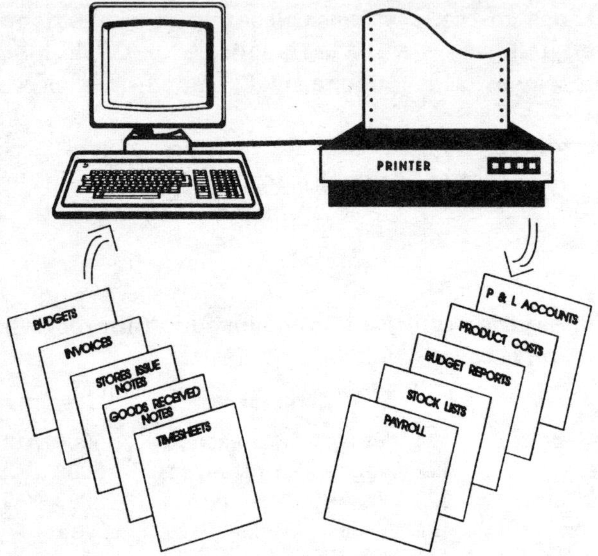

Figure 8.2 *Using a computer to process financial data*

Terminology

Like lots of subject areas, costing has a bit of jargon of its own. Most of it we will learn as we go but it is useful at this stage to concentrate on a few terms.

Cost centres

A cost centre is a physical location within an organisation. It is usually a whole department or a section of a department but it could just be one expensive machine. Usually, each cost centre's budgeted costs and actual costs are compared monthly, to feed useful information back to the manager concerned. This is why each cost centre needs its own unique location code. We explore 'budgetary control' in Chapter 12.

Cost units

A cost unit refers to something different. These are the products or services we either provide to others within our organisation or which we provide to outside customers. In a printing firm, for example, each bespoke print order from a customer will have its own unique job number and is a cost unit. In a mass-production industry, such as consumer durable goods, each washing machine or video player is a cost unit.

Direct and indirect costs

Costs can be split into two broad categories for costing and pricing purposes. These are known as direct and indirect costs. A *direct cost* is one that can readily be identified with, and charged to, a particular cost unit. In the printing firm just mentioned, direct costs will be the material costs of paper, card, and ink, together with the cost of machine time and the cost of labour expended on the preparation, printing, and finishing stages.

An *indirect cost* is more general in nature and cannot be specifically identified with a cost unit. These indirect costs, or overheads as we called them earlier, are first charged to cost centres and then shared out over the products and services produced. Indirect costs for the printing firm will include management and administration salaries, heating, lighting, rates, etc.

Fixed and variable costs

There is another way of looking at costs and classifying them into slightly different categories. This analysis is concerned with how a cost behaves when there is a change in the level of activity. Some costs stay the same total amount regardless of activity levels from week to week. Such costs are known as fixed costs, of which rent and rate bills are the classic example.

Other costs behave differently. If, say, the total cost of materials moves up or down in sympathy with the level of output, then this is called a variable cost.

The analysis of costs into fixed and variable categories is most useful when making decisions about the best course of action in circumstances where activity levels will change - say, the effect of cutting prices to increase sales volume. The main accounting technique that uses this analysis of costs into fixed and variable categories is called 'marginal costing', and is pursued in Chapter 10.

Costing labour, materials, and expenses

The resources firms use consist of three basic elements - labour, materials, and expenses:

- *Labour.* The cost of people employed by an organisation in both direct and indirect capacities.
- *Materials.* The cost of physical raw materials used directly in operations and other materials used in service activities.
- *Expenses.* The cost of bought-in services. Some are directly chargeable to customer products, eg subcontract or outwork. Other expenses relate to the multitude of fixed overhead costs, eg rates, electricity, legal fees.

We now want to look at the costing of each of these resources in turn, before showing later how they are used to help fix prices or estimates.

Labour costs

In some industries, such as education and health, labour costs may form more than half of the total running costs of an organisation. Other service industries, such as financial services, are also very labour intensive but new technology is gradually reducing the manual tasks here as well as elsewhere.

Manufacturing industries used to be very labour intensive with control of direct labour costs justifiably getting a high profile. With the coming of automation and robotics this is no longer the case, resulting in attention shifting to machine costs, material costs, and indirect labour costs.

Nevertheless, labour costs are still significant in all organisations and need to be carefully costed and controlled. To do this we need documentation, which usually takes the form of timecards and/or timesheets.

A timecard is clocked into a time-recording machine to verify attendance and record the hours worked. A timesheet (as in the example shown in Figure 8.3) can be used for the same purpose and, in addition, records both work done and cost unit/cost centre numbers. This would all need checking by a supervisor to maintain accuracy.

Other documents in use – in manufacturing particularly – are a piecework ticket (if remuneration is based on output) and a job card (if work is done by more than one operative or moves from one department to another).

All these documents – timecards, timesheets, job cards, and piecework tickets – will be used by accounting staff to prepare the payroll and to charge labour costs to appropriate cost units and cost centres.

Direct labour, including any bonuses and premium rates, can be directly charged to the products/services worked on. Indirect labour, however, is first channelled to cost centres and then absorbed into

Weekly Time Sheet

Name							Clock no			
Dept or Cost centre							Week ending			
Job or code no	Description of work	Hours taken					Hours	Rate per hour	Cost £
		Mon	Tue	Wed	Thu	Fri			
Signed (Worker)									
Signed (Foreman)									

Figure 8.3 *A typical time sheet*

product/service costs by using overhead recovery rates. There are a number of different payment systems to choose from when considering how to reward direct labour for their efforts.

Payment systems

The remuneration paid to employees can be based on the number of hours worked or on output achieved or some kind of combination of the two. The main types of payment systems are as follows:

- *Time-based system.* Pays a basic hourly rate for normal hours but enhanced rates after that. An example would be £6 per hour up to 38 hours and £9 per hour (time and a half) for each hour in excess of 38 per week.
- *Measured day work.* Pays high basic rates for high output and high-quality effort with agreed targets.
- *Incentive scheme.* Relates pay directly to output with certain safeguards for workers when output is restricted for reasons beyond their control. Piecework is the name given to an incentive system where a set amount is paid for each unit of output.

- *Premium bonus system.* Pays normal hourly or daily rates plus a bonus for any time saved relative to the time allowed.

Regardless of payment method, the cost of direct workers is charged directly to the products or services (cost units) on which they work. This cost will usually be enhanced by employer's contributions to National Insurance, holidays, and any other remuneration-related overhead.

Similarly, the pay of indirect workers (enhanced by these employee-related overheads) can be charged to the cost centres where they work. Overheads accumulated in each cost centre are then charged out to cost units benefiting from its services. This overhead-recovery process is described later.

Material costs

Firms may hold stocks of materials or components in their stores for issue at a later date. The purchase and subsequent issue of these materials is also documented at various stages to ensure that volumes and values are known and charged to the right cost units and cost centres.

Typical documents are as follows:

- *Purchase requisitions.* These are raised internally as soon as the reorder point is triggered. A requisition specifies the quantity, quality, and time requirements.
- *Purchase orders.* These are sent out for the economic order quantities to the selected suppliers who meet the requirements.
- *Goods received notes.* Made out after materials are received and matched with purchase orders and specifications.
- *Goods returned notes.* Raised only if any materials need to be returned to suppliers.
- *Invoices from suppliers.* Checked against goods received notes before payment is made.
- *Stores requisitions.* When duly authorised these are the only means of obtaining materials from store.
- *Stock records.* Kept manually by storekeeper and/or kept by computer recording all receipts and issues. The individual stock records are checked by a physical stocktaking on a continuous rotating basis.

All these documents and records have a part to play in the bookkeeping and costing systems for materials.

If materials are ordered for a specific purpose, the invoice can be specifically charged to the cost unit and/or cost centre concerned. What is not quite so straightforward is what charge to make for materials that have been held for some time and are subsequently issued from store.

Bases for pricing stores issues

A problem arises because purchase prices vary over time. The value placed on stores issues therefore affects the remaining stock value as well as the value of the materials issued. In turn this affects the cost of materials that are charged against income so that profit is also affected.

The options for pricing stores issues are as below:

- *First in first out (FIFO).* A popular method that issues oldest materials first at old prices. Remaining stock is therefore valued at recent prices for balance sheet purposes.
- *Last in first out (LIFO).* More popular in the US but not accepted as a valid basis by the Inland Revenue in the UK.
- *Standard price.* All similar materials are held in store at the one predetermined standard price specified and are issued at that value. Purchases at non-standard prices are still valued at this standard price but the cost variances are written off to the profit and loss account immediately.
- *Weighted average price.* This is a compromise between FIFO and LIFO values, issues stores and materials remaining in store at the same average price.

Example

A firm bought 200 units of material at 60p per unit in May and a further 400 units at 50p in August. The standard purchase price specified for this material is 60p. What is the cost of 300 units of this material issued in September under each of the different stores pricing systems?

Each pricing method gives a different answer, being £170, £150, £180, and £160 respectively. The calculations are:

FIFO	200	at 60p	+ 100 at 50p	= £170
LIFO	300	at 50p		= £150
Standard	300	at 60p		= £180
Average	100	at 60p	+ 200 at 50p	= £160

Over the whole life-span of any one company there will be no difference between these four methods of pricing stores issues. The total cost of all materials purchased is the same under all four and the profit made by the company over its whole life is therefore identical.

However, this is not true when we consider a month or a year in the life of that same company. The profit made in any one period will differ according to which method of stores pricing was used.

The FIFO method of pricing stores issues flatters profit when the price of materials is rising. The weighted average method similarly flatters profit when material prices are rising, but less so. The standard cost basis is the most realistic, provided the specified price is updated for changes in market prices of each material.

Once materials have been valued, direct materials can be charged out to the cost units by using the relevant job number. Indirect materials are charged to the cost centre incurring them, to be charged to cost units later as part of the total overhead recovery.

Expenses

We can dispense with direct expenses rapidly. These may occur if, say, a special piece of equipment is hired to do a job or if work is sent out on a subcontract basis. The invoice for such expenses can be charged to the cost unit concerned in much the same way as direct labour and direct material costs are coded with the job number concerned.

Indirect expenses, however, have no direct connection with cost units and are consequently charged to cost centres along with indirect labour and indirect materials. The treatment of all these three indirect costs is the story of overhead recovery, which we tackle next.

Overhead recovery

Overhead is just another word for indirect cost. Overheads are usually just as essential a cost as direct costs but they sometimes get tagged as non-productive costs. This is patently untrue as all the production in the world is useless without a sales force to sell it, accounts staff to pay wages, and suppliers and administrative staff to deal with other paperwork.

From a costing viewpoint overheads are a challenge. Although there is no direct link with the end product going to customers, overheads still have to be charged to cost units if we are to know their total costs. The total cost of a product is needed for stock valuation, pricing, and estimating purposes, and to know if we are making a profit at the selling price charged.

The question posed for managers and accountants is – how much overhead to charge to different product lines and to each cost unit? There are three broad solutions to this problem:

- Use a global overhead recovery method.
- Use a departmental overhead recovery method.
- Use an activity-based overhead recovery method.

Consider how a local garage charges each customer with a share of its overheads. Normal practice is that it combines overheads with labour, and charges an enhanced hourly rate to recover the cost of mechanic's time and overheads – and an element of profit!

This obviously is an easy and cheap way to deal with the costing of overheads. At the beginning of a year the garage estimates the cost of all its overheads and the number of mechanics' hours it will normally be able to charge out. The hourly overhead charge is worked out by dividing the estimated overheads for the year by the number of mechanics' hours in that same time.

Example
A garage estimates that its total overheads for the coming year will amount to £200,000. It also estimates that chargeable hours will come to 20,000. The overhead charge/recovery rate is £10 per hour.

If all customers were having similar work done then this system is likely to be as fair as any other. Many overheads accumulate with time as does rent, rates, office salaries, heating, etc. But in some circumstances this might not be regarded as a fair way to charge customers for different kinds of work.

What this global overhead recovery system does not allow for is that some customers may need the use of special equipment for a certain kind of repair while other customers do not. If the overheads include charges for the depreciation and maintenance of this equip-

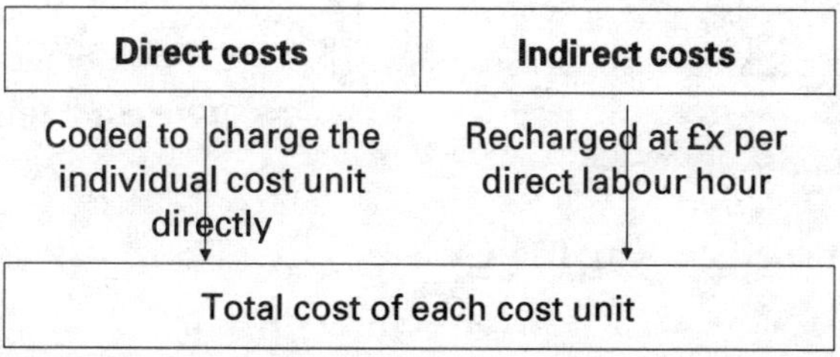

Direct costs | **Indirect costs**

Coded to charge the individual cost unit directly

Recharged at £x per direct labour hour

Total cost of each cost unit

Figure 8.4 *Global method of overhead recovery*

ment then the first customers are being subsidised by other customers who are being overcharged.

Many small firms use the above approach of putting all overheads into one big pot and then charging them out to cost units at an hourly rate according to the direct labour hours going into each product. This approach is shown in Figure 8.4.

Larger organisations with diversified products and more diverse production or operation systems find the global approach to overheads inappropriate. They cannot afford to undercharge some products, so gaining market share on less profitable lines, and they overcharge others, so losing market share on the more profitable lines.

For this reason they channel all overheads into their relevant cost centres where they arise. Cost centres providing a service to other operational cost centres have all their overheads recharged to them on the basis of the amount of service provided. All overheads are now in operational cost centres, which charge them out to cost units but

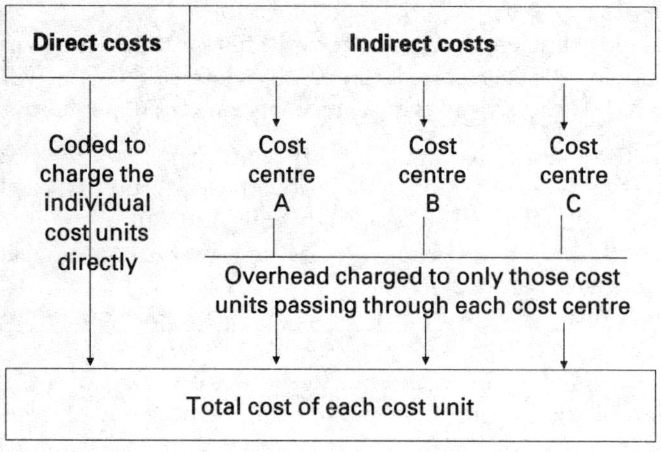

Figure 8.5 *Departmental overhead recovery method*

only those passing through that cost centre. In this way equity is established between different products. This more equitable system is illustrated in Figure 8.5.

Activity-based costing (ABC)

A subtly different means of overhead apportionment has appeared in recent years. This takes the view that activities are the cause of overhead costs and may arise in more than one cost centre for any one activity. For example, the obtaining of orders is an overhead cost that could entail the services of design, technical, and sales departments – three cost centres all contributing to the one overhead activity.

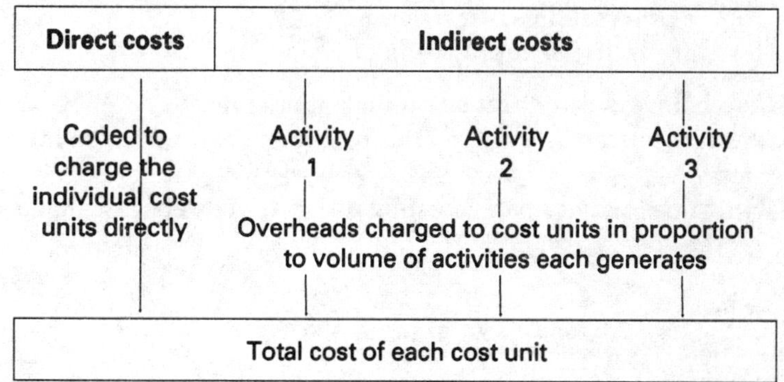

Figure 8.6 *ABC method of overhead recovery*

Various activities and their associated cost drivers are identified in this way and their overhead costs accumulated for each one. Appropriate overhead recovery rates are then used to channel each activity's overheads to products. Figure 8.6 illustrates this third and final approach to overhead recovery.

We can now see how the total cost of any product or service is built up. Direct labour, direct material, and direct expenses can all be coded with a job number to identify a particular cost unit. Indirect labour, indirect materials, and indirect expenses have to be shared out over cost units in a way that does not favour one product line at the expense of another.

The next chapter continues the costing story by examining the way businesses use cost information to help fix their prices.

Further reading

Costing, T Lucey, DPP.
Management Accounting for Decision Makers, G Mott, Pitman.
Principles of Cost Accountancy, A Pizzey, Cassell.
Costing, C Drury, Chapman & Hall.

Self-check questions

1 Is costing primarily concerned with revenue or capital costs?
2 Which documents typically convey basic cost data to accountants in an organisation?

3 Distinguish a 'cost unit' from a 'cost centre'.
4 Define indirect costs.
5 Give an example of a variable cost for:

(a) a leisure centre;
(b) a firm making cosmetics; and
(c) an electricity supply company.

6 In what ways can direct labour be remunerated?
7 What bases can be used to price materials drawn from an internal store?
8 How does activity-based costing differ from a departmental overhead recovery system?

9
Cost-based pricing

All organisations need to know the total cost of each product or service they provide to their customers for these reasons:

- To value work-in-progress and completed work as current assets in the balance sheet.
- To know what cost of sales to enter in the profit and loss account.
- To control product costs by comparing them with a predetermined target or standard cost.
- To know what profit is made at any particular selling price.
- To fix selling prices based on total cost, although there are many other non-cost influences on prices.

When prices are cost based, this calculation usually takes place before the order is received from the customer. This is the case when an estimate or quotation is requested for one-off or purpose-built items.

Where standardised products are concerned, the normal selling price is usually based on the total cost incurred on producing the product or providing the service. An element of profit is added in both cases for profit-seeking enterprises.

Sometimes work may be undertaken on a cost plus basis, meaning that the supplier will be reimbursed for all legitimate direct costs plus an agreed percentage for overheads plus a further agreed profit percentage. Some government contracts are let out on this basis. The selling price in these cases can only be worked out after the event.

The costing procedure for working out the selling price of any product or service is the same, irrespective of whether it takes place before or after the work is completed. This procedure is called 'absorption costing' by accountants, and is often referred to as 'full cost' or 'total cost' pricing.

Absorption costing

This term was chosen to describe the approach whereby products each absorb a share of the total overhead costs in addition to their direct costs. We can therefore say:

Selling price	=	Direct costs	+	Share of overheads	+	Profit

Example
A jobbing printer receives an enquiry for 100,000 leaflets of A5 size printed in black ink. The cost estimator has prepared the following estimate of resources required to do the job:

Direct costs:
- Paper – 204 reams of A4 at £3 per ream
- Ink – 2 litres at £9 per litre
- Machine/labour time – 2 hours at combined rate of £50 per hour

Indirect costs:
- Selling, distribution, and administration overheads are recovered by charging £40 per hour

Profit:
- An extra amount is added for profit, equal to one ninth of the total costs, to equate with a 10% profit on the selling price

The quoted selling price can be computed as follows:

	£
Direct costs:	
Paper	612
Ink	18
Machine time	100
Indirect costs:	
Overheads	80
Total cost	810
Profit	90
Selling price	£900

The precise methods used, and overhead recovery rates charged, vary from one organisation to another but the basic approach to full cost pricing is the same the world over.

In larger firms, a number of departmental overhead-recovery rates may be needed to determine total costs.

Example
The following details have been assembled to work out the price for a job in response to a customer's request:

Direct materials: 7.5 kilos at £10.50 per kilo

Direct labour:	*Department*	*Hours*	*Rate per hour*
	Machine shop	2.0	£8
	Assembly dept	1.0	£6
	Packing shop	0.2	£5

Overheads: These are recovered by means of separate hourly recovery rates for each of the above departments and then by an oncost of 25% to the works cost to cover selling and administration costs plus an element of profit.

The annual budgets for overheads for the above three departments are:

Department	*Hours*	*Overheads*	*Hourly rate*
Machine shop	1,000	£50,000	£50.00
Assembly dept	1,500	£22,500	£15.00
Packing shop	800	£26,000	£32.50

The price quotation can now be prepared as follows:

		£	£
Direct materials:	7.5 kilos at £10.50		78.75
Direct labour:	2 hours at £8	16.00	
	1 hour at £6	6.00	
	0.2 hours at £5	1.00	23.00
Overheads:	2 hours at £50	100.00	
	1 hour at £15	15.00	
	0.2 hours at £32.50	6.50	121.50
Total works cost			223.25
25% oncost for selling and administration overheads plus profit			55.81
Selling price to quote to customer			£279.06

Profit margins

Profit margins vary between organisations and industries. To understand why they vary we need to look at the relationship of three key accounting ratios – return on capital, profit margin, and turnover of capital.

Most profit-seeking firms set financial objectives in the form of a return on capital. If a firm had £2 million capital invested in business assets then it might regard a pre-tax annual profit of £400,000 as reasonable. This equates to a return on capital of 20% pre-tax.

If this annual profit of £400,000 was earned on sales of £4 million, this gives a profit margin of 10%. These sales of £4 million, when related to the capital employed of £2 million, result in a turnover of capital of two times, ie each £1 of capital generates £2 of sales in the year.

These three ratios are related to each other as follows:

Return on capital	=	Profit margin	×	Turnover of capital
20%	=	10%	×	2

Not all firms earn a 20% return on capital. Some earn more and some less, depending on the state of the economy and the quality of their management. In the long run a reasonable return on capital is essential for a firm to be able to attract new capital.

Firms also differ in the size of the other two ratios. Some industries have a high profit margin to compensate for a low rate of turnover of capital, as will be found with capital intensive activities, such as electricity generation and distribution. Other industries have a low profit margin compensated by a high turnover of capital rate, as found in construction, civil engineering, and food retailing.

The conclusion from all this is that there is no one profit-margin percentage that applies to all firms. Each firm sets its own target in the light of what is achievable in its own industry and circumstances. The 10% profit margin used in the estimating example may or may not be typical of the printing industry. We would have to look at the results of surveys carried out by their trade associations, or business monitoring organisations, to know what was the norm.

A survey of large manufacturing and service companies in 1986 by Mills and Sweeting showed that cost-related pricing methods were the most popular with approximately 70% of respondents. A similar proportion also selected full/absorption costing as the primary cost method used.

This does not necessarily mean that profit-seeking companies stick rigidly to prices determined by total costs. Companies use absorption costing as a long-term guide to what they need to sell at to earn a reasonable rate of return.

Some industries are dominated by one or just a few large suppliers. Small firms in these industries may have to be price followers rather than price determiners, unless they can differentiate their products on service or quality grounds.

In the short term, companies often trim their prices to suit market conditions. This can be disguised by the use of discounts as opposed to an overt price cut. This angle is explored more in the following chapter where the concept of 'contribution' is introduced.

Costing methods

Working out the total cost of a product may not be quite as straightforward as it sounds, depending on the method of production or operation used. There are a number of costing methods specifically designed to suit the way a particular product is made or service provided.

These costing methods go under various names, such as job costing, batch costing, contract costing, process costing, and service costing. Essentially, these five methods are based on only two main forms – job costing and process costing. We now look at the distinguishing features of each costing method.

Job costing

This applies where an individual job is carried out to a customer's specification, either at the supplier's premises or at the customer's premises. Jobbing printing and repairs to domestic appliances are relevant examples. The earlier examples (building up costs to quote a price) illustrated job costing.

Each job is given its own unique number in the cost coding system. This number is inserted on timesheets, stores issue notes, and invoices so that all direct costs related to the job are specifically charged to it. Overheads are added later in line with the recovery methods and recovery rates used by that firm. In this way the total cost of each job is built up.

This information can all be recorded by computer but in some firms a job card may accompany the work through its various stages and departments. Resources consumed are logged on to the job card as the work progresses.

Batch costing

Where a number (batch) of identical cost units are produced at one time they are often treated as one job in total and costed as such. The unit cost is therefore the total cost divided by the number of cost units in the batch.

Example
A batch of 1,000 washing machines was produced by a factory last week. Direct costs of labour and material parts charged to the job number for this batch amounted to £80,000. Overheads attributable to this production were a further £70,000.

$$\text{Unit cost} = \frac{\text{Total cost}}{\text{No of units}} = \frac{£80{,}000 + £70{,}000}{1{,}000}$$

$$= £150 \text{ per unit}$$

Contract costing

This applies to any very large job, usually associated with the construction industry, and often carried out at the client's site or premises. This is another variant of job costing, so that each contract, or part of a contract, will have its own job number. However, there are a number of special features of contract costing that distinguish it from job and batch costing.

Direct costs of labour and materials will still apply, but there may be additional direct costs for plant hire or work done by subcontractors. Site overhead charges can be specifically charged to an individual contract so the only overhead apportionments needed are those that relate to head office charges.

Example

Contract No 123

	£
Site wages	20,400
Site salaries	18,600
NI, pensions, etc.	6,200
Subcontract work	17,000
Internal plant hire	3,500
External plant hire	7,000
Materials delivered to site	46,000
Site overheads	5,300
Head office charges	2,750
Total contract costs to date	£126,750

Progress payments, assessed on the value of work done, help to offset the amount of working capital needed to finance contract work. This system of payment allows contractors and civil engineering firms to carry out multi-million pound schemes with only a relatively small amount of capital.

Process costing

This system of costing applies to a continuous and ongoing process that never, or rarely, stops. In such circumstances the unit cost cannot be separately recorded as in job costing. The unit cost in process costing is found by dividing the total costs for a period of time by the output over that period.

Example
The total of all direct and indirect costs for running a coal mine for a week amounted to £6 million. Output during this time amounted to 200,000 tonnes.

$$\text{Cost per tonne} = \frac{\text{£6m}}{\text{200,000 tonnes}} = \text{£30 per tonne}$$

In some process industries, for example oil refining, products may be produced either jointly or as a by-product of the main process. The costing treatment of by-products is that their resale value goes to offset the costs of the main product.

However, when products are produced jointly, the common costs incurred up to the separation point are apportioned pro rata to either their physical quantities or to their market values.

Service costing

This system of costing applies to any service industry where a uniform or standard service is provided to customers. It is similar to process costing in that the total costs of providing the service over a period of time is divided by the quantity of services provided to get a unit cost.

Example
The running costs of a local swimming-pool amount to £6,000 per week. Last week 8,000 people used the pool. The average cost per swim is therefore 75p.

In a similar way, transport or generating organisations could divide their total costs for a period of time by the activity taking place during that time to lead to the average cost per passenger mile or the cost per kWh respectively.

The actual unit cost of a service is used to help fix prices or other charges, but can also be used as a basis for cost control. For example, comparisons can be made with past unit costs or with targets, or with other organisations.

Inflation

When estimating future costs to establish an overhead recovery rate, full allowance for the anticipated rate of inflation should be made. Similarly, when actually quoting estimates or fixing selling prices, the up-to-date cost of materials and depreciation should be used. To do otherwise will not result in sufficient profit being made to replace the resources consumed at today's prices.

Further reading

Management Accounting for Decision Makers, G Mott, Pitman.
Pricing Decisions in Practice: How They are Made in UK Manufacturing and Service Companies, R W Mills and C Sweeting, CIMA.
Costing, T Lucey, DPP.
Management and Cost Accounting, C Drury, Van Nostrand Reinhold.

Self-check questions

1 Prepare a price quotation for the jobbing printer (mentioned early in the chapter) who has now received an order for 10,000 A5 menu cards. Direct materials are estimated at £180 and machine time will take three hours. All other cost and profit information is as before.
2 What size profit margin is required to give a return on capital of 30% when the turnover of capital is two times?
3 What costing method is most suited to oil refining?
4 How would a local authority know if its unit cost for providing a particular service was high, low, or indifferent?

10
Marginal costing

The previous chapter described the full cost of a product or service as a combination of direct costs and a share of the indirect costs. Marginal costing is a technique which also divides costs into two categories, but of a somewhat different nature. In this case costs are identified as being either fixed or variable, relative to the quantity of output:

Total cost	=	Variable costs	+	Fixed costs

A fixed cost is so called because it does not vary in total when output fluctuates. Rent and rates for a factory, shop, or office are good examples of fixed costs. Variable costs are those whose total (not unit cost) varies pro rata with the volume of output. The value of direct materials used on the product or service sold to customers is a typical variable cost.

It is possible to express fixed and variable costs in the form of a diagram or graph as shown in Figure 10.1. The similarity of variable costs to direct costs, and fixed costs to indirect costs, is sometimes a

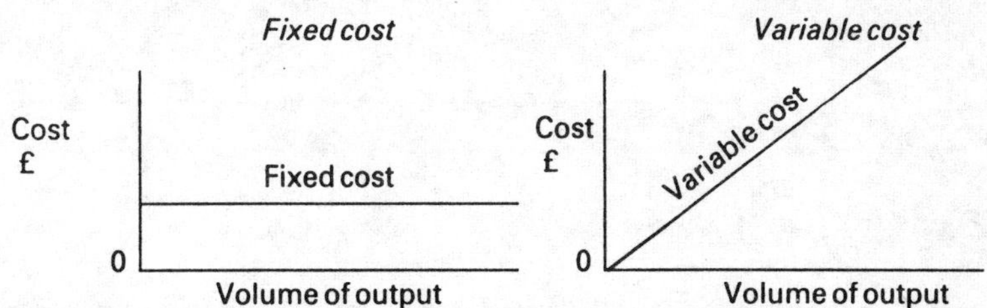

Figure 10.1

source of confusion. They are not quite the same for a number of reasons. Direct costs usually include the cost of direct labour and materials used on the product itself. Direct material is a variable cost because its cost varies exactly in proportion to the number of products made. This is not always the case with direct labour, particularly in the short term. For example, if a direct labour force is on a guaranteed weekly wage, we cannot say the cost is variable when there is a contractual agreement to pay them a fixed sum irrespective of the level of output achieved. Fixed costs will all be classified as overheads or indirect costs, but some overheads vary pro rata to output. Power, quality inspection, and some distribution costs are examples of variable overheads.

We can often use simple graphs to express the relationship of costs to output and use the graphs as an aid to decision-making. Take the example of two car hire firms. Firm A offers a car at a fixed rate of £20 per day plus 20p for every mile. Firm B charges only £12 per day but 30p for every mile. The two alternatives can be drawn on one diagram as in Figure 10.2. The total cost of using either car comprises the daily fixed charge plus the mileage cost, which varies according to miles run.

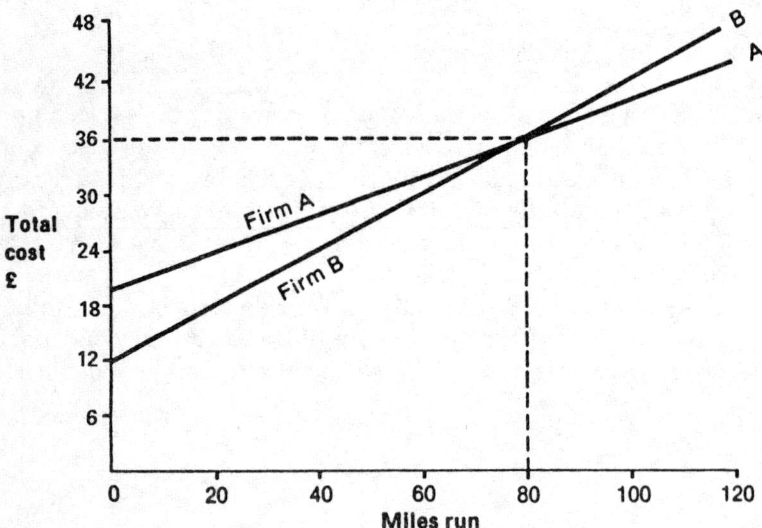

Figure 10.2 *Car hire costs*

We can conclude from the graph that firm B is the one to patronise if the daily mileage is expected to be less than eighty miles, while firm

A should be chosen for mileage in excess of that figure. The total cost is equal where the two lines cross and is called the break-even point.

Break-even analysis

This idea is also used by firms to depict costs, sales revenue, and output when the break-even point is that level of output where sales revenue just equals total cost. The firm makes neither a profit nor a loss at this point - hence the use of the term 'break even'.

Example
A firm makes only one product, which sells for £10. The variable cost per unit is £5 and fixed costs total £75,000 pa. Maximum capacity is 25,000 units pa but the firm is presently operating at 80% capacity.

Figure 10.3 shows the break-even chart drawn from this information.

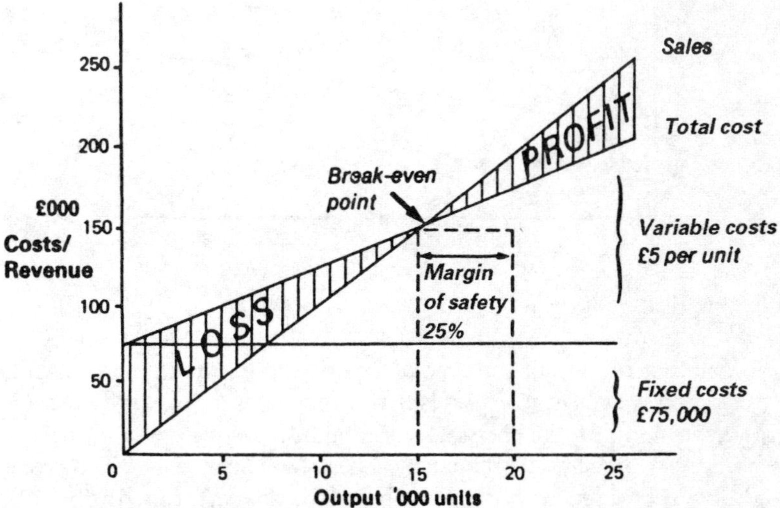

Figure 10.3 *Break-even chart*

Break even is reached at 15,000 units when sales just equals total costs of £150,000. Output of less than this amount results in a loss, while greater output makes a profit. The size of profit or loss at any output can be read off the graph at a glance, being the vertical distance between the total cost line and sales line. Also represented on the graph is the margin of safety which represents the proportionate fall in output which can take place before a loss is incurred. In this example, the present level of output of 20,000 units can fall by 25% to 15,000 units before a loss commences. Therefore the margin of safety is 25%.

Although the theoretical distinction between fixed and variable costs is easily understood it is not so easy in practice to separate them. Some costs fall into an in-between category called semi-fixed or semi-variable, where there is a fixed amount of cost plus an element that varies with output. One way to separate total costs into fixed and variable types is to graph total costs against the relevant levels of output. If the data covers a number of years the total costs should be updated to today's prices using relevant cost indices. The scattergraph is obtained from plotting total costs against level of output and drawing a line of best fit through the plots. Where the line intersects the vertical line at the origin approximates to the level of fixed costs. Figure 10.4 shows this approach which identifies fixed costs at approximately £200,000.

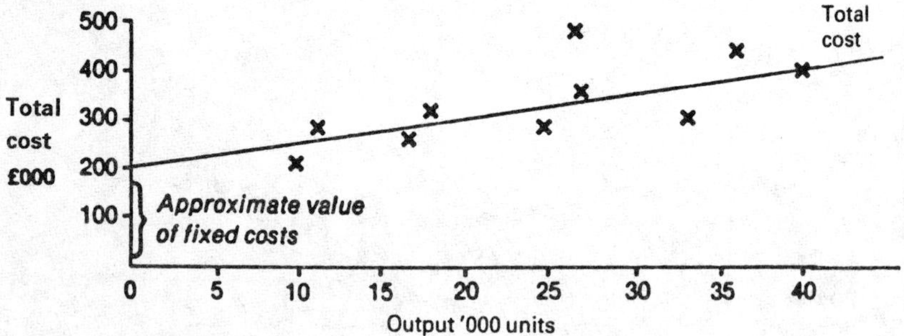

Figure 10.4 *Scattergraph*

Another reason for the practical difficulty in separating costs into fixed and variable categories is that such analysis varies with time. In the very long run all costs are variable because offices or plants can be closed down and then no further costs will be incurred. In the very short run of a few days, most costs are fixed, apart from direct materials, power, and possibly some wages, depending on the contracted method of payment.

Although we represent fixed costs as a horizontal line on a break-even chart it is not true to say that fixed costs will remain constant over a wide range of output levels. It could be that more supervisors or managers are required the higher the level of output, or more space or machinery is needed which result in increased rates or depreciation. Therefore fixed costs may increase in steps as output increases

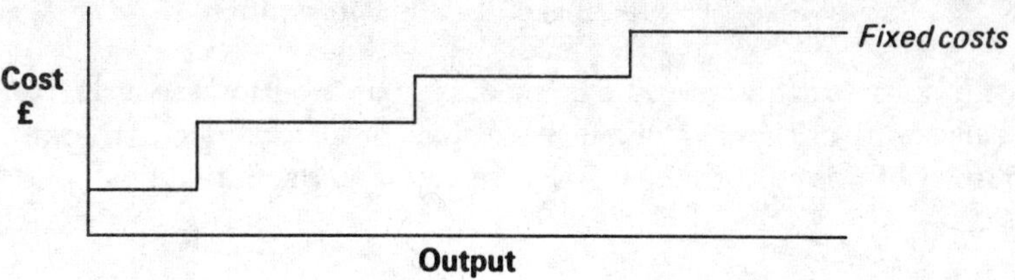

Figure 10.5 *Stepped fixed costs*

and may correspond more to the picture in Figure 10.5 than the horizontal line shown in previous diagrams.

Break-even charts are a useful way of depicting profit or loss at varying levels of output. They can be drawn for a firm as a whole or for one product only. In the latter case the fixed costs are those specifically applicable to the product together with a share of the total to be apportioned over all products.

Limitations of break-even charts

It is probably true that break-even charts are seen more often in textbooks than in real life. This is because the charts have some severe limitations. Clearly, costs do not move in a linear fashion across a wide range of activity levels. Nor does the product mix ratio stay constant in a multi-product firm. Any change in the mix will invalidate a chart as total sales value and total variable costs will vary with the mix. Finally, a chart cannot predict how many sales will be achieved at a certain price – that can only be attempted by market research.

Contribution

It is possible to draw a break-even chart in a slightly different manner. If the variable cost is drawn first and then the fixed cost on top, the resultant total cost is the same as if we had represented costs in the original reverse order. The reason for changing the order is to bring out what is known as the 'contribution'. This term is used to describe the difference between sales value and variable costs only. It is therefore an intermediate level of profit before fixed costs have been charged.

Sales	–	Variable costs	=	Contribution

We refer to different products making a contribution towards fixed costs and profit, by which we mean that they contribute to the common pool from which fixed costs are paid and profit remains.

Contribution	–	Fixed costs	=	Profit

Using the same basic data as for Figure 10.3, the break-even chart which identifies contribution as the shaded area is shown in Figure 10.6.

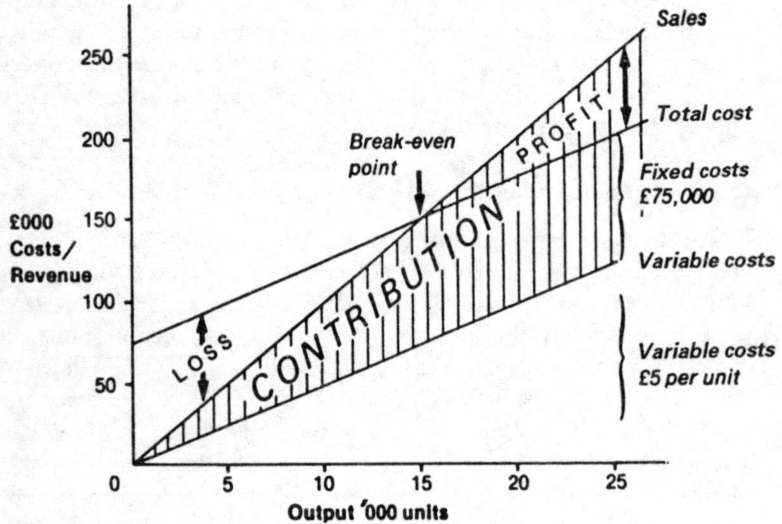

Figure 10.6 *Contribution break-even chart*

The profit and loss areas are still identifiable and break-even point remains the same. A most important use of the concept of contribution occurs when decisions have to be made concerning product profitability.

Example

Imet Ltd manufactures three products, A, B, and C, of which the first two have been making acceptable profits but C has been losing money for some time. The most recent results for last month are as follows:

Product	*A*	*B*	*C*	*Total*
	£000	*£000*	*£000*	*£000*
Sales	60	120	90	270
Less Total costs	42	99	93	234
Profit (loss)	18	21	(3)	36

The directors have considered a number of possible courses of future action but meanwhile have no new products available. Nor can they sell more of products A or B without dropping the selling price. The immediate decision is whether to drop product C and apparently save £3,000 per month.

On investigation by the accountant it is found that the total costs of the products includes £54,000 of fixed costs apportioned £12,000, £24,000, and £18,000 respectively. The fixed costs of £18,000 presently borne by product C will continue irrespective of whether that product is made or discontinued.

A more helpful analysis of the situation is to set out the contribution made by each product to the total fixed costs incurred by the firm and the overall profit achieved. This is shown in Figure 10.7.

Product	*A*	*B*	*C*	*Total*
	£000	*£000*	*£000*	*£000*
Sales	60	120	90	270
Less Variable costs	30	75	75	180
Contribution	30	45	15	90
Less Fixed costs				54
Profit				36

Figure 10.7 *Contribution analysis by products*

The directors of Imet Ltd can now conclude that it is better to continue selling product C for the moment because it is making a contribution of £15,000 towards fixed costs. If product C is discontinued the contributions from the remaining two products will not change, neither will the fixed costs incurred by the firm. Profit will therefore fall by £15,000 to only £21,000. So discontinuing product C immediately is not advisable.

Contribution ratio

Another use of the concept of contribution is when measuring the profitability of products. If the profitability is measured by expressing the net profit as a percentage of sales, product managers may argue about the unfairness of the apportionment of fixed costs to their own product. Because of the general nature of most fixed costs there is no direct link between them and individual products. One way around this endless debate is to express the contribution as a percentage of sales by calculating what is known as the profit/volume ratio or contribution ratio:

$$\text{Contribution ratio} = \frac{\text{Contribution}}{\text{Sales}} \%$$

Using the information in Figure 10.7 the contribution ratios for the three products are calculated as follows:

Product	*A*	*B*	*C*	*Total*
	£000	*£000*	*£000*	*£000*
Sales	60	120	90	270
Contribution	30	45	15	90
Contribution ratio	50%	37½%	16⅔%	33⅓%

Product C is seen to be the least profitable product on this basis.

Product mix

Sometimes firms need to know the particular mix of products which will make the best profit. This situation arises when there are capacity constraints which do not allow the firm to make all the products it can sell. The approach to this problem is to make those products which bring in the highest contribution per unit of scarce resource. Production is allocated to products in their descending order of profitability as measured by *'£ contribution per unit of scarce resource'*, be that space, skilled labour, raw materials, or any other scarce resource.

Example

A firm makes only three products and has no space to expand further. Its management want to know which products are the most profitable so they can plan their sales promotion activities accordingly. The following information is available:

Product	*A*	*B*	*C*	*Total*
	£000	*£000*	*£000*	*£000*
Sales	300	150	400	850
Less Direct labour	20	20	30	70
Direct materials	100	60	100	260
Variable overheads	30	10	30	70
Allocated fixed overheads	75	25	155	255
Total costs	225	115	315	655
Profit	75	35	85	195
Space occupied (sq m)	3,000	1,000	6,000	10,000

In this situation the scarce resource is space and, therefore, the firm should make the most profitable use of that space. This will be achieved by ranking products according to their contribution (not profit) per square metre.

The above information should therefore be presented in a marginal costing format to arrive at the contribution per square metre on each product as follows:

Product	*A*	*B*	*C*	*Total*
	£000	*£000*	*£000*	*£000*
Sales	300	150	400	850
Less Variable costs	150	90	160	400
Contribution	150	60	240	450
Contribution ratio	50%	40%	60%	53%
Space occupied (sq m)	3,000	1,000	6,000	10,000
Contribution per sq m	£50	£60	£40	£45

Normally, we would rank the three products in order of their contribution ratio, CAB. When we take account of space being a scarce resource, the contribution per square metre ranks the products in the different order, BAC. This firm should endeavour to switch production away from product C to product B, or failing that, from C to A.

Pricing

The previous chapter explained how firms can fix selling prices based on the total cost of a product plus the profit margin required to earn an acceptable rate of return on capital. An alternative approach is to set the profit/volume ratio required to recover total fixed costs and leave the required profit. For instance, a firm has fixed costs of £200,000 pa, a profit target of £50,000, and budgeted sales of £600,000. The total contribution required is £250,000 on sales of £600,000 which yields a contribution ratio of about 42%. Selling prices can now be set for individual products at a level which leaves a 42% contribution after the variable costs have been deducted. As with full cost pricing there is no guarantee that firms will be able to charge these prices but they do indicate the level of prices needed to achieve a particular return.

Another situation arises in a recession where firms are not able to obtain orders at reasonable prices. Intense competition for scarce orders may result in firms quoting prices which do not fully cover costs. Ship-repairing is sometimes a case in point, being a very cyclical industry. Some repair jobs are very quickly completed so in this situation the only significant variable costs are those for direct materials. Any price in excess of these variable costs will make a contribution towards fixed costs which, in this instance, will even include direct wages if the labour force are on a guaranteed week.

Obviously no firm can survive very long quoting prices below full cost, or obtaining work whose contribution does not recover fixed costs. In the short term, firms do price work on a less than full cost basis if the alternative is no work at all and even bigger losses!

Changes in volume of output

When calculating product costs on a full cost basis the fixed costs are apportioned over the budgeted volume of output at £X per unit. At higher or lower levels of output the fixed cost per unit is lower or higher respectively, even though fixed costs in total remain the same. It is therefore advisable, when considering changes in output, to leave fixed costs aside and use the contribution approach.

Let us take as an example M Ltd whose directors are considering a 10% reduction in the price of one of their products to increase market share. They wish to maintain profit at the present level by offsetting the volume gain against the price reduction. The present situation is as follows:

Sales of 10,000 units at £20 each	£200,000
Variable costs of £15 per unit	£150,000
Fixed costs	£40,000
Profit	£10,000
	£200,000

The increased volume of sales required at the now lower price of £18 can be calculated from the number of contributions per unit needed to make up the total contribution required:

Contribution per unit	=	selling price – variable cost
	=	£18 – £15
	=	£3
Total contribution required	=	Fixed costs + Profit target
	=	£40,000 + £10,000
	=	£50,000
Required volume of sales	=	$\frac{\text{Total contribution}}{\text{Contribution per unit}}$
	=	$\frac{£50{,}000}{£3}$
	=	16,667 units

Therefore to make the same total profit an increase of 67% in volume sales is needed to offset the proposed 10% price reduction.

Further reading

Management Accounting for Decision Makers, G Mott, Pitman.
Principles of Cost Accountancy, A Pizzey, Cassell.
Management and Cost Accounting, C Drury, Van Nostrand Reinhold.

Self-check questions

1 Draw a break-even chart to decide from which firm you would hire a car. Firm A charges £25 per day plus 14p per mile while firm B charges £18 per day plus 20p per mile.
2 Draw the break-even chart shown in Figure 10.3 and read off the amount of profit made when output equals 18,000 units.
3 Referring to the information in Figure 10.7, would you advise the directors of Imet Ltd to discontinue product C if they could use the same resources to produce 80% more of product A? (Assume same cost and selling price per unit.)
4 Your repair yard has been asked to tender for an immediate repair to a damaged ship, which will provide work for the next few weeks. The yard is short of work, with many workers idle, although being paid a guaranteed wage. You have heard that another firm has already tendered on the basis of direct costs only, without any contribution to overheads or profit. Will you still put in a bid? Give reasons for your answer.
5 A firm sells a product for £25 which has a variable cost of £14. Fixed overheads amount to £800,000 in total and the firm requires a return of 20% on the £1.5 million capital employed. How many products need to be sold?
6 A firm has sales of £200,000, £300,000, and £400,000 for its three product lines X, Y, and Z and variable costs of £100,000, £180,000, and £280,000 respectively. Due to a skilled labour shortage,

production will have to be cut back next month to the 650 hours that will be available. The three product lines currently consume 350, 350, and 300 hours respectively. Advise the firm on the most profitable product mix to adopt until full production can be restored.

11
Standard costing

Financial information does not always have to be looked at after the events have taken place. It can also be used in a forward planning context. Standard costing is an accounting technique used for the planning and control of costs. The standard cost of a product (or service) is the total cost of labour, materials, and overhead apportionment that should be incurred in the production process. When production takes place the actual costs of the batch are compared with the predetermined standard cost for that quantity. Inevitably differences, now called variances, will occur and these are examined for their causes in order to improve future performance. Figure 11.1 illustrates this sequence of events as a control cycle.

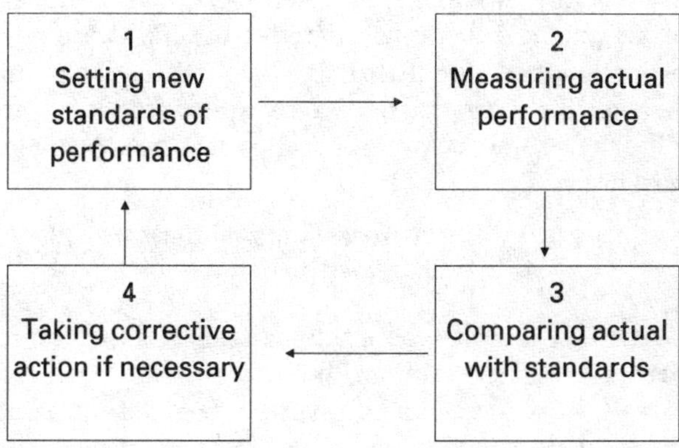

Figure 11.1 *The control cycle*

Firms use standard costing techniques for a variety of reasons. The actual setting-up of the standard cost specification involves determining the most suitable materials and methods of operation from the viewpoints of both firm and consumer. Once set, a standard becomes a yardstick against which performance can be measured. It also engenders cost consciousness in employees who know that costs are being monitored, and, it is hoped, acts as a motivator if the standards are realistically set. Top management can stand back from the day-to-day management which they can delegate and control by investigating only significant variances from standard. Finally, a standard cost is a firm base from which to price products.

Ratios

Before going into the detailed analysis of variances it is useful to look at some measures of company performance associated with the standard costing technique. Central to these measures is the concept of the 'standard hour' which represents the amount of work which can be done in one hour under standard conditions. The standard hour is a useful common denominator with which to aggregate different operations and different products. With this definition we can measure the operating efficiency of a firm by relating the standard hours equivalent of the work produced to the actual hours taken:

$$\text{Efficiency ratio} = \frac{\text{Standard hours}}{\text{Actual hours}} \times \frac{100}{1}\,\%$$

For example, last week a firm took 500 actual hours to produce goods equivalent to 450 standard hours. Its efficiency ratio for last week is therefore 90%, being adverse compared to the 100% target.

Another ratio is used to measure the level of activity as opposed to the above level of efficiency. The activity ratio relates the actual work produced to the budgeted work for that period, both being expressed in standard hours:

$$\text{Activity ratio} = \frac{\text{Actual standard hours}}{\text{Budgeted standard hours}} \times \frac{100}{1}\,\%$$

Taking the same example where actual standard hours were 450, let us assume the budgeted standard hours were 475. The activity ratio is therefore 94.7% which again is adverse when 100% is achievable.

A third ratio measures capacity usage by relating actual hours worked in a period to the budgeted standard hours:

$$\text{Capacity ratio} = \frac{\text{Actual hours}}{\text{Budgeted standard hours}} \times \frac{100}{1}\ \%$$

Using the same figures from the previous illustrations, when 500 actual hours are expressed as a percentage of 475 budgeted standard hours, the capacity ratio is 105.3%. This indicates a favourable variance achieved by somehow working more hours than planned.

Standard cost specification

When applying standard costing to any product the starting point is to specify quantities and grades of the labour and material elements and include an apportionment of budgeted overheads to arrive at total standard cost. The setting of labour and material standards involves determining the best layout, methods of operation, and most suitable materials which may lead to economies over previous practice. Management science plays a part here with the application of such techniques as method study, work measurement, value analysis, and value engineering. An example of a standard cost specification is given in Figure 11.2.

Product: A B Fittings		*Batch size:*	100 units	
	Quantity	*Unit price*	*Standard cost*	
Materials			£	£
Metal A	40kg	£2.50 per kg	100.00	
Packing cartons	1	25p	25	100.25
Labour				
Operator 1	8 hours	£3.00 per hour	24.00	
Operator 2	12 hours	£2.50 per hour	30.00	
Packer	1 hour	£2.20 per hour	2.20	56.20
Overheads (standard allowances)				
Variable overheads	21p per unit		21.00	
Fixed overheads	84p per unit		84.00	105.00
Total standard cost				261.45
Standard profit				28.55
Standard selling price				£290.00

Figure 11.2 *Standard cost specification*

Periodically, the actual costs of production are compared with the predetermined standard as laid down in the specification. Variances will be thrown out where the actual cost of some, or all, elements will differ from the standard cost for the quantity actually produced. These variances could be expressed as a + or a – representing an adverse or favourable result or the symbol letters A or F used instead. Variances are capable of further analysis, as we shall see, to identify their cause and allow management to take remedial action if necessary. In practice the specification and actual costs are all computerised so that no laborious calculations are required in multi-product firms.

Basically there are only two main types of variance – those relating to resource prices and those relating to volume. Referring back to Figure 11.2 let us assume a batch of 100 fittings was made recently using 45kg of metal which had just been purchased for £2.30 per kg. The total material cost variance for metal is the difference between the actual cost and standard cost:

Actual cost		Standard cost		Material cost variance
45kg × £2.30 = £103.50	–	40kg × £2.50 = £100	=	£3.50 (A)

This £3.50 variance results from two causes and not just one. On the one hand extra costs are incurred through using 5kg more metal than specified, resulting in a material usage variance of 5kg × £2.50 = £12.50 (A). On the other hand the firm bought the metal more cheaply than it expected and thus saved 20p × 45kg = £9 (F) which is the material price variance. To summarise:

Total material cost variance		£3.50(A)
Material usage variance	£12.50(A)	
Material price variance	£9.00(F)	£3.50(A)

Variances for other costs and sales can be similarly divided into two main types and the full list is shown in Figure 11.3.

Price variances	*Volume variances*
Material price variance	Material usage variance
Labour rate variance	Labour efficiency variance
Variable overhead expenditure variance	—
Fixed overhead expenditure variance	Fixed overhead volume variance
Sales price variance	Sales volume variance

Figure 11.3 *Price and volume variances*

Before looking at a more comprehensive example it is necessary to define each variance carefully and explain it in more general terms.

Material

Material price variance represents the difference in purchase cost caused by a variation in the unit price of the material. It is calculated from the difference between the actual and standard price per unit of material multiplied by the actual quantity purchased.

Formula: (AP–SP) AQ

Material usage variance represents the difference in the cost of material used caused by more or less efficient use of that material. It is calculated from the difference between the actual and standard quantity used evaluated at the standard price. In some situations it is possible to analyse this further into mix and yield variances. (Note that any variation from the standard price is contained in the price variance itself.)

Formula: (AQ–SQ)SP

Labour

Labour rate variance represents the difference in labour cost caused by any variation from normal rates of pay. It is calculated from the difference between the actual and standard rate per hour multiplied by the actual number of hours paid. Formula: same as material price variance, the rate per hour being the price of labour.

Labour efficiency variance represents the difference in labour cost caused by the degree of efficiency in the use of labour compared with the specified standard. It is calculated from the difference between the actual hours taken and the standard hours allowed evaluated at the standard rate per hour. Formula: same as material usage variance, ie (AQ–SQ)SP.

Variable overheads

These are overheads whose total cost varies pro rata with the level of production, as opposed to fixed overheads whose total cost does not vary with the production level.

Variable overhead expenditure variance represents the difference between the actual cost and the total amount recovered at the standard rate per unit of output. It is calculated from the difference between actual variable overheads and the quantity of output multiplied by the standard recovery rate per unit. (Note that when variable overheads are recovered on a labour basis, as opposed to a product basis, then a variable overhead efficiency variance can arise.)

Formula: AC – (AQ × SR)

Fixed overheads

Fixed overhead expenditure variance represents the difference between the actual cost and the estimated or budgeted cost.

Formula: AC–BC

Fixed overhead volume variance represents the under- or overrecovery of fixed overheads caused by the actual volume of production being different from the budgeted volume on which the recovery rate is based. It is calculated from the difference between actual and budgeted volume multiplied by the standard recovery rate per unit.

Formula: (AQ–BQ) SR

Sales

Sales price variance represents the profit lost or gained by selling at a non-standard price. It is calculated from the difference between actual and standard selling price multiplied by the actual quantity sold.

Formula: (AP–SP) AQ

Sales volume variance represents the profit margins on the difference between actual sales and budgeted sales. It is calculated from the standard profit margin multiplied by the difference between actual sales volume and budgeted sales volume.

Formula: (AQ–BQ)standard profit

A note of caution should be sounded here. It should not be assumed that all standard costing systems will use the same basis as that shown above. In certain industries using chemicals, the material cost variances are capable of further analysis, as are labour and overhead variances in many other industries. The basis of overhead recovery can also influence the precise method of overhead variance calculation. It is also possible to base a standard costing system on marginal costing principles as briefly outlined at the end of this chapter. Notwithstanding these exceptions, the above analysis of variances provides a very good grounding for most practical systems. A brief example is now taken to demonstrate the calculation of basic material and labour variances.

Example
The standard cost of an article comprises:

Material X	2 kg per article at £5 per kg
Labour	6 hours per article at £3.50 per hour

Last week 400 articles were produced and the actual costs were:

Material X	850 kg at £4.50 per kg
Labour	2,300 hours at £3.50 per hour

From this information we can calculate the material cost variance and the labour cost variance together with their respective price and volume variances:

Actual cost	–	Standard cost	=	Material cost variance
850 × £4.50 = £3,825		2 × 400 × £5 = £4,000		£175 (F)
Material price variance	=	(AP – SP) AQ		
		(£4.50 – £5) 850 = £425 (F)		
Material usage variance	=	(AQ – SQ) SP		£175(F)
		(850 – 800) £5 = £250 (A)		

The saving of £175 in material costs has two causes. Material X was bought more cheaply than standard, thus saving £425. Possibly because the cheap material was substandard, excessive waste occurred costing £250. Overall the company saved £175; therefore the precise reasons are worth investigating with the purchasing officer and production supervisor respectively.

Actual labour cost	–	Standard labour cost	=	Labour cost variance
2,300 × £3.50 = £8,050		6 × 400 × £3.50 = £8,400		£350 (F)
Labour rate variance	=	(AP – SP) AQ		
		(£3.50 – £3.50) 2,300 = £NIL		
Labour efficiency variance	=	(AQ – SQ) SP		£350(F)
		(2,300 – 2,400) £3.50 = £350 (F)		

There is no rate variance, so the saving in labour cost of £350 is all due to the workforce being more efficient than the standard set. Again this is worth investigation with production supervisors to see if lessons can be learned for future occasions.

The ratios and variances mentioned rely on the preparation of budgets detailing planned levels of output, costs, and income. This also means that a firm operating a system of standard costing should be able to predict the profit that it will make in a future period from its trading operations. The actual profit it makes will be the same as the budgeted profit if there are no sales or cost variances. Any adverse variances will reduce the actual profit relative to that budgeted, while favourable variances will enhance the actual profit. A profit and loss account can be prepared on standard costing lines. This does not show the absolute values of income and expenditure, but the detailed variances which affect the budgeted profit and reconcile it with the actual profit. A more comprehensive example now follows to illustrate this approach.

Example
Carr Chemicals Ltd are a one-product firm. The company uses a standard costing system and prepared the following budget for last week which was expected to result in a profit of £7,000:

Budget for one week

	£	Units	£
Sales at £3 per unit		10,000	30,000
Direct materials			
10,000 kilos at 50p per kilo	5,000		
Direct labour			
5,000 hours at £2.40 per hour	12,000		
Variable overheads			
10,000 units at 25p each unit	2,500		
Fixed overheads			
£3,500 per week (35p each unit)	3,500		
Total cost of sales		10,000	23,000
Budgeted profit at 70p per unit			£7,000

Unfortunately they did not sell as many products as they had planned, as the actual results show, but yet a greater profit was achieved.

Actual result for one week

	£	Units	£
Sales at £3.10 per unit		9,000	27,900
Direct materials			
9,500 kilos at 45p per kilo	4,275		
Direct labour			
4,500 hours at £2.45 per hour	11,025		
Variable overhead	2,000		
Fixed overhead	3,250		
Total cost of sales		9,000	20,550
Actual profit			£7,350

We can now draw up a statement reconciling the actual profit with the budgeted profit by detailing the adverse or favourable variances for the week. This shows how the extra profit is achieved:

Profit and loss account for the week	£	£	£
Budgeted profit			7,000
Variances:	(F)	(A)	
Sales price variance (£3.10–£3.00)9,000	900		
Sales quantity variance (9,000–10,000)70p		700	
Material price variance (45p–50p)9,500	475		
Material usage variance (9,500–9,000)50p		250	
Labour rate variance (£2.45–£2.40)4,500		225	
Labour efficiency variance (4,500–4,500)£2.40	—	—	
Variable O/H expenditure variance 2,000–(9,000 × 25p)	250		
Fixed O/H expenditure variance (£3,250–£3,500)	250		
Fixed O/H volume variance (9,000–10,000)35p		350	
	£1,875	£1,525	350(F)
Actual profit			£7,350

(Note that the standard quantities used in the labour efficiency, material usage, and variable overhead expenditure variances are based on the actual production level of 9,000 units.)

Standard marginal costing

It is possible to use a marginal costing approach to standard costing when a standard contribution is determined instead of the standard profit used in a full cost system. The contribution price variance will be identical with the sales price variance representing the profit lost or gained by selling at a non-standard price. Where the two systems differ is that the sales and fixed overhead volume variances are replaced by one contribution volume variance, being the contributions lost or gained on the difference between budgeted volume and the actual volume of activity.

Inflation

The standard cost specification should be based on current prices of the relevant costs. This may lead to periodic revisions of the standard cost and selling price.

Further reading

Management Accounting for Decision Makers, G Mott, Pitman.
Management and Cost Accounting, C Drury, Van Nostrand Reinhold.
Costing, T Lucey, DPP.
Principles of Cost Accountancy, A Pizzey, Cassell.

Self-check questions

1 What is a standard hour?

2 Define the activity ratio.

3 Name some management techniques which may be used when setting a standard cost specification.

4 Variances are either favourable or ...?

5 Define and give the formula for the labour efficiency variance.

6 The standard cost specification for a product is as follows:

Selling price		£31
Less Factory costs		
Direct material – 12 kg at 50p	£6	
Direct labour – 4 hours at £3	£12	
Variable overhead per product	£2	
Fixed overhead per product	£5	
		£25
Standard profit per product		£6

A firm budgeted to produce and sell 1,100 products last week. Actual production and sales was only 900 and other information is as follows:

Selling price – £32
Direct material – 12,600 kg at 55p
Direct labour – 3,200 hours at £3
Variable overheads £2,100
Fixed overheads £5,700

Produce a statement reconciling the budgeted profit with the actual profit by disclosing all possible variances.

7 The standard material cost of fabric specified for a particular garment is £4.50, comprising three metres at £1.50 per metre. Last week, 1,000 garments were made using 3,200 metres of fabric bought in at £1.40 per metre. Calculate the total material cost variance and analyse further into the material price variance and material usage variance.

12
Budgetary control

There are many similarities between a system of budgetary control and the standard costing technique discussed in an earlier chapter. They are both concerned with planning and control involving the setting of targets and the later comparison with actual results. Differences, hereafter called variances, arising from such comparisons are identified so that corrective action can be taken as required.

Much detailed preparatory work is common to both budgetary control and standard costing as they are both concerned with detailed costs and revenues. Where the two systems differ is in the unit of application. A standard cost specifies the selling price and cost of a product while a budget is prepared for a function or a department. Standard costs are not based on departments because the standard overhead recovery includes costs from all departments, even when the direct costs are incurred in only one department. Budgets and budgetary control are applicable in all organisations, whether manufacturing or service industries, whether profit seeking or not.

Purpose

The main purpose of budgetary control is to plan and control the firm's activities. Corporate and strategic planning are concerned with the long-term broad objectives of the firm. Budgetary control, however, is an expression of financial plans to meet objectives in the coming accounting year. These short-term objectives may be to earn X% return on capital or achieve a certain level of turnover or market share. In some organisations the objective may simply be not to overspend, ie to keep spending within a grant or other budget allocation. Although budgets are plans for action in the very near future they must be compatible with what the firm is trying to achieve in the longer term.

Using this system senior management can delegate responsibility to departmental managers and so concentrate solely on deviations from plans without getting overwhelmed by day-to-day activities that are running smoothly. They are therefore practising the principle of management by exception.

Preparation of budgets

Top management should specify broad objectives to a budget committee comprising representatives of both directors and functional managers. The committee then interprets these objectives into outline plans for each departmental head who in turn submit their detailed proposals. This process may continue a number of times to get the necessary integration and coordination of the individual budget proposals.

Essentially, this is a 'bottom-up' approach with managers retaining ownership of their budgets, as opposed to imposed or 'top-down' budgets, where ownership and some motivation is lost.

When finally accepted by the budget committee, the functional budgets are aggregated into a master budget. This consists of a budgeted profit and loss account for the year, broken down into months, and a projected balance sheet at the year end. If approved by the board this becomes the policy to be pursued for the coming year.

In many firms this procedure, outlined in Figure 12.1, is assisted by an accountant or budget officer, who provides information and

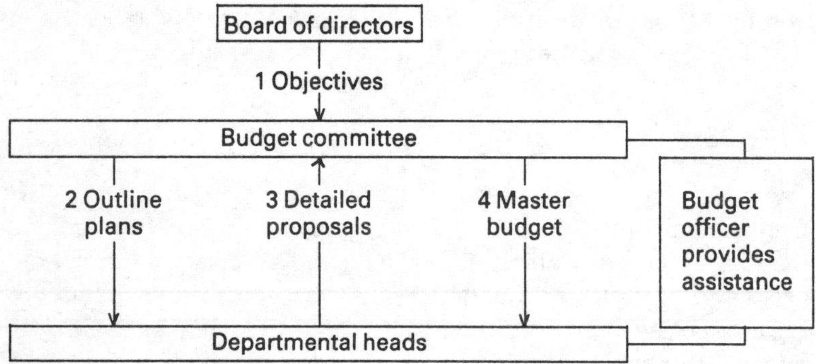

Figure 12.1 *Budget preparation*

advice to all concerned. Very small firms may not need a formal committee structure but would do well to set plans down on paper to integrate the functions and see the overall effects in terms of profit and capital requirements.

Incremental or zero-based budgets?

Thought must also be given when setting budgets whether to base them on previous years' experience or start afresh with a clean sheet. The former approach is referred to as incremental budgeting. Last years' figures are taken as a base and then adjusted for expected changes in prices, costs, and activity levels. A frequent criticism of this approach is that it does not encourage fresh thinking and may perpetuate existing inefficiencies.

A more recent approach is to start with a clean sheet – a zero base. This ignores previous experience and requires a manager to justify all the resource requirements expressed as costs in his or her budget. Each item of expense is therefore questioned, first, as to whether it should exist at all, and only then, as to its precise level.

Zero-base philosophy may be restricted to certain administrative functions where it is particularly relevant in questioning redundant clerical procedures. It is, however, applicable in all functional areas. A major objection may be the time and effort needed to run a zero-based system compared to the quicker incremental budgeting approach. For this reason, some organisations require a zero-based budget from each department every few years, using an incremental approach in the intervening years. In this way only some departmental budgets are given the closest of scrutinies in any one year.

Identification of key factor

The starting point with budgeting is to identify the key factor which limits the firm's growth at this moment in time. In many firms this key factor will be sales volume but it could be a shortage of space, machinery, or materials. In many organisations, money itself will be the limiting factor, as is the case with local authorities and other grant-funded bodies.

Assuming sales is the key or limiting factor for a firm, this places the major responsibility for budgeting on the shoulders of the sales manager or director. The sales team will have to consider the present level of business, anticipate future trading conditions, obtain feedback from sales representatives and market research to come up with a sales budget. This budget is not just one total sales figure for the coming year but must be analysed by customers, by markets, by sales area, and by months.

Having specified sales the production budget comes next. The level of production must equate with budgeted sales except when stock levels change. Where stocks are not required, or are kept at a constant level, production and sales volumes will be identical.

Therefore the starting point for budgeting production is the sales budget after taking into account possible changes in stock levels or the use of subcontractors. Production levels must fall within existing capacity as otherwise production would have been identified as the key or limiting factor rather than sales. The production budget specifies the products to be made, when production is to take place, which departments are to be used and the cost of labour, materials, and machine time consumed.

Departmental overhead budgets are then prepared based on the level of service needed to allow the sales and production functions to meet their budgets. The production department overheads will be geared to the production levels specified for those departments. Similarly, the selling and distribution costs will be geared to the level of the sales budget while the various administrative departments' budgets will be determined by the overall level of activity. Research and development also has a budget but this is more a long-term investment of funds not closely related to short-term needs and is very similar to the capital budget mentioned below.

In this way the various functional and departmental budgets are prepared which facilitate the composition of subordinate budgets for material purchases and manpower planning. The functional budgets form the basis for a master budget in the form of a budgeted profit and loss account and projected balance sheet. It is this master budget which goes to the board for approval and, if not satisfactory, the marketing/production mix must be thought through again.

There are two other budgets which it is necessary for accountants to prepare using their professional skills and applying them to the vast store of financial information prepared in the budgeting process. First, the cash budget quite literally is a monthly budget of cash inflows and outflows which are expected to arise from the plans expressed in the functional budgets. Details of its preparation and uses are contained in the later chapter on the control of working capital.

Second, a capital budget is a collation of planned capital expenditures on both replacement and new assets. It is partly influenced by

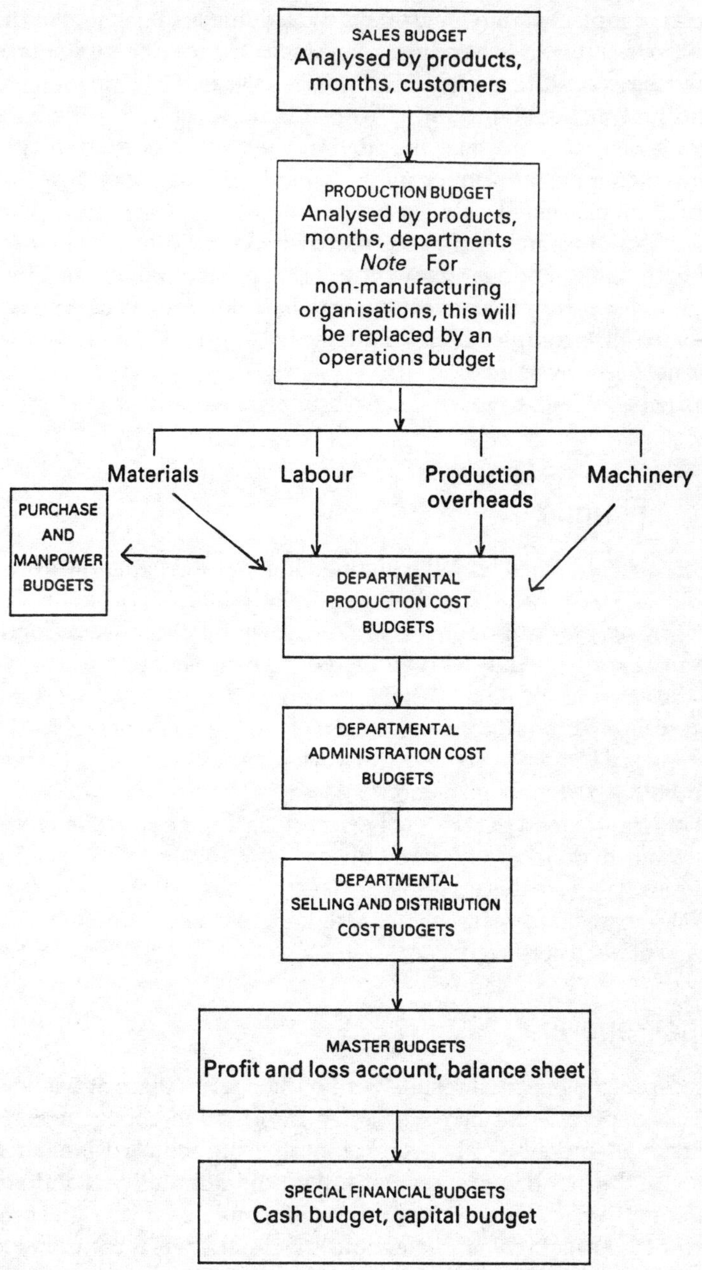

Figure 12.2 *The budgeting process*

the need to replace or buy new assets to facilitate achievement of the coming year's functional budgets. Also included may be capital projects whose expenditure started in a previous year. The total planned expenditure must be within the firm's financial capacity otherwise the available capital must be allocated to the most important categories and most profitable investments. Chapter 14 describes how this profitability is assessed.

Once projects have been approved their progress must be monitored in the capital budget reports by comparing actual costs against those budgeted for the proportion of the work completed. An estimate of 'costs to completion' is also included to give early warning of anticipated cost overruns.

A schematic diagram of the budgeting process is shown in Figure 12.2.

Budget periods

Budgets are concerned with the planned income and expenditure for the coming year. The accounting year is the natural choice for the budgeting process, although it is broken down into months for regular comparison of actual with budgeted figures. These months may be of the calendar or lunar variety, or some other constant working period to avoid distorted comparisons due to the incidence of works and statutory holidays. Some firms work on a rolling year, adding a new month's budget as each month passes.

Other firms extend the budget horizon by asking for detailed forecasts of out-turn up to two years ahead, with looser forecasts for a further few years. In this way, top management start to build a picture of what the next five years' results will look like and can adjust their strategic plans accordingly.

Budget reports

The comparison of actual results with budget takes place at two levels. Each departmental manager is fed information about the costs (and income) under his or her control, comparing actual costs against budget for the month under review and for the cumulative months of the accounting year so far expired. An example of this is given in Figure 12.3. Sometimes a distinction is made between controllable costs and costs reallocated to a department although not wholly within the manager's control.

A line and subtotal may be drawn after controllable costs are listed. This indicates to the manager concerned achievement against budget for items he or she has both responsibility for and authority over. If other overheads are then listed over which the manager has responsibility but no authority, care must be exercised in how this information is used to monitor that manager's performance.

Month..Dept..							
Cost code	*Description*	*Current month*			*Cumulative*		
		Budget	*Actual*	*Variance*	*Budget*	*Actual*	*Variance*
	Controllable	£	£	£	£	£	£
320	Salaries etc.	3,600	3,400	200 F	23,000	24,300	1,300 A
	Non-controllable						
710	HO charges etc.	1,000	1,100	100 A	7,000	7,700	700 A

Figure 12.3 *Monthly budget report*

At a higher level in the organisation the budgeted profit and loss account is compared with the actual results achieved and reported to the board of directors. When a firm uses a standard costing system the list of variances will link the budgeted profit with the actual profit achieved in the month. Where standard costing is inappropriate to the firm's products, the monthly profit and loss account will compare budgeted costs and revenues with the actual costs and revenues respectively, to disclose the variances.

Very small firms will tend to use the approach of comparing budget and actual profit and loss account items although there is no reason why they should not use standard costing where standardised products are concerned. This is particularly true now that computers are so widely available for such routine tasks.

Packages are available, or dedicated software can be written to produce monthly budget reports for each department which integrates with the total financial results. Much budgeting work can now be performed on standard spread sheets, such as Lotus 1-2-3 without having to go to additional expense.

Significance

There is no point in drawing trivial variances to the attention of departmental managers or directors. Limits may be set as to what counts as a significant variance, being either a percentage of the budgeted figure and/or a certain sum of money. In this way time is not wasted on insignificant events and explanations are only required when a variance is deemed to be important.

Behavioural implications

Motivation to achieve targets is a key feature of budgetary control. This is why ownership of a budget by the budget holder is most important, and is not forthcoming when budgets are imposed from on high without consultation.

Human nature, being what it is, may lead managers to 'pad' their budgets or leave in 'budget slack' so that budget variances are always favourable. Therefore, budgets must be realistic targets to aim at, being neither too optimistic to please the boss, nor too tight to be attainable.

Although run by accountants because of their access to the information required, budgets should not be seen as an accountant's tool. Budgetary control is a management tool and its motivating appeal will be diminished if it does not have the support of the chief executive and fellow directors.

Budget reports must be timely and contain information relevant to the recipient. If too much time elapses after the period end before issuing a budget report, then interest in, and explanation of, variances will suffer. A frequent reason given for delays is 'waiting for invoices'. This can be overcome by getting managers to 'accrue' expenditure for which no invoice has been received or to adopt a formal system of 'commitment accounting'.

Inflation

Budgets should be prepared on the basis of estimated costs and income over the period, including the size and timing of the anticipated rates of inflation on the various constituents. Should inflation have unforeseen consequences or occur at totally unexpected rates it may be necessary to revise the original budget at a later date. Such action will be a rare event as frequent budget revisions ensure that targets are met!

Flexible budgeting

The system of budgeting described above is based on fixed budgets which remain unchanged irrespective of the actual level of activity achieved. If the actual level is significantly different from the budgeted level there will be significant 'volume' variances. When standard costing is used, the difference in profit caused by the different level of activity is particularly quantified in the sales volume and fixed overhead volume variances.

In the absence of a standard costing system the solution to the problem of variable levels of activity lies in the use of a flexible budget. This is defined by the Chartered Institute of Management Accountants as a 'budget which is designed to change in accordance with the level of activity attained'. Essentially the flexible budget consists of not one budget, but a series of budgets, each being based on a different level of activity within the expected range. For example, if a firm never expects activity to fall below 70% it can prepare four budgets of income and expenditure at 70%, 80%, 90%, and 100% levels of the maximum capacity. Should the actual level turn out to be, say, 83%, then the budget for that level can be derived by interpolating the 80% and 90% budgets. Comparison of actual results can then be made with the budget for the same level of activity. The resulting variances are of a controllable nature as the change in volume has been eliminated.

Flexible budgeting obviously entails the analysis of costs into fixed and variable categories to forecast expenditure at different levels of activity. This is not the same analysis as indirect and direct costs because some indirects vary with the level of activity and some directs, possibly wages, are fixed.

The example in Figure 12.4 contrasts the variances arising under a fixed budget system with those obtaining in a flexible budget system. Under the fixed budget system, variances arising from a drop in the level of activity appear as favourable variances. When the budget is 'flexed' to the actual level of activity, actual costs are compared with budgeted costs for the same level of activity. The variances resulting from this comparison are of a controllable nature because, by very definition, a flexible budget obviates volume or uncontrollable variances.

Firms may use a mixture of fixed and flexible budgets for different departments. Essentially, the choice is that of fixed budgets fully integrated with a standard costing system to disclose volume variances or flexible budgets where standard costing is inappropriate.

1. Illustration of a fixed budget report

Activity	*Fixed budget for month* *100%*	*Actual results for month* *85%*	*Variances* *15% (A)*
	£	£	£
Direct labour	33,000	31,000	2,000 (F)
Direct materials	27,000	23,700	3,300 (F)
Overheads	36,000	34,100	1,900 (F)
Total	£96,000	£88,800	£7,200 (F)

2. Flexible budget for the same month

Activity	*70%*	*80%*	*90%*	*100%*
	£	£	£	£
Direct labour	27,000	29,000	31,000	33,000
Direct materials	18,900	21,600	24,300	27,000
Variable overheads	10,500	12,000	13,500	15,000
Fixed overheads	21,000	21,000	21,000	21,000
Total	£77,400	£83,600	£89,800	£96,000

3. Flexible budget report for the same month

	Flexed budget *85%*	*Actual results* *85%*	*Variances* —
	£	£	£
Direct labour	30,000	31,000	1,000(A)
Direct materials	22,950	23,700	750(A)
Variable overheads	12,750	12,600	150(F)
Fixed overheads	21,000	21,500	500(A)
Total	£86,700	£88,800	£2,100(A)

Figure 12.4 *Comparison of fixed and flexible budget systems*

Planning, programming, and budgeting systems (PPBS)

This form of budgeting applies to public service organisations, such as local authorities and hospitals. These organisations will run short-term departmentally based budgeting systems to control expenditure within a financial year, in the same way as profit-seeking enterprises.

PPBS, however, differs from ordinary budgeting. First, it plans further than just one year ahead. Second, it transcends departments. PPBS is about how resources are going to be allocated to achieve the various objectives of the organisation, for example, the care of the elderly. Once the objectives have been established, programmes are identified to meet those objectives and the costs/benefits of alternative programmes are assessed.

The chosen programmes form, in effect, a long-term plan to be pursued over a number of years. Each programme budget will disclose the cost of providing a service to satisfy an objective, broken down into time periods. It therefore informs management in a manner allowing them to make judgements about such effectiveness, that would not be possible if programmes were fragmented in the departmental budgets concerned.

Further reading

Management and Cost Accounting, C Drury, Van Nostrand Reinhold.
Management Accounting for Decision Makers, G Mott, Pitman.
Principles of Cost Accountancy, A Pizzey, Cassell.

Self-check questions

1 What is a key or limiting factor in budgeting?
2 What factors would you consider when fixing the sales budget for the coming year?
3 What is a cash budget?
4 What is a flexible budget?
5 What have budgetary control and standard costing systems got in common?
6 A firm has 350 kg of a raw material in stock at the beginning of a budget period. Production will use 10,000 kg of the material during the period and the firm wants the stock level to increase to 750 kg at the end of that time. What quantity must be purchased?
7 How does PPBS differ from budgetary control?

Part 3

Financial management

The way in which a company finances its assets has an effect on the return on owners' capital and the overall cost of capital. Gearing up the capital structure together with tax allowances on interest payments can enhance the return on shareholders' funds but carry risks if taken too far. Many companies, including some household names, went bust in the 1989–92 recession as a result of overgearing.

Capital is invested either in fixed assets or in working capital. This part of the book examines the techniques of investment appraisal which assist in the decision of whether, when, and where to deploy scarce resources. Some research findings on the appraisal methods actually used by firms are also briefly discussed. The management of stocks, debtors, and cash which make up working capital is also explored, together with such new developments as MRP, JIT, and factoring.

Both the raising of capital and its use affect the share price of a private-sector company through the impact on reported profit. Different ways of valuing company shares are discussed before examining their role in merger/takeover situations, and the growing interest in MBOs.

Finally, the taxation of business profits is outlined under the system of corporation tax for limited companies and income tax for self-employed persons. The UK is a predominant trader with other countries and the accounting peculiarities of overseas, as opposed to home, trade are reviewed.

13
The cost of capital

Capital is not free. The owners of firms and financial institutions require a return on their investment in the company. In turn the company must earn a return on assets at least equal to this cost of capital. To do otherwise will not satisfy the providers of that capital and will make the raising of future capital more difficult, if not impossible.

Firms need to set a minimum required rate of return against which the profitability of proposed new investments is measured. This required rate must at least be equal to the cost of the different types of capital used in the business.

There are two main sources of new capital for new investments. Firms can either borrow the money, usually from a financial institution, or they can obtain it from the owners. In this latter case new equity capital can be obtained in one of two ways. Companies occasionally sell new shares to existing shareholders on a 'rights' issue. This may be unpopular as it tends to depress the existing share price on the Stock Exchange. The other way companies obtain new capital from the owners is by not paying out all the profits earned as dividends. By this means companies are assured of the extra capital they need and they save the expense of issuing new shares.

Most firms use a mix of borrowed and owners' capital and the relationship between the two is known as 'capital gearing'. A company is said to be highly geared when it has a large amount of borrowed capital relative to owners' capital. It is lowly geared when the proportion of borrowed capital is small. Strictly speaking gearing is the use of any prior charge capital including preference shares. The relationship between these two sources of capital is also expressed by

	(a) *Low gearing*	*(b)* *High gearing*
Owners' capital (share capital + retained profits)	90%	50%
Borrowed capital	10%	50%
Total capital	100%	100%

Figure 13.1 *Example of high and low capital gearing*

calculating each source as a proportion of the total capital. The two situations in Figure 13.1 illustrate different levels of gearing.

There is no one particular level of capital gearing that is regarded as satisfactory for all companies. Each firm is examined on its past record, future prospects, and the security of the interest and capital repayments. In most industries the 50% borrowed capital indicated in Figure 13.1(b) would be regarded as very high, although much higher rates are not uncommon in the rather special case of property development. Even here, after the slump in property in the early 1990s, financial institutions may be more wary in future of lending too high a proportion of development capital.

It is possible to find examples of companies with no borrowed capital, resulting from a policy decision by management to finance growth internally from retained profits. Such companies eliminate the risks of defaulting on the loan or interest repayments, or having to reduce dividends to make interest payments when profits fall. On the other hand they miss the opportunity of increasing the return to ordinary shareholders by investing borrowed capital to earn more than the cost of the interest, as Figure 13.2 shows.

When a company has no gearing the change in the profit results in the same proportionate change in the return on shareholders' funds. In the *nil* gearing example, doubled profits also double the return to the owners from 10% to 20%. The doubling of the same profit in the high gearing example more than doubles the return on ordinary shareholders' funds from 12% to 29%.

Most firms decide that a judicious amount of borrowed capital is beneficial and try to adhere to a target level of gearing over the years. It may be that in any one year the target is exceeded because conditions in the capital markets do not allow a particular kind of funding to take place. This can be redressed as soon as market conditions allow.

New projects must be financed by new capital, as opposed to existing capital which has already been spent on existing projects. We therefore need to look at the cost and the mix of new capital to calcu-

	Nil gearing	*High gearing*
	£000	*£000*
Capital structures		
Ordinary shares of £1	2,900	1,400
Retained profits	1,000	1,000
10% loan stock	—	1,500
	3,900	3,900
Profit of £600,000:		
Profit	600	600
Interest	—	150
	600	450
Corporation tax at 33%	200	150
Earned for ordinary shareholders	400	300
Return on ordinary shareholders' funds	10.25%	12.5%
Profit of £1,200,000:		
Profit	1,200	1,200
Interest	—	150
	1,200	1,050
Corporation tax at 33%	400	350
Earned for ordinary shareholders	800	700
Return on ordinary shareholders' funds	20.5%	29.2%

Figure 13.2 *Illustration of the effects of capital gearing*

late the minimum required rate of return on new investments. Also we must bear in mind the effects of taxation and inflation on each type of capital as they differ in certain respects. We will first examine the cost of borrowed capital, then the cost of equity, and weight the different proportions to get an overall cost.

The cost of borrowed capital

The rate of interest which has to be paid on new loans to get them taken up by investors at par can be regarded as the cost of borrowed capital. Such rates of interest vary over time in sympathy with interest rates obtainable on alternative investments. They also vary slightly according to the size of the loan and the degree of risk attached to the particular firm.

An alternative approach can be used to find the current cost of borrowing for a firm which has existing quoted loans or debentures. If the fixed rate of interest on such loans is less than the current going rate, these securities will have a market price of less than the par value of the stock. This means investors will obtain an annual return from the interest payments and a capital gain on the eventual repayment of the stock at par.

Suppose X Ltd has a 10% loan stock standing at £83 per £100 nominal value, repayable at par in five years' time. An investor today is therefore willing to pay £83 for the right to receive £10 yearly interest for the next five years and his or her £100 back at the end of that time. We can approach this in the way we calculate the discounted cash flow (DCF) yield on industrial investments as explained in the next chapter. Figure 13.3 shows this to be 15%.

Year	*Cash flow*	*PV factors at 15%*	*PV*
	£		£
0	–83	1.000	–83.00
1	+10	.870	+8.70
2	+10	.756	+7.56
3	+10	.658	+6.58
4	+10	.572	+5.72
5	+110	.497	+54.67
			+£0.23

Figure 13.3 *Calculation of the DCF yield on the investment of £83 in £100 of 10% loan stock repayable in five years' time*

The DCF yield of 15% obtained by an investor buying the company's existing loan stock can be regarded as the current cost of interest on new loans issued at par. It represents the money or nominal cost of new loans, which is used to calculate the target rate of return in nominal terms. The real cost of loan capital will be significantly less as investors are not compensated for the fall in the value of their capital. This is the reason for the 'gearing adjustment' in the inflation-adjusted profit and loss account. In the 1970s this real cost of loan capital was negative after allowing for both inflation and the tax relief next mentioned.

In the later 1980s and the early 1990s, the real cost of capital turned positive again, due to high interest rates relative to low inflation rates. A 10% base rate, for example, coupled with a 4% inflation rate equates to a 6% real cost of borrowing for firms with the best credit rating. Very small firms could expect to pay another 3–5 points.

Interest on loans, debentures, and overdrafts is deductible from profits before calculating the corporation tax charge, whereas dividends are not. In effect tax relief is granted on interest payments which, with corporation tax at 33%, reduces the rate of interest by about one third. Figure 13.4 illustrates this point.

	Company A (no gearing)	Company B (50%) gearing
Shareholders' funds	£10m	£5m
10% loan	—	£5m
Total capital employed	£10m	£10m
Profit before tax and interest	£2,000,000	£2,000,000
Interest on loan	—	£500,000
Profit after interest	£2,000,000	£1,500,000
Corporation tax at 33%	£660,000	£495,000
Tax saved	£165,000	

Figure 13.4 *Illustration of tax relief on interest payments*

It can be seen that two companies with identical total capitals and annual profits do not pay the same tax charge. Company B which financed half of its capital requirement from a 10% loan saves £165,000 of the £500,000 interest cost through tax relief. The effective rate of interest on the loan is therefore only 6.7% $\left(\frac{\text{£0.335m}}{\text{£5.000m}} \times \frac{100}{1}\%\right)$. It is not surprising that firms find gearing attractive when they compare the after-tax cost of loans with the cost of equity capital!

The cost of equity capital

The equity of a company is its risk capital, embracing ordinary share capital and retained profits which can be regarded as having the same cost. Companies retain profits to short-circuit paying out all profits with one hand while asking shareholders to buy new shares with the other. There is clearly a saving in administrative costs and professional fees by retaining profits, so this alternative will be slightly cheaper in practice.

Put simply, the cost of equity is the return shareholders expect the company to earn on their money. It is their estimation, often not scientifically calculated, of the rate of return which will be obtained both from future dividends and an increased share value. Unfortunately, simple concepts are not always so easy to apply in practice and the cost of capital is a favourite battlefield for academics with no one agreed practical solution.

It is possible to calculate the cost of equity as the DCF yield achieved from the estimated future dividends and the increased share value at a future point of time. This corresponds to the approach used to calculate the cost of borrowed capital in Figure 13.3. An alternative approach is to take the current dividend yield for a company and add the expected annual growth. For example, Graham Ltd currently pay a net dividend of 10p on each ordinary share which is quoted at £2 on the Stock Exchange. Growth of profits and dividends has averaged 15% over the last few years. The cost of equity for Graham Ltd can be calculated as:

$$\text{Cost of equity capital} = \frac{\text{Current net dividend}}{\text{Current market price}}\% + \text{Growth rate }\%$$

$$= \left(\frac{10\text{p}}{£2} \times \frac{100}{1}\%\right) + 15\%$$

$$= 20\%$$

With this method, dividends are assumed to grow in the future at the constant rate achieved by averaging the last few years' performance. This growth is best calculated from profits after tax, rather than dividends, as changes in company dividend policy or government controls over dividend payments can distort short-term trends. No residual share price is included as it is assumed that dividend payments continue to perpetuity. The 20% cost of equity capital above is a nominal rate rather than a real rate of return to investors. It is an after-tax return as dividends are paid from taxed profits, unlike interest payments which are allowed against tax.

Another way to calculate the cost of equity is to calculate the 'earnings yield' which was a popular method in the past. The term 'earnings yield' is akin to the dividend yield but in this case it refers to profit irrespective of whether it is paid out as dividend or retained by the company.

For example, Graham Ltd made a profit of £20 million last year, which is expected to be maintained. There are 50 million ordinary shares in issue and they currently sell at £2 each on the Stock Exchange. The earnings yield and therefore the cost of equity at 20% can be calculated from:

$$\text{Earnings per share} = \frac{\text{Profit for year}}{\text{No of ordinary shares}} = \frac{£20\text{m}}{50\text{m}} = 40\text{p}$$

$$\text{Earnings yield} = \frac{\text{Earnings per share }\%}{\text{Market price}} = \frac{40\text{p}}{£2} = 20\%$$

A more recent approach to the cost of equity tries to take the risk element into account. Known as the 'capital asset pricing model', a particular company's share performance is measured against the whole market performance for a period of years. In both cases the risk-free return earned on short-dated government securities is excluded so that the risk premium or discount against the market generally can be ascertained. The nominal cost of equity capital for any one company therefore comprises the after-tax risk-free return plus the company risk premium relating to the degree of risk attaching to an investment in that particular share.

It is unlikely that all the above techniques will coincide but it is also unlikely that there will be very wide divergence. We must always remember that a precise calculation will only really matter for marginal projects rather than the vast majority of schemes which are either more than marginally profitable, or totally unviable. Having decided on the cost of equity we can reassure ourselves by conducting a few simple tests. The cost of equity should be more than the pre-tax cost of borrowed capital because of the greater element of risk. Taken over only one year this does not appear to be the case as evidenced by the 'reverse yield gap' which measures the excess of the current fixed interest rate over the current dividend yield on shares. As dividends can increase in future years whereas interest remains fixed, this results in the cost of equity exceeding the cost of borrowed capital when taken to perpetuity.

Another comparison we can make is to look at the shareholder's opportunity cost of making alternative investments. If the cost of equity appears lower than the return achievable on other financial securities of equal or lesser risk, we should go back to the drawing board. Either the calculation of the cost of equity is incorrect or we cannot justify investing more equity capital to achieve a lower return than shareholders expect.

New projects are financed by a mix of borrowed capital and equity capital. Having determined their separate costs we now need to combine them together to calculate the weighted average cost of capital at the desired level of capital gearing.

Weighted average cost of capital

Let us assume Canny Ltd attempt to keep their gearing ratio of borrowed capital to shareholders' funds in the proportion of 15:85. The nominal cost of new capital from these sources has been assessed, say, at 10% and 20% respectively. We now need to take account of the tax relief on interest, the cost of each type of new capital, and the mix of types to calculate the overall cost as in Figure 13.5.

Type of capital	*Proportion*		*After-tax cost*		*Weighted cost*
10% loan capital	0.15	×	6.5%	=	1.0%
Shareholders' funds	0.85	×	20.0%	=	17.0%
	1.00				18.0%

Figure 13.5 *Calculation of the nominal weighted average cost of capital*

The resulting weighted average cost of 18% is the minimum rate which Canny Ltd will accept on proposed investments. Any investment which is not expected to achieve an 18% return is not a viable proposition for this firm. When firms weight the cost of capital for risk by adding a risk premium, this may result in a substantially higher target being set for some projects.

New investments are financed from a pool of funds rather than from one particular source, except in the case of particularly large projects. This pool is composed primarily of borrowed and owners' capital together with depreciation and other retained profits. We can think of depreciation as retained profit for the specific purpose of helping to replace any assets that have worn out during the year. Such asset replacements allow those projects to continue to earn a return provided this is still satisfactory. When we appraise replacements we can use the current cost of capital to choose between alternative replacements and to decide when the replacement should take place.

The next chapter discusses how firms appraise new investments.

Further reading

Investment Appraisal, G Mott, M & E (Pitman).

Principles of Corporate Finance, R A Brealey and S C Myers, McGraw-Hill.

Investment Decisions and Financial Strategy, R Pike and R Dobbins, Philip Allan.

Self-check questions

1 What is meant by a high level of 'gearing'?

2 Using the illustration in Figure 13.2, calculate the return on ordinary shareholders' funds in the high gearing case when the profit is £1,000,000 and the tax rate is 50%.

3 What is the current cost of interest on a new loan if a firm has an existing 8% loan repayable in three years' time and quoted at £75 per £100 nominal value?

4 What is the after-tax cost of interest for a company paying 35% rate of corporation tax if it pays 12% interest on a bank loan?

5 Canny Ltd ordinary shares sell at £1.50 at the present time and the

growth of profits and dividends has averaged 10% pa in recent years. What is its cost of equity capital if the latest dividend was 8p net?

6 What is the 'reverse yield gap'?

7 Calculate the nominal weighted average cost of capital in Figure 13.5 when the proportion of loan capital to shareholders' funds is 0.4:0.6.

14
Capital investment appraisal

Investment appraisal is concerned with decisions about whether, when, and how to spend money on capital projects. Such decisions are important ones for the companies involved because often large sums of money are committed in an irreversible decision, with no certain knowledge of the size of future benefits.

Suppose a printing firm is considering buying a binding machine for £10,000, which will reduce labour costs on this activity by £3,000 every year for each of the five years the machine is expected to last. What the management of this firm have to consider – and this is no easy task – is whether a return of £3,000 every year for five years justifies the initial investment of £10,000.

The essence of all investment appraisals is to measure the worthwhileness of proposals to spend money, by comparing the benefits with the costs. If this measurement is done badly, it can hamper a firm's growth and employment prospects for years to come, and may lead to an inability to attract new investors. Financial institutions and individuals provide firms with capital in the expectation of a reasonable rate of return. If a firm invests that money in projects which do not yield a reasonable return then investors will be wary of that company in the future. The minimum return required on new investments will be the cost of capital as calculated in the previous chapter.

We measure the worthwhileness of investment proposals by building simple financial models of the expected events. Using the binding machine example above we can set out the expected events as cash inflows or outflows for each year of the machine's life, as in Figure

14.1. These cash flows start at year 0, which is the beginning of the first year when the project is initiated.

	£
Year 0	−10,000
Year 1	+ 3,000
Year 2	+ 3,000
Year 3	+ 3,000
Year 4	+ 3,000
Year 5	+ 3,000
Total profit	+£5,000

Figure 14.1 *Financial model of the binding-machine project*

Types of investment situation

There are a number of basic situations where an appraisal takes place:

- *Expansion* – assessing the worthwhileness of expanding existing product lines requiring additional investment in buildings, plant, stocks, debtors, etc.
- *New product/diversification* – assessing the viability of the more risky investment in totally new products.
- *Cost saving* – assessing the profitability of a cost-saving scheme; for example, when an investment in a new machine automates an existing manual process.
- *Replacement* – deciding whether and when to replace an old machine with a new one to save operating costs or reduce wastage.
- *Alternative choice* – deciding between alternative investments to achieve the same ends; for example, choosing between two or more machines with different financial characteristics.
- *Financing* – comparing the cost of purchasing an asset outright with the alternative cost of leasing.

All the above investment situations have the same common approach. In each case we must decide whether the benefits we get from the initial investment are sufficient to justify the original capital outlay.

There may be some investment situations where no benefits are quantifiable in money terms. For example, the government may require firms to invest in fire detection and alarm systems in all their premises. In this case firms have no choice and, although there will be benefits in employee welfare, these are not readily quantifiable in cash terms. Even in this kind of situation an appraisal technique could be used to help us make the choice between competing systems which have different financial characteristics. In the case of the fire detection and alarm system, one supplier's equipment may have a high capital cost but a low maintenance cost over a long life. An alternative supplier's equipment may have a low capital cost but high maintenance costs over a short life. We would need to formalise this information to make a rational judgement.

All appraisal methods require an estimate of the yearly cash flows attributable solely to the project under review. Typically there will be an initial cash outflow on a project, being the cash spent on the physical assets, such as buildings, plant, vehicles, machinery, and the like. If any of these items need replacing before the project ends, then a cash outflow will also occur in that later year. Other cash outflows may occur through the firm building up stocks or giving credit to its customers. These working capital items will be cash outflows at the beginning of the project or at some subsequent date if increased in amount. At the end of a project the working capital is released and becomes a cash inflow at that time.

Cash inflows occur, for example, from sales revenue less their wage and material costs. No deduction from such income is made for depreciation as the total asset cost is shown as a cash outflow. Where cost-saving projects are concerned, the cash inflow each year is the value of these cost savings, again without charging any depreciation. The cost of the investment will be shown in full as a cash outflow at the time of acquisition. It is worth emphasising at this point that profits which accrue from cost-saving investments are just as valuable as profits from investments extending the firm's output.

At this stage all cash flows are expressed in £s of year-0 purchasing power and inflation is ignored. A brief description of how to cope with inflation follows later but first a review is needed of the four main methods used to appraise investment projects.

Investment appraisal methods

Two of the methods are relatively crude measures of the worthwhileness of an investment and this sums up their weakness. The remaining methods are much more precise as they are both based on yearly interest calculations. They are easy techniques to understand and with the help of computers and calculators are not difficult to implement. In recent years more and more firms have been adopting these interest-based methods of appraisal although some firms may retain a payback requirement in addition. It should be appreciated that only these latter methods can adequately incorporate taxation, inflation, and uncertain future events.

Payback method

Simplicity is the keynote of this investment appraisal method. Payback measures the number of years it is expected to take to recover the cost of the original investment.

As an illustration let us assume that the board of directors of the printing firm mentioned in Figure 14.1 set a maximum period of three years within which any investment must be paid back. Payback in this example will take just over three years to complete and the investment will be rejected. One disadvantage of this method is that cash received after payback is completed is totally ignored. Another disadvantage is that no attempt is made to relate the total cash earned on the investment to the amount invested. The payback method does not attempt to measure this total profitability over the whole life of the investment and other methods have to be introduced to do this. However, payback is still used and can yield useful information as an indicator of risk, but is best used in conjunction with other methods.

Rate of return method

The rate of return used to be the main method of investment appraisal as it purports to measure exactly what is required, namely, the annual profit as a percentage of the capital invested.

An average profit is calculated by taking the total profits earned on the investment over the whole of its life and dividing by the expected life of the project in years. Profit in this context is after charging the total cost of the investment or wholly depreciating it in accountants' terminology. This total profit is more easily understood as the total cash inflows less the total cash outflows. The average investment is normally regarded as half the original investment on the grounds that it will be wholly depreciated by the end of its useful life. Referring again to Figure 14.1, the average profit is £1,000 and the average investment £5,000, giving a rate of return of 20% pa for five years.

A disadvantage of this method is that the calculation can give misleading results. Provided total profits were £5,000 over the five years, the return will be 20% irrespective of whether the cash flows increased, decreased, or stayed constant as in the example. The method does not take timing into account. Nor will it help rank projects whose lives vary, as the rates of return cannot be directly compared in this case.

At a later stage it will also become apparent that the average investment is a statistical illusion. One reason is that the cost of the investment is often quickly reduced by the early receipt of tax allowances. If these benefits are averaged out over the life of the investment they will not be shown at their true worth to the firm.

True rate of return

The profitability of an investment should be measured by the size of the profit earned on the capital invested. This is what the rate of return method attempts to do without perfect success. An ideal method will not rely on averages but will relate these two factors of profit and capital employed to each other in every individual year of the investment's life.

A useful analogy can be made with a building-society mortgage. In this situation the borrower pays to the society a sum of money each year. Part of this sum is taken as interest to service the capital outstanding, leaving the remainder as a capital repayment to reduce the capital balance. The profitability of the investment from the society's viewpoint can be measured by the rate of the interest payment, assuming that the yearly capital repayments have paid off all the mortgage.

Figure 14.2 sets out the yearly cash flows of a typical building-society mortgage of £20,000 repayable over ten years with interest at 12% pa on the reducing balance. The small surplus remaining at the end of ten years is negligible given the size of the annual cash flows.

This building society is getting a true return of 12% pa on the reducing capital balance of the mortgage.

Present value

The calculations involved in proving the building society's return on investment to be 12% are somewhat laborious. A simpler method is used in practice based on the principles of compound interest. Suppose £1 was invested one year ago at interest of 10% pa. After one year the sum has grown to £1.10. If the £1 was invested two years ago it would have grown to £1.21 with the first year's interest reinvested. Compound interest measures the *future value* of money invested sometime in the past. It is equally possible to look at money in the reverse direction, namely, the *present value* of money receivable at a future point in time. The present value of a future sum of money is

	Annual cash flow	Interest payment at 12% pa	Capital repayment	Capital balance outstanding
	£	£	£	£
Year 0	–20,000			20,000
1	+3,540	2,400	1,140	18,860
2	+3,540	2,263	1,277	17,583
3	+3,540	2,110	1,430	16,153
4	+3,540	1,938	1,602	14,551
5	+3,540	1,746	1,794	12,757
6	+3,540	1,531	2,009	10,748
7	+3,540	1,290	2,250	8,498
8	+3,540	1,020	2,520	5,978
9	+3,540	717	2,823	3,155
10	+3,540	379	3,161	6 (surplus)

Figure 14.2 *£20,000 mortgage at 12% pa repayable over ten years*

the equivalent sum now that would leave the recipient indifferent between the two amounts. The present value or equivalent sum to £1 receivable in one year's time is that amount which, if invested for one year, would accumulate to £1 in one year's time. Using a 10% rate of interest, £1 receivable in one year's time has an equivalent value now of £0.909 because £0.909 invested for one year at 10% will accumulate to £1.

Figure 14.3 is an extract from the present value table shown in Appendix 4 compared with the compound interest factors at the same rate of interest.

	Present value of £1 receivable in a future year with interest at 10%	Future value of £1 with compound interest at 10%
Year 0 (now)	1.000	1.000
1	.909	1.100
2	.826	1.210
3	.751	1.331
4	.683	1.464

Figure 14.3

The relationship between the factors is that one is the reciprocal of the other for the same year. For example, for year 4 $\frac{1}{.683}$ = 1.464

Returning to the building-society mortgage illustrated in Figure 14.2, this was shown to have a true rate of profitability of 12%. This can now be proved using the simpler present value approach as in Figure 14.4. To do this the cash flows are tabulated yearly and brought back (discounted) to their present value by the use of present value factors. In effect, interest is deducted for the waiting time involved. The remaining cash is therefore available to repay the original investment. The profitability of the investment is measured by the maximum rate of interest which can be deducted, while leaving just enough cash to repay the investment. This rate of interest is the same 12% as found in Figure 14.2. The surplus of £3 is negligible given the size of the annual cash flows.

	Annual cash flow	*Present value factors at 12%*	*Present value*	
	£		£	£
Year 0	−20,000	1.000		−20,000
1	+3,540	.893	+3,161	
2	+3,540	.797	+2,821	
3	+3,540	.712	+2,520	
4	+3,540	.636	+2,251	
5	+3,540	.567	+2,007	
6	+3,540	.507	+1,795	
7	+3,540	.452	+1,600	
8	+3,540	.404	+1,430	
9	+3,540	.361	+1,278	
10	+3,540	.322	+1,140	+20,003
				+£3

Figure 14.4 *Calculation of the rate of profitability of a £20,000 mortgage repayable over ten years with interest of 12% pa using present value factors*

The rate of profitability on this investment is 12%.

The effect of using present value (PV) factors on the future cash flows is to take compound interest off for the waiting time involved. If a higher rate of interest than 12% was applied in Figure 14.4 then not all the capital would be repaid over the ten-year life. If a lower rate of interest than 12% was used, the capital repayments would be larger each year as the present values would be larger. This would result in the mortgage being repaid in less than the ten years stipulated.

Both the methods of calculation explained above in Figures 14.2

and 14.4 arrive at the same conclusion, although at first sight they may not appear related. That they are related can be seen by comparing the capital repayments in Figure 14.2 with the inverted present values in Figure 14.4 which are almost identical apart from rounding off differences. This will always be the case in examples with constant annual cash flows. The present value approach will also give correct results with any fluctuating pattern of annual cash flows.

Net present value method

We can use this present value approach to assess the profitability of investment projects. For example, the directors of E Ltd are considering investing £150,000 on a press to make and sell an industrial fastener. Profits before charging depreciation (ie cash inflows) are expected to be £60,000 for each of the first four years tapering off to £40,000 in year 5 and only £20,000 in year 6 when the press will be scrapped. E Ltd normally require a minimum rate of return of 20%.

The cash flows can be set out and multiplied by the present value factors at 20% to demonstrate whether this project meets the 20% required rate as in Figure 14.5.

	Annual cash flow	*PV factors at 20%*	*PV*		
	£		£		£
Year 0	−150,000	1.000			−150,000
1	+60,000	.833	+49,980		
2	+60,000	.694	+41,640		
3	+60,000	.579	+34,740		
4	+60,000	.482	+28,920		
5	+40,000	.402	+16,080		
6	+20,000	.335	+6,700		+178,060
				NPV	+£28,060

Figure 14.5 *Calculation of the net present value at 20%*

The net present value (NPV) surplus of £28,060 means that the rate of return is more than the 20% rate of interest used. This is because the annual cash flows are big enough to allow more interest to be deducted and still repay the original investment.

The word 'net' in net present value means the sum of the negative and positive present values and this method of investment appraisal is widely known as the net present value method or NPV method for short.

Discounted cash flow yield method

The NPV method answers the question of a project's viability when tested against the required rate of return of that particular company. This required rate is alternatively referred to as the criterion rate, or cut-off rate, being 20% in the above example for E Ltd. Sometimes managers want to know not just whether a project is viable, but what rate of return they can expect on a project. To answer this question the NPV method is taken a stage further. The annual cash flows in E Ltd are discounted again at a higher trial rate of interest. Such trial is an educated guess but a higher rather than a lower rate is chosen because of the NPV surplus which previously occurred.

Assuming a trial rate of 30% was chosen, then the annual cash flows can be discounted by the present value factors at 30% as in Figure 14.6.

	Annual cash flow	*PV factors at 30%*	*PV*	
	£		*£*	*£*
Year 0	−150,000	1.000		−150,000
1	+60,000	.769	+46,140	
2	+60,000	.592	+35,520	
3	+60,000	.455	+27,300	
4	+60,000	.350	+21,000	
5	+40,000	.269	+10,760	
6	+20,000	.207	+4,140	+144,860
			NPV	−£5,140

Figure 14.6 *Calculation of the net present value at 30%*

As there is a deficit net present value of £5,140 the rate of return is less than 30%. This is because too much interest has been deducted to allow all the capital to be repaid. If instead of going to an estimated trial rate of 30% the annual cash flows had been repeatedly discounted at 1% intervals from the 20% required rate then a zero net present value would have been found at about 28%. This is the true rate of return on the project and is known as the discounted cash flow yield. In other words, the DCF yield is the solution rate of interest which, when used to discount annual cash flows on a project, gives an NPV of zero. The DCF yield is also known as the IRR.

Interpolation

It would be a tedious task to adopt the above method of successive discounting at 1% intervals but fortunately this is not required. The

NPV calculation at 20% and 30% yielded a surplus of £28,060 and a deficit of £5,140 respectively. This provides sufficient information to estimate the DCF yield reasonably accurately by interpolation, which can then be proved by calculation. The interpolation shows:

$$20\% + \left\{ \frac{28{,}060}{28{,}060 + 5{,}140} \times (30\% - 20\%) \right\} = 28.5\%$$

Another interpolation method takes the form of a simple graph with the rate of interest on the vertical axis and the net present value on the horizontal axis. The NPVs from the trial at the company's required rate and the further 'guesstimate' are then plotted against their respective interest rates and the two plots joined by a straight line. The approximate DCF yield is where the straight line intersects the vertical axis at a zero NPV. If the two plots are far removed from the actual rate of return the interpolation may not be quite accurate and it should be proved by a final calculation.

It is possible to calculate the DCF yield to one or more decimal places. Although one decimal place may be justifiable there is usually no case for further precision. This is because the basic data on which the calculations are performed are only estimates of future events. To calculate the DCF yield to, say, three decimal places gives an impression of precision which is illusory.

Other short cuts

The interpolation techniques described earlier are obvious short cuts in the search for the solution rate of interest. Some managers may have access to calculators or computers which can rapidly answer the question of a project's rate of profitability. Another short cut is applicable where there is a constant annual cash flow in every year of the project's life. This method is based on the principle that if a constant cash flow is multiplied by individual PV factors the total present value will be the same as if the constant annual cash flow had been multiplied by the sum of the individual PV factors.

If the sum of the individual PV factors had to be arrived at by literally adding up the individual factors this might be thought to be a long short cut! Fortunately a table exists with all the adding up done for the reader and the total of any number of individual year factors can be read off at a glance. Such a table is shown in full in Appendix 5 as the present value of £1 receivable annually or, put more simply, a cumulative PV table.

Such cumulative PV tables can be used as short cuts to both the

NPV and DCF yield. Because the cumulative table applies only to constant annual cash flows this technique is usually used for rule-of-thumb calculations on a project's profitability. Very often managers or industrial engineers want a quick guide as to whether it is profitable to pursue a certain course of action. This can easily be done using a cumulative PV table when the cash flows are relatively constant. A more comprehensive evaluation incorporating taxation, grants, working capital changes, etc., can be done later.

Take for example a proposal to introduce a fork-lift truck to handle palletised stock in a warehouse at a cost of £50,000. This can be expected to yield an annual saving in labour costs less truck running costs of £18,500. The equipment is expected to last six years and the company regards a 25% return before tax as a minimum requirement.

	Annual cash flow	*Cumulative PV factors at 25%*		*PV*
	£			£
Year 0	–50,000	1.000		–50,000
1–6	+18,500	2.951		+54,594
			NPV	+£4,594

Figure 14.7 *Calculation of the NPV on a fork-lift truck project*

The project satisfies the required rate of 25%.

The above method quickly solves the NPV but can be used to even greater effect in finding the DCF yield. Here we require the cumulative PV factor to be first calculated and then looked up on the line of the relevant year of the cumulative PV table, in this case year 6. Continuing with the fork-lift truck example, the cumulative PV factor which gives an NPV of zero must be equal to £50,000 ÷ £18,500. This is the cost of the investment divided by the constant annual return which equals 2.703. On the year-6 line of the cumulative PV table, 2.703 almost exactly equates with the cumulative factor of 2.700 at 29%, which is therefore the size of the DCF yield.

Comparison of appraisal methods

Four methods of investment appraisal have been discussed so far and useful conclusions can be drawn by comparing these four methods on the same projects. Figure 14.8 sets out three projects with different lives and different patterns of cash flow and appraises them by payback, rate of return, NPV, and DCF yield methods.

	Project A (£)		*Project B (£)*		*Project C (£)*	
Year 0		−200,000		−200,000		−200,000
1	+20,000		+80,000		+60,000	
2	+40,000		+60,000		+60,000	
3	+60,000		+60,000		+60,000	
4	+60,000		+40,000	+240,000	+60,000	
5	+60,000				+40,000	
6	+68,000	+308,000			+20,000	+300,000
Total Profit		+108,000		+40,000		+100,000
Payback period (ranking BCA)		4⅓ years		3 years		3⅓ years
Rate of return (ranking ACB)		18%		10%		16.7%
NPV @ 12% (ranking CAB)		−£884		−£12,580		+£15,100
DCF yield (ranking CAB)		12%		8.5%		15%

Figure 14.8 *Appraisal methods compared*

The payback method selects project B as the most attractive investment but ignores the short life remaining after payback is completed. This is taken into account however by the DCF yield method, which shows up project B in its true light as the least profitable of all three projects.

The rate of return method selects project A as the most profitable simply because the average profit per year is more than in the other two projects. When the timing of those profits is taken into account then project A is shown to give a DCF yield, or true return, of only 12% compared with its rate of return of 18%. Such inaccuracies have persuaded many firms to abandon the rate of return method and use the DCF yield method to appraise projects.

When project A is compared with project C on the DCF yield method the extra £8,000 profit on project A does not compensate for the slow build-up of the project. Even though total profit is £8,000 less on project C the project is more profitable than project A because discounting emphasises the value of the earlier high returns.

In short, payback can yield useful information but must not be used by itself. Either discounting method will give more accurate results than the rate of return method when assessing the profitability of an investment over its whole life. Firms may sometimes calculate the rate of return expected in the first year of operation and compare this with the actual return earned for monitoring purposes. This monitoring or post-audit appraisal is an important part of project investment. However, the complexities of taxation, grants, working capital, and other items reduce the validity of the rate of return method in many cases.

Research findings

A study of the investment practices of 100 large UK companies during the 1970s and 1980s (conducted by R Pike and M Wolfe) and its implications for the 1990s was published by the Chartered Institute of Management Accountants in 1988. This showed a greatly increased use of discounting techniques such that in 1986 three-quarters used the IRR/DCF yield technique and two-thirds used the net present value method. Payback measurement increased to over 90% while half of the companies used the average rate of return.

Obviously firms are using multiple appraisal techniques, but when asked to select their primary evaluation criteria, payback and IRR/DCF yield came out well ahead of average rate of return or the net present value method.

Ranking of projects

There are two ways to rank projects in order of attractiveness when using discounting techniques. The simplest is to rank them by the size of their DCF yields. When firms use only the NPV method the size of the NPV surplus is not related to the amount of capital invested to earn that surplus. To compare the relative profitability of projects on the NPV method we go a step further and calculate a profitability index by dividing the NPV inflow by the NPV outflow. Taking project C in Figure 14.8 as an example, the NPV inflows totalled £215,100 and the NPV outflow £200,000 giving a profitability index of 1.0755. Any project is viable when the profitability index exceeds 1.000 but its relative profitability against other projects can be measured by the size of the index number.

Care must be taken when ranking in the two special situations of capital rationing and the choice between alternative projects. The selection of projects when capital is insufficient must be based on the profitability index of the competing projects for those scarce funds. When a choice has to be made between alternative projects which are mutually exclusive it should be based on the highest NPV surplus.

Taxation

When appraising the worthwhileness of any investment in the private sector, the effects of tax must be taken into account. The payment of tax on profits is offset to some extent by tax allowances on certain new assets acquired. These tax transactions must be incorporated into the yearly cash flows after allowing for the time lag on the payment of tax. Tax allowances reduce the tax liability of the company as a whole, and are therefore subject to the same time lag as tax payments. The timing of tax payments and the size of tax allowances is explained in Chapter 18.

Let us take as an example a firm which buys a machine for £100,000 which is expected to last four years. Taxable profits are estimated at £45,000 each year being sales less operating costs without charging depreciation. The firm pays tax at 33% and gets 25% pa capital allowances on the machine on a reducing balance basis. The cash flows for this project can be set out as in Figure 14.9 and discounted in the normal way.

Year	*Investment*	*Taxable profit*	*Tax paid at 33%*	*Capital allowance*	*Tax saved on allowance*	*Net cash flow*
	£	£	£	£	£	£
0	−100,000					−100,000
1		+45,000		25,000		+45,000
2		+45,000	−14,850	18,750	+8,750	+38,900
3		+45,000	−14,850	14,063	+6,563	+36,713
4		+45,000	−14,850	42,187	+4,922	+35,072
5			−14,850		+14,765	−85

Figure 14.9 *Cash flows incorporating 33% tax*

Uncertainty

In most industrial investment appraisals there is no certainty that the eventual outcome will be exactly as predicted at the time of the appraisal. There are some crude methods we can use to minimise the risks involved. These methods include rejecting all projects which do not recover the initial investment in a specified number of years or varying the required rate of return according to how risky we view the project. Another method uses two further sets of cash flows based on optimistic and pessimistic assumptions. These set parameters within which we would expect to find the actual DCF yield.

More scientific methods can be used on important project appraisals where the capital to be spent is significant given the size of that particular company. Computers have an important contribution to make here when repetitive calculations are involved. One of these more sophisticated methods is to test the sensitivity of the return on investment to inaccuracies, or variations, in any one item of the cash flow while holding the other items constant.

Another method is to draw a decision tree which shows diagrammatically the various stages of a sequential decision process. Alternative courses of action open to the firm are depicted as branches of a tree and are assigned probability factors according to the likelihood of their occurrence. The value of each possible outcome is calculated by multiplying the benefit by its probability. The highest profit (or least cost) tells us which course of action to select.

Inflation

Up to this point the investment appraisal techniques discussed have implicitly ignored the existence of inflation and its effects on the future cash flows of projects being appraised.

Inflation brings additional problems to project appraisals. It increases the uncertainty and makes more difficult the estimation of the future cash flows including sales revenue, operating costs, and working capital requirements. It also influences the required rate of return through its effects on the cost of capital.

In the context of investment appraisals it means that two aspects of the value of money must be considered. The time value of money has already been catered for by the use of present value factors which deduct interest for the time elapsed when waiting for future cash receipts. The other aspect is the change in the value of money itself, not because of the time lapse, but because the inflationary process decreases its purchasing power.

When describing how to allow for inflation in investment appraisals, and cope with both these aspects, it is useful first to distinguish between the real rate of return on a project and its nominal rate of return. A simple example may clarify this difference between real and nominal rates of return.

Suppose an investor receives an income of £100 pa on an investment of £1,000. His or her nominal rate of return is 10%. If inflation is zero then the real rate of return will also be 10%. If, however, inflation is running at 6% pa then the real rate of return is approximately the nominal rate minus the rate of inflation which leaves only 4%:

$$\underset{0.04\ (4\%)}{\text{Real rate of return}} = \left\{ \frac{\text{Nominal rate of return } 1.10}{\text{Rate of inflation } 1.06} \right\} - 1$$

$$or\ \underset{0.10\ (10\%)}{\text{Nominal rate of return}} = \left\{ \underset{1.04}{\text{Real rate of return}} \times \underset{1.06}{\text{Rate of inflation}} \right\} - 1$$

Again, if inflation is running at 15% pa then his or her nominal rate of return of 10% is swamped by inflation and the investor gets a negative real rate of return of about 5%. This experience was all too vivid for small investors in the 1970s and some of the 1980s when the rate of inflation frequently exceeded the rate of interest received on bank or building-society deposits or other similar investments.

Turning to an industrial context a company's return on investment is the annual after-tax profit expressed as a percentage of the capital employed in the business. This is a nominal rate of return. The real return on investment will be this nominal return less the rate of inflation and it should be recognised that the real rate of return for British industry generally has been in single figures in many recent years.

The real and nominal rates of return referred to here for the whole company are not strictly correct because the concept of profit is not identical with that of cash flow. This is because profit ignores the timing of cash receipts and payments and can arise when cash is not even received. It is important to recognise that the company's one-year return on investment is conceptually different from the whole life project return based on the timing of cash flows. It is far from uncommon for a wholly satisfactory project with a high estimated return to have an adverse effect on the company profit and loss account, particularly in the first year or two. This is because the initial investment costs show as depreciation and interest charges before revenue starts to flow and profits are earned.

In the case of individual project appraisals the nominal rate of return is the apparent DCF yield found when discounting future cash flows that have been inflated to take account of anticipated inflation. The real rate of return on such a project however is this nominal rate of return minus the rate of inflation. If future cash flows on a project have been expressed in the constant value of year-0 purchasing power, then the solution DCF yield is the real rate of return.

At appraisal time we are therefore faced with a choice whether to express future cash flows at their inflated values and find the nominal rate of return or alternatively to express them in the constant purchasing power as at year 0 and find the real rate of return. What influences us as to which choice to make depends on how top management express the target rate of return, and whether we see the future cash flows keeping pace with inflation or not. Most firms will probably express the target rate of return in nominal rather than real terms. This is because the target rate is often based on the nominal costs of borrowing or the opportunity cost of alternative financial investments.

Use of computers

Any manager having to carry out investment appraisals on a regular basis will find a personal computer indispensable. Either a dedicated program to a specific company application or a general spreadsheet will perform the required calculations in no time at all. The hardest task will be to enter the cash flow information. When repeated runs on varied assumptions of cash flows are required, financial modelling as it is termed, a computer can recalculate NPV and DCF yields almost instantly, so saving hours of manual effort.

Spreadsheets lend themselves to the matrix layout needed to set out cash flows over the life of an investment. Years go along one axis and the various cash flow items down the other. This forms a grid in which the values are entered in relevant cells. In this way, information in any cell can be subjected to arithmetical and discount calculations, which are built-in functions on most spreadsheets, without having to key in present value factors.

A simple example of a spreadsheet approach might be as shown opposite:

	Year 0 (£)	Year 1 (£)	Year 2 (£)	Year 3 (£)	Year 4 (£)
Investment:					
Fixed assets	(17000)			(3500)	500
Working capital	(21000)	(2000)	(3000)	2000	24000
	(38000)	(2000)	(3000)	(1500)	24500
Costs:					
Cost of sales	—	(4000)	(5000)	(4200)	(2000)
Wages/salaries	—	(10000)	(10500)	(11000)	(11200)
Other expenses	—	(3000)	(3200)	(3500)	(3900)
		(17000)	(18700)	(18700)	(17100)
Sales:					
Cash	—	13000	16000	14000	6500
Credit	—	22000	28000	22000	11000
	—	35000	44000	36000	17500
Net cash flows	(38000)	16000	22300	15800	24900
NPV at 15%	(38000)	(24080)	(7221)	3175	17418
IRR/DCF yield					35%

Note: Brackets denote negative cash flows.

Further reading

Capital Budgeting for the 1990s, R H Pike and M B Wolfe, CIMA.
Investment Appraisal, G Mott, M & E (Pitman).
Principles of Corporate Finance, R A Brealey and S C Myers, McGraw-Hill.
Investment Decisions and Financial Strategy, R Pike and R Dobbins, Philip Allan.

Self-check questions

1 What are the situations where an investment appraisal is relevant?
2 What is the payback period for the annual cash flows contained in Figure 14.2?
3 What is the present value of £4,000 receivable in three years' time if the cost of capital is 12%?
4 What is the net present value of an investment of £20,000 now, with an annual cash return of £5,000 for ten years, if the cost of capital is 15%?
5 What is the DCF yield on the example in Question 4?
6 Interpolate the DCF yield when the NPV surplus is £45,000 at 15% and the NPV deficit is £25,000 at 20%.
7 Is it worth buying a new machine costing £10,000 if it is expected to

save £3,000 each year over a five-year life? The cost of capital is 14% and the company is not subject to corporation tax.

8 Differentiate between a 'real' and a 'nominal' rate of return.

9 What is the real DCF yield on an investment of £30,000, expected to produce an annual return of £8,000, rising in line with inflation, over its six-year life?

15
Managing the working capital

The capital of a company is employed in two distinct areas. Some of it goes to provide the permanent or fixed assets, such as buildings, plant, and vehicles. The remainder goes to provide the working capital necessitated by having to pay for the cost of goods and services before recovering the money from customers.

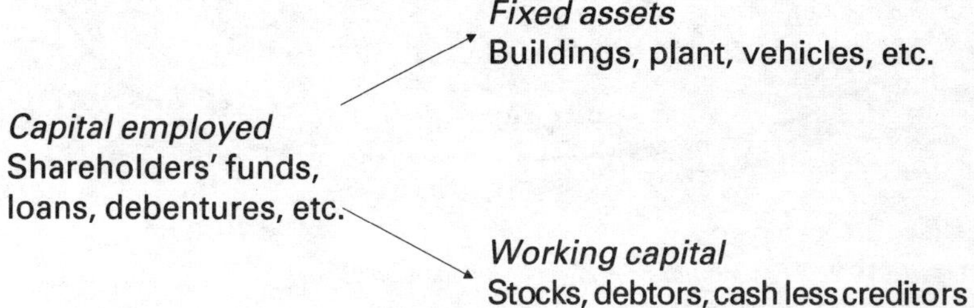

Figure 15.1 *The employment of capital*

Working capital is the value of all the current assets less the value of the current liabilities. It therefore includes the cost of stocks of raw materials, work-in-progress and finished goods together with the amount owed by customers, less the amount owed to suppliers:

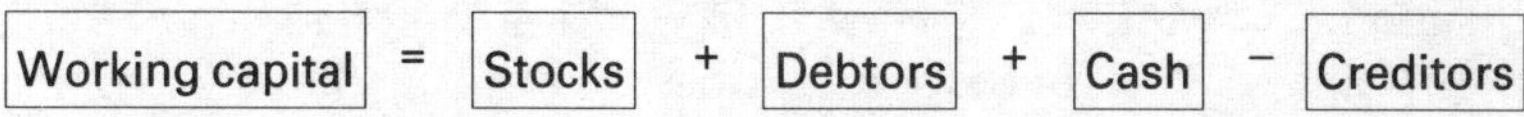

The key to managing working capital successfully is to find the right balance between liquidity and profitability. A firm needs to be liquid enough to pay the wages and other bills when required, but on the other hand it needs to carry sufficient stocks so that production is not unduly disrupted nor customers dissatisfied with 'stock-outs'. Both these requirements can be met given unlimited working capital but much of it would be idle for long periods of time. This means that profit would be lost due to the extra holding costs of large stocks and the interest costs of the capital involved. Therefore we have to strike a balance between profitability and liquidity recognising that they pull in opposite directions.

How much working capital is needed is obviously related to the volume of business, namely, the level of sales. If we divide the annual sales by the amount of working capital we find out how many times the working capital went round or circulated during the year. For example, if sales last year were £2 million and the average working capital was £0.5 million then working capital circulated four times

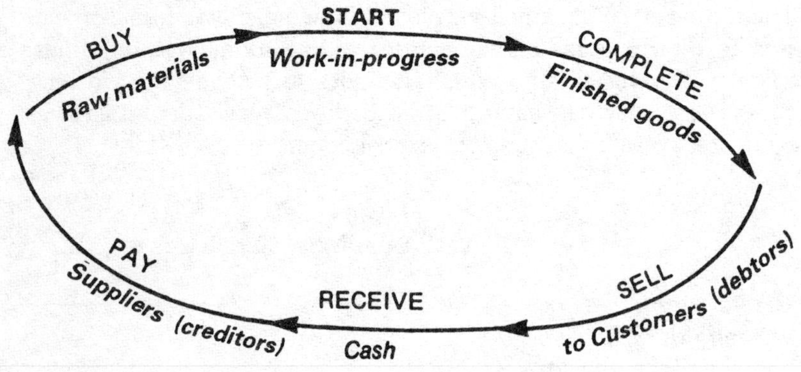

Figure 15.2 *The working capital cycle of a manufacturing firm*

during the year. This circulation process is shown in Figure 15.2.

For an existing company we can find the working capital requirement from the relationship of working capital to sales. In the example mentioned above, working capital represented 25% of annual sales. Put another way, the firm needed 25p working capital for every £1 of sales. If this is typical of that firm's experience during the year and not an atypical year-end situation, we can say that for every £1 change in sales there will be a 25p change in working capital requirement. This may seem a crude relationship but it will give accurate enough results for some practical purposes.

Another way the working capital requirement can be determined is from the length of the 'operating cycle'. This term refers to the length of time between the company first paying out cash on materials, wages, and overheads and the eventual receipt of cash from the sale of the goods or services produced. An example is given in Figure 15.3 with hypothetical figures to illustrate the point.

	Weeks
Average time raw materials stay in stock	7
(–) Credit period granted by suppliers	(6)
	1
(+) Average time taken to produce the goods/services	3
(+) Average time finished goods stay in stock	2
(+) Average time customers take to pay	7
= Total length of operating cycle	13

Figure 15.3 *Length of the operating cycle*

Having determined the length of the operating cycle a firm can calculate the maximum working capital requirement from the sales forecast for that length of time. Using the above example of a thirteen-week cycle, if sales are forecast at £2 million for the coming year, then £0.5 million (ie $\frac{13}{52}$ × £2m) working capital will be required. This ignores the possibility of seasonal fluctuations when the £2 million sales would not be evenly spread over the year. Similarly the working capital required will also fluctuate in advance of the fluctuation in the level of sales. Also ignored is the possibility of a change in stock levels.

The above calculation exaggerates due to the profit element in sales. Strictly speaking, the proportion $\frac{13}{52}$ should be applied to the cost of sales and not the full selling price.

A guide as to whether a firm has sufficient working capital and a viable mix of constituent items can be obtained from a look at two ratios previously met in Chapter 6.

The 'current ratio' of current assets to current liabilities looks for a norm of about 2:1, ie there should be £2 of current assets for every £1 of current liabilities. It may appear that this is an arbitrary figure but it has long been regarded by business people as reasonable. The premiss is that half of the current assets are stocks and therefore not quickly turned into cash to pay the current liabilities.

Excluding stocks from current assets leaves us with liquid assets and here we look for the obvious 1:1 ratio. Notwithstanding, it is quite easy to find examples of companies operating quite successfully on ratios below this or below the 2:1 current ratio. One reason is that bank overdrafts are included in current liabilities but unless they are called in they are not a current liability in the normal sense of the word. Also firms may have unused overdraft facilities with which to counter an apparently unsatisfactory liquidity position.

In some particular industries it is quite usual to meet 'adverse' current ratios of less than 2:1 and this may be due to their individual circumstances. An example of this occurs in both food retailing and construction if stocks or work-in-progress are turned into cash before trade creditors have to be paid. In the past, supermarket operators have financed the acquisition of new premises from the credit obtained from food manufacturers, whose produce they have sold for cash before the manufacturers' invoices were due to be paid.

There are other reasons why the longstanding norms for current and acid test ratios may not be so relevant. This relates to the moves to JIT with regard to purchasing stocks, and the increasing use of factoring customer debts. Both these topics are discussed later in this chapter.

Having looked at working capital requirements in total, let us now examine how each constituent part is best managed.

The management of cash

There are two key instruments for managing cash – the cash budget and the forecast cash flow statement. The former is the more detailed statement showing all the cash receipts and payments for the coming year broken down into monthly intervals. A typical example appears in Figure 15.4 containing the cash transactions we might expect to find in a manufacturing business. The layout illustrated makes it easier to compile and ensures rapid assimilation of the information.

Month	1	2	3	4	5	6	7	8	9	10	11	12
Cash inflows												
Sales												
Grant												
Total												
Cash outflows												
Wages												
Purchases												
Salaries												
Services												
Capital expenditure												
Tax												
Dividends												
Total												
Monthly +/–												
Cumulative +/–												

Figure 15.4 *A cash budget for a manufacturing firm*

When compiling the cash budget it is essential to allow for the time lags on transactions. If a firm finds that credit customers take an average of eight weeks to settle their account, then sales that take place in month one will appear as a cash inflow in month three. Similarly, purchases will not be paid for in the month of purchase but in a later month depending on the credit period obtained from suppliers. Note also the absence of depreciation which is not a cash expense.

The other instrument which helps to manage cash is the forecast cash flow statement. It might be thought that this is similar to the cash budget but there are important distinctions. If we refer back to Figure 7.2 in Chapter 7, the cash flow statement is a summary of the detailed cash transactions. The first entry, for example, shows the cash flow from operating activities, of which profit is the main constituent item. The cash budget, however, details the individual items of income and expenditure as they are paid for, not when they were initially incurred. The cash flow statement is therefore very useful in identifying the *causes* of the change in the liquid position. It highlights *changes* in stocks and debtors and in the level of investing activities or new financing for example, which are not obvious from the cash budget which records the actual receipts and payments of cash.

Armed with these two statements we should now know the size, duration, and causes of potential surpluses or deficits of cash. Short-term cash surpluses of a few months' duration should be invested short term to earn more profit while being capable of being turned back into cash when required. Examples are the purchase of tax reserve certificates, Treasury bills or other short-dated government stocks or investment on the London money market. The taking of cash discounts for early payment to suppliers may be advisable if the annual rate of interest so earned exceeds that available on financial investments. If a surplus is disclosed that is expected to continue in later years, thought must be given to using this in the expansion or diversification of the existing business or in the acquisition of new businesses.

Forecast cash deficits obviously pose more of a problem than cash surpluses. A short-term deficit lasting only a few months will be disclosed in a cash budget and explained in the forecast sources and applications of funds. If the cause is a seasonal increase in stocks and debtors then the evidence of these statements will usually persuade the bank manager to extend overdraft facilities. Failing this, the firm may have to trim stocks, renegotiate credit terms, defer capital expenditure, and somehow level out the peak cash outflows.

Long-term cash deficits are caused by a move to an increased volume of business, large capital expenditure programmes, or simply the effects of inflation which require more cash to finance the same activities. Such events have to be met by introducing new long-term capital. This may take the form of a rights issue of new shares or a loan or debenture repayable over a number of years or in a lump sum on redemption. Sale and leaseback of valuable premises may be a 'one-off' way of releasing funds for other uses but the rent will reduce profits in much the same way as would interest on a loan.

The management of debtors

Apart from retail shops, most UK companies sell on credit so their managers must decide whom to sell to, on what terms, and how to follow up late payments. When another firm applies for credit as a potential customer it would be rash indeed to agree credit without checking on credit worthiness. This can be done by employing a suitable agency like Dun & Bradstreet, or it can be carried out by the firm's own staff. Checks should include talking to other suppliers who have been quoted as trade references and checking bank references. Unfortunately the latter may say little more than the length of time the account has been operated. Sales representatives may form an opinion by calling at the potential client's premises and they may also hear valuable information on the informal grapevine. A copy of the client's annual accounts can be requested and perused using ratio analysis techniques to look at the profitability, liquidity, and debt capacity. If an existing customer requests a higher credit limit, then his or her track record on prompt payment, or otherwise, can easily be checked.

Having decided whom to sell to, a firm must now decide the terms of sale, being the length of the credit period and whether to offer cash discounts for early payment. The length of credit period is often settled by the normal terms for that particular industry. Firms compete with one another for custom and it would be difficult for one firm to impose a shorter credit period than its competitors, unless it had some compensating advantages. Typical credit terms demand payment by the end of the following month to that invoiced, which means between four and eight weeks' credit.

Cash discounts are a way of stimulating early payment, thereby reducing the amount of working capital required. The disadvantages lie in the cost and administrative burden. If a cash discount of 2% is offered for payment of invoice within two weeks, this may persuade customers to accept instead of taking a further four weeks' credit. A discount of 2% for four weeks is equivalent to an annual rate of 26%. If credit customers would have taken a further six weeks to pay after the expiry of the discount period then the 2% discount is equivalent to an annual rate of 17%.

Early payment induced by cash discounts will reduce profits but it may be largely compensated by not having to borrow so much capital. The effective annual rate of cash discounts can therefore be compared with the cost of bank overdrafts or loans, which would be needed to finance the longer credit period taken when discounts are not offered.

The other factor to consider is administration and the loss of goodwill when disputes arise. Customers may claim cash discounts even though the cash is received after the end of the discount period. Sorting out this kind of problem can negate some of the advantages of early payment.

Some firms offer a tapering discount/penalty scheme where the cash discount reduces in steps as the normal credit period shortens, but after that a stepped penalty is added to the invoice value according to the lateness of payment. An example of this approach would be:

Payment within		2 weeks	of	invoice	3%	discount
"	"	4	"	"	"	2%	"
"	"	6	"	"	"	1%	"
Payment after		6	"	"	"	1%	penalty
"	"	8	"	"	"	2%	"

Having sold to credit customers and specified the payment terms we must consider what follow-up procedure to adopt with late payers. Many firms use a monthly statement, both as a reminder and for the customer to check the balance on his or her account. If payment is not forthcoming in the stipulated time a reminder letter should be sent followed by a more strongly worded letter about a fortnight later. Should payment still not be received, consideration should be given to terminating supplies and instituting legal action and the customer informed accordingly.

Legal action for the recovery of the debt is appropriate where the debt is small or where the sale was subject to an unresolved dispute and the client's ability to pay is not in doubt. Where the debt is large and the customer's ability to pay is now in doubt, it may be more appropriate to bring matters to a head by applying to have the company wound up. A 'retention of title' (Romalpa) clause in the contract of sale may help to recover goods not yet paid for. Consideration can also be given to taking out some kind of trade indemnity insurance against bad debts as a matter of policy.

Use of computers

In this era of information technology, firms should have all the necessary information about customers' debts to hand. The overall debtor's position can be judged by the age analysis of invoices shown in Figure 15.5.

It can be seen that 14% of total debtors have exceeded the stipulated time allowed. Not all of this will be deliberate slow payment or potential bad debts, but will be partly caused by inflexible payment procedures in the client firms. This overdue proportion (14%) can be monitored against previous experience to identify trend movements and indicate a change in follow-up policy.

Apart from the overall debtors picture a print-out of individual overdue accounts is essential, with indicators of the follow-up stage reached in each case. Of particular concern will be the seven accounts which are more than three months old.

Duration from invoice date	% of total debtors	Cumulative total %	Number of accounts
0–14 days	28%	28%	264
15–28 "	25%	53%	205
29–42 "	19%	72%	147
43–56 " Due date	14%	86%	82 Due date
57–70 "	7%	93%	38
71–84 "	4%	97%	16
85–98 "	2%	99%	20
99+ "	1%	100%	7

Figure 15.5 *Age analysis of debtors' invoices*

If an age analysis is not available, a rough guide to the credit period can be found by using the ratio $\frac{\text{Debtors}}{\text{Sales}} \times 365$ days, which will indicate the efficiency of credit control when compared with the period allowed.

Factoring and invoice discounting

This is a specialist finance service that provides working capital secured against the client's customers' invoices. Factors will typically pay up to 80% of invoice value immediately, with the balance, less fees and interest charges, after the customer settles the invoice in due course.

The main advantages of entering into a factoring/discounting arrangement are:

- to ease cash flow by substantially reducing the working capital requirement for credit sales;
- to finance the expansion of the business. Apart from the above reason, when factoring is first undertaken, it may release some working capital for reinvestment in fixed assets;
- to ease the administration and management of customers' accounts and debts; and
- to provide cover against possible bad debts.

Factoring is the term used when the service provided embraces full management of customer accounts as well as the provision of finance against customer invoices. It can be either recourse or non-recourse factoring depending on whether the bad debt risk is borne by the client or by the factor. Charges may be up to 3% of invoice value plus interest charges on the money advanced.

Invoice discounting is limited to the provision of finance against customer invoices, often without the clients' knowledge - hence the term confidential invoice discounting. Fees for this service may be up to 0.5% of invoice value plus interest charges on the money advanced, somewhat similar to bank overdraft rates.

The management of creditors

Trade creditors are debts owed to suppliers of goods and services in whose books they appear as debtors. The policy for dealing with creditors is very straightforward and mirrors that of debtors. If no cash discounts are offered then the full credit period should be taken. To do otherwise, by making an earlier payment, would reduce the profit by increasing the amount of working capital which had to be financed by borrowed capital with consequent interest payments.

If cash discounts are offered then the decision, like debtors, is whether the effective *annual* rate of interest earned by the discount exceeds the cost of capital used up by the early payment. Taking the example of a 2% cash discount for payment one month earlier than normally allowed, this equates to an annual rate of 24%. Provided the cost of available overdrafts, loans, or other sources of capital is less than 24% it will be beneficial to take the cash discount.

An overall check on the period of credit taken can be found from the ratio relating trade creditors to purchases, namely $\frac{\text{Trade creditors}}{\text{Purchases}} \times 365$ days. If creditors were £80,000 and the year's purchases £320,000 this equates to 91 days' credit taken from suppliers. This will serve as a reasonable guide provided the creditors figure is not abnormally high or low at this time.

Problems arise when examining other companies' published accounts with a view to calculating this creditor's payment period. First, the figure of 'trade creditors' has to be found in the appropriate note to the accounts relating to all creditors due for payment within one year. This trade creditors figure should now be divided by 1.175 to eliminate VAT, if relevant.

The next step is to derive a purchases figure as this is unlikely to be disclosed, even in the most detailed notes accompanying the accounts. An approximation of the cost of buying-in materials and services can be calculated by subtracting value added from sales. Both these figures would usually exclude VAT in the published accounts, so no adjustment is necessary. See Chapter 7 if you need to recapitulate on value added!

The management of stocks

When looking at the current ratio we saw that the assumption is made that stocks represent half of current assets. There are three possible kinds of stocks – raw materials, work-in-progress, and finished goods. In manufacturing industry all three types are likely to be present unless the product is to a customer's 'one-off' specification, when completed work is not usually held in stock. In service industries physical stocks are not so prevalent but work-in-progress in the form of wages, salaries, and overheads may be very significant. Architects, for example, are rewarded pro rata to the value of building work done, but many months of work are put in at the design stage when no money is received from clients.

In an ideal situation firms would need no stocks. Raw materials would be delivered daily; production would be completed the same day and the finished goods would immediately be sold and delivered to customers. This situation is most unusual in practice because firms buy in bulk to reduce the unit cost of purchases and to hold some stock as an insurance against non-delivery. Production is not completed the same day in some industries. In many cases work-in-progress may consist of a number of stages when the need for buffer stocks and economical production runs leads to an abundance of components. Diverse product ranges result in larger stocks of work-in-progress and finished goods than found in a single-product company.

To ensure that production is never halted for lack of materials or component parts, and that customers are never dissatisfied, might entail holding very large stocks. The working capital tied up in this way ensures that firms produce and sell efficiently, but profits are offset by the costs of warehousing, possible deterioration, and, most significantly, the interest on the capital tied up in stocks.

Managing stocks requires balancing these conflicting factors. It means setting stock levels to allow for normal delivery times plus a small buffer stock for safety. This is achieved by calculating the reorder level which on normal usage will reduce the buffer stock level by the time delivery has been achieved. For example, if a firm uses 200 kg of material X per week and delivery takes three weeks then the reorder level will be the buffer stock plus 600 kg. The other balancing act occurs when setting the economic order quantity (EOQ). When buying in large quantities, extra discounts and reduced ordering and handling costs will be achieved, but these advantages are offset by the increased interest and storage costs. Conversely, if frequent orders are placed, interest and storage costs will be reduced but ordering, handling, and the unit purchase cost will increase. A formula is available for solving EOQ, where

A = annual usage in units,
S = ordering/handling cost per order,
i = cost of carrying stock as a %,
C = unit cost of the stock item:

$$EOQ = \sqrt{(2AS/iC)}$$

Sometimes firms have to cut their cloth according to the finance available for stocks. Many firms these days simply cannot afford stock levels which ensure continuous production in large runs or 100% customer satisfaction. This is the reason for the move towards 'just-in-time' (JIT) ordering systems, which, as the name implies, means holding little in the way of buffer stocks and passes the stockholding costs on to the supplier.

Material requirements planning (MRP)

The above formula for EOQ assumes demand is reasonably constant whereas in fact it may fluctuate considerably. This means that stock levels are much higher than they need be for considerable periods of time. Instead of estimating demand from past experience, material requirements planning is based on what needs to be purchased or manufactured to fulfil the planned level of production, to meet actual or expected orders from customers. The demand for components to satisfy production needs is reduced by the stock-in-hand, and the net balance, when compared with the supply picture, determines when to initiate the order. Unwanted stock is not kept for long periods under this MRP system and the reduction in finance, storage, and obsolescence costs can be considerable. Computers make the operation of this system feasible even when large numbers of components are involved.

Just-in-time and EPOS

Stock levels can be reduced by developing closer relationships with key suppliers. Long-term contracts can be negotiated with suppliers whereby very frequent deliveries of small quantities are made, just sufficient to meet immediate production requirements.

Both parties can benefit from this. Suppliers can plan ahead with greater certainty when they possess a long-term contract. They are also likely to receive payment on time, when the transfer of funds may be linked to delivery dates plus an agreed credit period.

The buyer also gains from introducing just-in-time systems of procurement. Safety stocks can be reduced or eliminated; stockholding costs are reduced if delivery is made directly to the point of production; savings also arise if the onus is placed on the supplier to meet specified quality standards, hence eliminating inspection and testing costs for the buyer.

In the retail sector similar changes have occurred with the use of 'electronic-point-of-sale' (EPOS) systems. These use computers allied to bar-code readings at the tills to record the movement of stocks.

In this way stock levels can be monitored at any time or the process taken a stage further to trigger automatically and place orders to replenish those stock items that have fallen to reorder levels.

Further reading

Principles of Corporate Finance, R A Brealey and S C Myers, McGraw-Hill.

Self-check questions

1 Define 'working capital'.

2 How can a firm determine the extra working capital required if sales are expected to increase by £100,000 next month and stay at that level?

3 Draw a pro-forma cash budget for the firm of your choice using the layout in Figure 15.4.

4 What checks would you undertake before granting credit to a new trade customer?

5 What is the annual cost of granting cash discounts of 2% if it results in payment five weeks earlier?

6 How many days credit are being taken by customers when debtors are £57,000 and annual sales are £250,000? Ignore seasonal fluctuations.

7 Name the three possible kinds of stock.

8 What decisions do firms have to take to ensure they do not run out of stocks of materials?

9 What benefits might a buyer expect from moving to just-in-time arrangements with its suppliers?

16
Share values

Share capital is provided by the owners of limited companies and therefore relates to the private sector. We saw in Chapter 3 that there are two main types of shares – preference shares and ordinary shares. Preference shares carry the right to a fixed rate of dividend before ordinary shareholders receive any dividend. Usually preference shareholders have no further right to an increased dividend, irrespective of the level of profit attained by their company.

Value of preference shares

The value of preference shares is therefore dependent on the rate of dividend attached to those shares and its relationship with the rate currently offered on new shares. Where there is a risk of non-payment of dividend it will depress the market price of the shares. This will be very marked if the situation is expected to last some years and the arrears of dividend are not allowed to be accumulated over this period.

Ignoring the possibility of non-payment, let us take as an example the 7% £1 preference shares in XYZ Ltd when the current rate of dividend being offered on similar new shares is 10%. Obviously no one will pay £1 for existing shares giving them a 7% return when they can buy new shares offering a 10% return. The price of the 7% shares will fall to a level where the holder receives a 10% return.

$$\text{Preference share value} = £1 \times \frac{7\%}{10\%} = 70\text{p}$$

Where special voting rights attach to preference shares or where repayment is drawing close then the share price will reflect these factors. For tax reasons mentioned earlier, preference shares are now uncommon and our main concern is with the value of a company's ordinary shares.

Convertible preference shares

A special form of preference share came to prominence in the 1980s called a 'convertible preference share'. Such shares start their life as conventional preference shares but carry the right to be converted into a specified number of ordinary shares at a later date(s). Convertible preference shares provide an element of gearing into the capital structure and are often used to reduce the dilution of earnings for ordinary shareholders after a takeover of another company.

Value of ordinary shares

There are a number of possible reasons why ordinary shares need to be valued. When a public limited company first offers its shares to the public it needs to fix a price at a small discount to what the shares are thought to be worth. If a company is taken over its shares are bought by another company, or an individual, and those shares have to be valued to fix the cash purchase price or the value of any shares issued in exchange.

There are two taxes relating to the wealth owned by individuals. *Capital gains tax* applies to profits on the sale of shares, while *inheritance tax* applies to the value of shares given or bequeathed to another person. Normally the relevant value is the stock market price at the time of sale or transfer. In the case of private limited companies which are debarred from a stock market quotation, some other means of valuing shares has to be found.

There are two main approaches to valuing ordinary shares. We can either value them according to the assets they own or according to the profits earned on those assets.

Assets basis of valuation

Let us take as an example EZ Engineering Ltd whose balance sheet reads:

	£000	£000
Fixed assets:		
Land and buildings		350
Machinery, vehicles		700
		1050
Current assets:		
Stocks, work-in-progress	400	
Debtors	250	
	650	
Creditors due within a year:		
Trade creditors	150	
Bank overdraft	200	
	350	
Net current assets		300
Total assets *less* Current liabilities		1350
Creditors due after one year:		
1% Secured loan		400
Net assets		950
Capital and reserves:		
Called-up £1 share capital		500
Profit and loss account		450
		950

The value of the assets owned by ordinary shareholders is the £1.7 million value of total assets (£1.050m + £0.650m) less £0.750 million total debts to outsiders (£0.350m + £0.400m) making £0.95 million. This is of course the same as the value of shareholders' funds which represent the net worth or the equity. The asset value per share is the value of shareholders' funds or assets belonging to shareholders divided by the number of shares issued:

$$\text{Asset value} = \frac{\text{Shareholders' funds}}{\text{Number of shares}} = \frac{£950{,}000}{500{,}000} = £1.90 \text{ per share}$$

This £1.90 value is referred to as 'book value' because it is based on the balance sheet value of the assets. If the assets are valued at their current worth to the company as a 'going concern', this may lead to a different value of the shares. Suppose the land and buildings in EZ Engineering's balance sheet have just been professionally valued at £550,000. This increases the value of the shareholders' funds by £200,000 and consequently the individual share value to £2.30 on a going-concern basis.

A third approach to asset values is on a 'break-up' basis, as when the assets are sold off one by one. In this case, book values may not be realised for some assets.

Goodwill

When a company buys out another company it takes over the physical assets and debts of that other company. In addition, it takes over the established name of the company which has been built up over a long period of time. The value of that name and reputation is an intangible asset and is known as 'goodwill'. Most companies have their own goodwill but it is an impossible thing to value as we cannot say what specific amount has been spent on its creation.

Goodwill only appears in a balance sheet when it literally has been bought off another company. Usually this is done by taking over another company and paying more for the shares than the value of the physical assets acquired, less any debts assumed. The excess represents the payment for goodwill. In the case of EZ Engineering, £2.30 per share represents the current value of assets owned by shareholders. Assuming EZ's shareholders were paid £2.50 on a takeover, then the purchaser has paid £100,000 (ie 20p × 500,000) for goodwill.

If a company has gone into liquidation it may be possible to buy only the trade name from the liquidator, without taking over any physical assets. In this situation the whole payment represents the cost of goodwill.

Sometimes goodwill is calculated as X number of years' purchase of profits. This is not a scientific calculation so much as an attempt to measure the purchase cost of goodwill against the annual profit achieved. In the final analysis, goodwill is worth only the discounted future benefits accruing to the name and reputation acquired.

Even when companies pay out money for goodwill it does not always appear in their balance sheet. SSAP 22 recommends they write off such goodwill against their reserves immediately. This treats acquired goodwill in the same way as internally generated goodwill, so no goodwill appears in the balance sheet.

However, the standard does alternatively allow a company to treat acquired goodwill as an asset and to write it off over its expected useful life. This is similar to the depreciation process when an asset is reduced in value in the balance sheet by transferring some of its cost to the profit and loss account. It is not normally included in the list of trading expenses but shown as an exceptional item below the line where the normal trading profit is determined.

Brands

In the last few years a debate has been raging in the UK whether or not brand valuations should be included in the balance sheet. This relates both to 'acquired brands' on a takeover and to 'internally generated brands' that have been built up over a number of years.

A catalyst for this debate was the action by Grand Metropolitan plc to capitalise nearly £600 million of acquired brands in 1988. Some household names followed suit, with some going so far as putting a valuation on internally generated brands.

One view is that acquired brands are part of the goodwill being bought and should be capitalised initially, then written off over their expected useful life. The problem then remains of what value to place on internally generated brands as the costs have usually never been recorded for this purpose. Some brands date back to the previous century!

The new Accounting Standards Board see this whole topic of accounting for intangible assets as a priority for it to address. The current SSAP 22 dealing with goodwill favours the immediate write-off to reserves of any acquired goodwill/brand values. However, the relevant International Accounting Standard allows the capitalisation of goodwill and brands arising on acquisition. It will be interesting to see how the conflict of views between brand companies, accountants, and analysts is eventually resolved.

Earnings basis of valuation

The second main approach to valuing ordinary shares is based on the profit after tax attributable to each share. Such profit is referred to as the 'earnings per share' and represents the total profit (after charging interest, tax, and preference dividends) divided by the number of ordinary shares:

$$\text{Earnings per share} = \frac{\text{Profit attributable to ordinary shareholders}}{\text{Number of ordinary shares}}$$

In the case of EZ Engineering there were 500,000 £1 ordinary shares in existence. Let us assume that the profit after tax was £150,000, in which case:

$$\text{Earnings per share } \frac{£150{,}000}{500{,}000} = 30\text{p}$$

An earnings per share calculated from last year's profit may not be a good guide to the future maintainable profit if last year was in any way abnormal. Companies do occasionally make an annual loss in which case the earnings per share is negative. In both situations an estimate is needed of the future profit and hence the earnings per share that can be achieved in the coming year(s).

Assuming we know the earnings per share, this is translated into a share value by using a comparative price/earnings (p/e) ratio for other companies in the same field. A p/e ratio relates the earnings per share to the market value of the share as follows:

$$\text{Price/earnings ratio} = \frac{\text{Market price of the share}}{\text{Earnings per share}}$$

In the case of plcs with a stock exchange quotation these p/e ratios can be found in the financial press or calculated from the company's accounts using the current market price. With unlisted or private companies this market price is non-existent. A merchant bank or trade association can sometimes be approached to advise on a comparative p/e ratio for companies in the same industry with a similar profit record and prospects.

Referring back to EZ Engineering Ltd, we assumed that its earnings per share was 30p. If we now assume that similar small engineering companies have a p/e ratio of about 5 we can derive the share value for EZ Engineering by multiplying the earnings per share by this comparative ratio:

$$\text{Share value} = 30\text{p} \times 5 = £1.50$$

This is a smaller value than that obtained on the assets basis (£2.30) for the same company but it would be sheer coincidence if they were identical. This is because share prices tend to fluctuate from day to day, so therefore must the p/e ratios as the earnings per share is a constant figure until the next year's profit is known. Share prices based on earnings can also be higher than asset value, particularly in service industries where profits are more related to the skills of employees than the use of assets.

An examination of p/e ratios in, say, *The Financial Times*, will reveal wide disparities between apparently similar companies operating in the same industry. A favourite example of mine is to compare Marks & Spencer with other stores groups. Generally speaking, Marks & Spencer command a higher p/e ratio than most other store groups (ignoring special recovery situations) because of their proven management skills and track record. Consequently its shares are more highly regarded by investors who are willing to buy at a market price reflecting a much higher p/e ratio than they are prepared to pay for other stores' shares. Investors clearly expect that increased profits in future years will soon bring the p/e ratio down if calculated on the market price at the time of their original purchase.

Another reason why a p/e ratio may appear abnormal in comparison with other companies is when it is calculated on historic earnings per share, which are not expected to be maintained. A company can experience internal problems peculiar to itself, for example a strike. On the other hand, it may be about to launch a new product, as in the case of drug manufacturers whose share prices are very sensitive to new product announcements even though they may take some years to filter through into actual earnings. Rumours of an impending takeover may be another reason for an apparently high p/e ratio if earnings on assets are poor and the asset value per share considerably higher than the value based on earnings alone. After a prolonged recession, high p/e ratios may simply be discounting that recovery in profits is about to take place.

Discounted earnings basis of valuation

A theoretically sound approach to valuing ordinary shares is to calculate the present value of the stream of future earnings going on to perpetuity. This present value approach progressively reduces the worth of future earnings by deducting compound interest for the waiting time, as explained in Chapter 14. The sum of the present value for each year represents the current value of the shares. For any one firm the discount rate used will be its cost of capital, while for an individual it will be the opportunity cost of the return available on alternative investments. Although useful for valuing securities with a fixed rate of return, it is not so easy in practice for an outsider to estimate future earnings on ordinary shares for most companies.

This discounting approach to share values is at the heart of the concept known as 'shareholder value analysis', taking a company's true value as the present value of its future cash flows. SVA concentrates management's attention on closing the gap between the current share price and its true value by identifying areas to improve operating efficiency. Such measures to enhance shareholder value can be just as effective as expansion or increased gearing.

Stock exchange

The stock exchange is a market where financial securities are bought and sold and where, like any other market, the forces of supply and demand determine prices. There are markets in government stocks and foreign stocks and shares, in addition to the UK company stocks and shares which are our main concern.

The existence of the stock exchange allows companies to tap a wide body of investors. It also allows those investors the means to realise their capital at any time by selling their shares to someone else through the market, without the company being involved. These transactions in second-hand shares form the bulk of the activity in the market.

Another function of the stock exchange is as a barometer of business confidence through the movement of share prices. Various indices of share prices are available, the most famous being *The Financial Times* Footsie 100 index of share prices of 100 large companies.

Market makers quote two prices for each company's share they are willing to deal in. The higher is their selling price and the lower is their buying price with the difference representing their profit margin or 'turn'. They adjust these prices according to how many shares they hold as well as in anticipation of market movements.

Small investors cannot approach a market maker direct, but must deal through a broker who acts as their agent and tries to negotiate the best deal by comparing competitive quotes from the various market makers in that share.

Fluctuations in share prices

It should be noted that share prices reflect future expectations rather than current or past performance, with many investors looking up to a year ahead. Many factors influence share prices by working on the levels of supply and demand. General factors which affect share prices across the board are announcements of economic indicators, possible changes in government, wars, strikes, and even international events. More specific factors affecting the share price of only one company are announcements (or rumours) regarding profits, dividends, orders, changes in management, new share issues, and other happenings.

When a company announces its interim or final profit and dividend, there may not be any change in the share price, even when the figures are significantly different from the previous year. Only if the announcement is different from that expected, and already discounted in the share price, will there be any further price movement.

New issues

Invariably limited companies start off as private companies and gradually grow in size. A company goes public and gets a listing on the stock exchange when its capital needs are no longer met internally; when the owners wish to realise some of their investment; or get a value for tax purposes.

Both a merchant bank (issuing house) and a stockbroker are appointed to the company to help guide it through the lengthy process and value the shares at a realistic level. The price is fixed at the last possible minute to take account of the p/e ratios of similar companies and market conditions at the time. Underwriters agree to take up any unwanted shares for a small commission and this ensures the success of the venture whatever the market conditions on the day.

Very large companies that are already household names may succeed in going public by issuing a 'prospectus' and inviting investors to subscribe. These cases are very rare. More usually a company sells the shares to a merchant bank which in turn offers them to the investing public at a slightly higher price. This 'offer for sale' may be composed partly of new shares to raise capital for the company, and partly of existing shares where the original shareholders wish to realise some of their capital.

Small companies can avoid some of the advertising and other expenses by obtaining stock exchange permission for a 'placing'. Instead of offering shares to the general public by an offer for sale, shares are placed initially with clients of the broker and merchant bank handling the issue. Occasionally one hears of an 'introduction' when a company with a large number of existing shareholders, or with a listing abroad, gets a quotation on the London Stock Exchange. No new shares are involved necessarily, but sufficient shares must be made available to the jobbers to allow the market to function.

Offer by tender

When fixing the price of shares for an offer for sale or placing, account will be taken of the standing of similar companies with regard to financial yardsticks such as p/e ratio, dividend yield, and dividend cover. Occasionally a company comes to the market which is rather unique in the sense that no other companies in the same field already have a quotation. Such a company is a suitable candidate for the 'tender' approach. When the government privatised Amersham in 1981 it offered the shares at a fixed price, but considerably underestimated the substantial premium that investors were willing to pay for such a high-technology company. Attempts were made to persuade the government that any future issues would use the tender method but this was not implemented until 1987 with the partial tender offer for British Airports.

When an offer for sale is by tender, applications are invited from investors at or above a stated minimum price. All shares are eventually issued at the same striking price which represents the lowest price at which the last shares on offer are taken up. Those investors who are very keen to buy will offer a very high price hoping this will secure an allocation of shares at a lower striking price. Let us assume that company X offers 500,000 shares for sale at a minimum price of £2 each and gets the following tender bids:

Number of shares	*Tender price*
7,500,000	£2.00
1,350,000	£2.10
625,000	£2.20
300,000	£2.30
125,000	£2.40
50,000	£2.50
25,000	£2.80

Ignoring the possibility of large applicants being scaled down, the striking price would be fixed at £2.30, being the highest price at which all 500,000 shares can be sold. Applicants who tendered less than £2.30 would receive no shares.

Rights issues

Companies with an existing stock market quotation also issue new shares. When they issue them for cash it is known as a 'rights' issue, whereas when they are 'free' it is called a 'scrip' issue. It is important to understand the reasons for these issues and the effect on the share price of the company concerned.

The simplest to understand is a rights issue, when a company raises more capital either to finance more assets or to repay borrowed capital and so reduce its gearing. Existing shareholders are first given the right to buy the new shares pro rata to the number of shares they already own. For example they may be offered a 1 for 5 at £1.50 which means they can buy one new share at £1.50 for every five they already hold. The year 1991 was a bumper one for rights issues, well exceeding the £7 billion raised in 1987 at the height of the boom.

When a rights issue is first announced it may have a depressing effect on the existing share price. This is partly because of the threat of a larger than normal number of shares coming on to the market, due to some existing shareholders being unwilling or unable to put up more money. It is also a response to the size of the discount offered by the company, as the new shares will be offered at a price at least 10% lower than the market price to ensure the success of the issue.

After the rights issue has been effected the market price can be estimated from the following formula:

$$\text{Ex-rights price} = \text{Subscription price} + \left\{ \text{£ discount} \times \frac{\text{Number of shares pre issue}}{\text{Number of shares post issue}} \right\}$$

In the case of the 1 for 5 issue at £1.50 previously mentioned let us assume the market price stood at £1.74 before the issue was announced. After the issue the share price of both old and new shares should be:

$$\text{£}1.50 + \left\{ 24\text{p} \times \frac{5}{6} \right\} = \text{£}1.70$$

Very often share prices may not conform with the above pattern. This is possibly because at the time of the issue the company makes an updated forecast of future profits and dividends. If this is better, or worse, than market expectations then the share price will move accordingly.

Shareholders who do not wish to exercise their rights can sell them in the market provided the subscription price is less than the current market price. To reduce expenses for small investors, the company sometimes does this on their behalf after the expiry date.

Scrip issues

A scrip issue is a very different animal. Here the company issues new shares to existing shareholders on a pro-rata basis, but receives no cash for them. The mechanism of a scrip issue is to capitalise reserves, meaning that the issued share capital is increased while the reserves are decreased by the same amount. This is merely a book entry and may be thought of little purpose.

There are a number of reasons why scrip issues occur. Creditors or bankers may insist on it as a safeguard to their interests. Certain reserves can be used for dividend payments if cash is available and this could be at the expense of creditors who are owed money. Once reserves are made up into share capital, dividends can no longer be paid from this source.

Companies usually express dividends as *X* pence per share as opposed to the previous practice of declaring them as a percentage of the par value of a share. This can be misleading for employees in particular, who may not see that the dividend is a return on all shareholders' funds and not just the issued capital. Very often scrip issues are a public-relations exercise with employees and shareholders, based on their inadequate knowledge of company finance.

Small investors prefer low-priced shares to high-priced ones for psychological reasons. A £10 share is really just as valuable as ten £1 shares. Scrip issues have the effect of lowering the market price of a share pro rata to the size of the issue. Say, for example, a 1 for 1 scrip issue is made then the market price of shares should halve. If a 1 for 2 issue is made then the price should fall by one third leaving the investor no better and no worse off. Take two shares which stand at £3 each before a 1 for 2 scrip issue. After the issue a shareholder will still hold £6 (3 × £2) value as before.

As with rights issues, the share price may not respond as described if a dividend forecast accompanying the scrip issue does not equate with market expectations.

Dividend cover

We saw with preference shares that the market price was based on the size of the dividend payment. This is not the case with ordinary shares because very few companies pay out all their profit as dividends. A combination of inflation and growth means that firms need extra capital each year to finance the increased value of fixed assets and working capital. The prime source of this extra capital is retained profit.

The proportion of profit paid out as dividend is ascertained from the 'dividend cover' expressed as:

$$\text{Dividend cover} = \frac{\text{Earnings per share}}{\text{Dividend per share}}$$

Because of complications with irrecoverable advance corporation tax and overseas taxation there is more than one method of calculation of dividend cover. In essence, where earnings per share is 24p and the net dividend is 8p the dividend cover is three times, meaning that one third of the profit is paid out as dividends:

$$\frac{24p}{8p} = 3.0 \text{ times}$$

This financial ratio is used as a measure of risk to the dividend should profits decline in future years. It is also used to express the proportion of earnings retained, in this case two thirds.

Dividend yield

The dividend yield is the gross dividend expressed as a percentage of the current market price. Dividends are paid net by companies, as the advance corporation tax also satisfies the standard rate of income tax for the shareholder. Dividend yields are usually measured gross because any individual's tax liability is unknown, and also because the return offered on most other alternative investments is also expressed in gross terms.

In the above example of an 8p net dividend this is equivalent to a 10p gross dividend with the rate of tax at 20% ($8 \times \frac{100}{80} = 10p$). If the market price of the share is £1.60, then:

$$\text{Gross dividend yield} = \frac{10p}{160p} \times \frac{100}{1}\% = 6.25\%$$

This can now be compared with returns on other investments or other shares. It must be remembered that dividends are only part of the return received by investors. This is because retained profits are also expected to increase the market price of the shares over time. For this reason ordinary shares cannot be valued by reference to their dividend yield. All earnings should be taken into account irrespective of whether they are retained or distributed as dividends. A more valid approach is to use the comparative p/e ratio mentioned earlier to value ordinary shares.

Dividend policy

In the case of small private companies the shareholders are usually either directors or members of their families. The dividend policy of these companies takes into account the need to retain profits as additional capital, as well as considering the needs and tax status of the shareholders regarding dividend income.

Public companies with a stock market quotation must consider their shareholders when framing their dividend policy. We have seen that the dividend yield at any moment in time is not a means to valuing shares. Shareholders do expect their company to pursue a consistent dividend policy and not use retained profits as the sole source of new finance. Should a company have pursued a policy, say, of distributing one half of its profit over a number of years, then this policy will be expected to continue. Any reduction of dividends to fund high capital expenditure will be greeted by a sharp fall in the market value of the shares. Although this does not immediately have any effect on the company, it makes future 'rights' issues more difficult and could lead to a takeover bid.

An exception to this rule appeared in the severe recession of the early 1990s. In some instances, companies that still paid dividends but were perceived to be imprudent, found that their share price fell as a result. In other cases, companies that cut their dividends to affordable levels were rewarded by a rise in their share price.

Further reading

Principles of Corporate Finance, R A Brealey and S C Myers, McGraw-Hill.
Beginner's Guide to Investment, B Gray, Century Business.
Brand Valuation, edited by J Murphy, Business Books.

Self-check questions

1 What is the market value of a non-redeemable 11% preference share of £1 if the current rate of dividend on new shares is 9%?

2 What are the advantages and disadvantages to an investor of holding preference shares?

3 What are the three main ways of valuing ordinary shares?

4 What is goodwill?

5 Takeover activity often increases at times when share prices are high. Why is this so?

6 Differentiate between market makers and brokers.

7 Name the different ways a new issue can come to the market.

8 Why do shares often fall in value when a 'rights' issue is announced?

9 Why do companies make 'scrip' issues?

10 Define 'dividend cover'.

11 What is the dividend yield on a share with a market value of £1.60 when the net dividend is 9p and advance corporation tax is 30%?

17

Mergers, takeovers, and buy-outs

The terminology used in this connection is not as precise as first appearances might suggest. A merger is when two or more companies join together voluntarily under the umbrella of a newly formed holding company. The parties concerned have equal status in the discussions leading up to the merger even when the companies involved are unequal in size.

A takeover is when one company buys out the shareholders in another company. It implies the unwillingness of one party and the use of force by the other. Very often this is not the case, as with an 'agreed takeover'. This represents a merger in many ways, except that no new holding company is formed and the larger company buys the issued shares of the smaller company. Should the smaller company take over the larger company, this is known as a 'reverse takeover'.

In recent years 'buy-outs' have become more frequent. When a particular activity no longer fits into the corporate plan of a holding company, it may decide to divest itself of that subsidiary. Sometimes group overheads charged to the subsidiary result in an inadequate return on capital. Occasionally companies go into receivership with potentially profitable activities submerged by other loss-making subsidiaries. All of these situations yield potential candidates for a buy-out by their management and other employees. More recently, management buy-ins have occurred where a management team is brought together with the purpose of identifying a suitable company for them to acquire, usually in conjunction with venture capitalists and other financiers.

In the case of mergers and takeovers the reasons are somewhat different from those of management buy-outs. Any amalgamation should fit in with the corporate strategy of the principal company involved. The purpose is to make the combined companies more profitable, and stronger, than was the sum of their separate parts.

Very often economies of scale are cited as the justification for mergers and takeovers. These are described as technical, financial, marketing, managerial, and risk-bearing economies resulting from the integration of activities.

Integration can take three forms - vertical, horizontal, and lateral. Vertical integration occurs when two companies at different stages join together under common ownership. A company can integrate forward to the market outlets or backward to the raw material and component supplies. An example of forward vertical integration is a shoe manufacturer taking over a chain of shoe shops, while a manufacturer taking over a leather tannery represents backward vertical integration. The main economies will be financial, resulting from the coordination of production and marketing functions and the elimination of middlemen profits.

Horizontal integration occurs when two companies at the same stage combine together. The purpose may be to eliminate competition or to broaden the product range and geographical coverage. Many economies are possible in this situation including technical, marketing, managerial, and financial benefits.

Lateral integration is the third possibility, being a diversification from existing activities as when a construction company buys a shipping company. An attraction here could be if the particular industrial cycles do not coincide, so that risks are spread.

Occasionally a financial economy occurs through the workings of our tax system. If one company has accumulated tax losses or unclaimed capital allowances it may be possible for them to be offset against profits of another company. Although chancellors have tightened up the rules over the years, losses can be worth taking over and may be the main attraction to a predator.

Asset-stripping days seem to be behind us, but there will always be opportunist bids where a company appears to be lowly valued in the market. This may follow a particularly bad set of annual results or may be the result of years of poor management. New owners may be willing to take a long hard look at the component parts, weeding out unprofitable or misplaced activities. Money raised from such divestments, or from the sale and leaseback of properties, may go some way to funding the original purchase price.

Another reason for amalgamations of companies may be the need for management succession. Where the founder owners of a private company have no suitable successors within the family, they may seek a merger or takeover with a larger public company to safeguard their investment.

Valuation of a business

Control of a business rests with shareholders who own the voting shares. Where voting powers are vested in the ordinary shares the value of a business is the total value of these shares. Occasionally, voting rights are vested in preference or other special categories of ordinary shares, but these are rare occurrences.

In the previous chapter we saw that there are the following different approaches to valuing ordinary shares:

- *Asset value.* Each share is represented by a proportionate part of the assets owned by the company after allowing for the payment of all debts. If we value these net assets and divide by the number of issued ordinary shares we arrive at the asset value per share. An additional amount may be added for goodwill as discussed previously.
- *Earnings value.* The earnings per share is the amount of profit earned for each ordinary share after tax, interest, and preference dividends have been allowed. We try to find comparable companies and use their price/earnings ratio as a basis for valuing the shares of the company in question.
- *Stock market value.* This value is relevant in mergers and takeovers in the case of a public limited company with a quotation on the stock exchange. Very few bids succeed at the existing stock market price unless it has been pushed too high on takeover rumours, or major shareholders agree to sell at a lower price. A higher price than the pre-bid stock market value is needed because market prices are based on willing buyers and sellers at the margin. To tempt all existing shareholders to sell their shares may require substantially higher prices and 20–50% premiums are not uncommon, especially in boom times.

Tactics

The price a bidder is prepared to pay for another company depends on a number of factors. Obviously an assessment of the asset value and earnings value can be made bearing in mind the broad changes that the new management propose. As previously mentioned, no bid is likely to succeed at a price below stock market value where this exists. Any additional payment for goodwill over and above tangible asset value depends on the reason for the bid and the strengths of the two parties.

Tactics are not very relevant in a merger where the good faith of both companies' management is paramount. In a takeover, particularly if it is opposed, battle lines are drawn very much as in chess. Each side proceeds with caution, one move at a time, anticipating and countering the other side's move.

The bidder usually tries to gain a foothold by acquiring itself, or through associates, a stake in the other company. If this is done through normal market purchases the effect on the other company's share price may lead to speculation of an impending bid. This can be avoided by spreading such purchases over a long period of time but it is not possible to build up a large stake secretly due to preventive measures in the City Takeover Code.

Defending an unwanted bid depends on that management's record and the proportion of total shares under their control. If the company has just announced poor results and the directors own only a tiny proportion of the total issued shares then any price significantly above the present market price will be hard to resist. On the other hand a company with a good track record of profit and dividend growth, together with a substantial director interest in the shares, may be able to fight off an unwelcome bid or demand such a high price that the bidder withdraws.

Very few bids are either successful at the first attempt or withdrawn on first refusal. Sometimes three or four increased bids are made in response to the defending management's arguments, all of which are given space in the national financial press as well as being mailed personally to each shareholder. Once 90% acceptance of a bid has been achieved the remaining 10% can be compulsorily acquired at the same price. Even when 90% acceptance is not achieved, but voting control passes to the predator, the remaining minority shareholders should think their position over carefully. There is no guarantee that the new parent will follow dividend policies to their liking and it may be wiser to accept the bid rather than be 'locked in' without an effective voice.

Monopolies Commission

Mergers and takeovers are not allowed to take place without due regard to the public interest, particularly where a reduction in competition would result from the proposed amalgamation of companies. In cases where substantial assets are to be acquired, or where a monopoly of more than one third of the market would result, the Department of Industry can refer the proposal to the Monopolies Commission. Such a reference can effectively kill off a proposal as the necessary investigations may take up to six months and the resulting uncertainty causes difficulty in share dealings of the companies involved.

Consideration

This refers to the form in which the purchase price is paid. Possible types of consideration are ordinary or preference shares, loan stock, convertible securities, or cash itself. Only cash counts as a disposal for capital gains tax purposes and this may prove unpopular with large shareholders to whom it would apply. Gains of several thousand pounds are exempt in any tax year so small shareholders are not influenced in the same way.

Payment can be effected in preference shares or loan stock, both of which have a fixed rate of return. These will not be so popular with the ordinary shareholders being bought out, as their investment requirements are usually growth of dividend income and an increasing value of their capital. Neither preference shares nor loan stock participate in the changing prosperity of the parent company but they do enhance the gearing benefits for the latter company's ordinary shareholders.

A compromise often reached is to offer a mixture of securities and cash in exchange for the shares in the recipient company. Another alternative is to offer to pay in convertible loan stock. This starts its life as a conventional loan with a fixed rate of interest but carries the right to be converted into a predetermined number of ordinary shares in the parent company at a future date. From the bidders' point of view no dilution of equity is involved immediately, and a lower rate of interest can be offered than that acceptable on a pure loan stock. When conversion takes place at a future date it is anticipated that earnings from the company taken over will have grown sufficiently to offset any dilution of equity earnings in the parent company.

Sometimes the management of the two companies cannot agree on the value of the one to be taken over because of uncertainty as to the level of its future profits. This situation can be resolved by the offer of a performance-related purchase price when the initial down-payment is supplemented by later additional payments on achievement of agreed profit targets.

The following short case study illustrates the valuation of a company's shares in an agreed takeover context.

Example

A large public company has just been approached by the directors of EZ Engineering Ltd (a smaller private company) with a view to merging the two companies. The latest balance sheet of EZ Engineering Ltd showed:

Balance sheet as at 31 December 19X4.

	£000	*£000*
Fixed assets:		
Freehold land and buildings (at cost)		350
Plant and machinery (net)		600
Vehicles, etc. (net)		100
		1,050
Current assets:		
Stocks and work-in-progress	400	
Debtors	250	
	650	
Creditors due within a year:		
Trade creditors	150	
Bank overdraft	175	
Tax payable	125	
	450	
Net current assets		200
Total assets *less* Current liabilities		1,250
Creditors due after a year:		
6% debenture (repayable in January 19X6)		400
Net assets		850
Capital and reserves:		
Called-up £1 share capital		500
Profit and loss account		350
		850

The directors of EZ Engineering Ltd have also disclosed the following information:

- On a going concern basis the values of assets and current liabilities are all reasonable except that a recent professional valuation puts the freehold land and buildings at £550,000.
- In a liquidation, stock and work-in-progress would fetch only about £250,000 and redundancies would cost another £250,000.
- After-tax profits have been static in real terms over the last three years, being £150,000 in 19X4 and this level is expected to be maintained. The pretax figure was £275,000 and a normal return would be 20% on total assets.
- Public companies of a similar size to EZ Engineering Ltd have been averaging price/earnings ratios of 5 recently on the London Stock Exchange.

Calculate and discuss the various methods of valuing the ordinary shares of EZ Engineering Ltd on the basis that its directors are willing sellers, and state reasons for the valuation you think most reasonable to both parties.

Calculation of value of ordinary shares

	Book value	*Break-up value*	*Going concern value*
	(£)	*(£)*	*(£)*
A Asset basis			
Fixed assets	1,050,000	1,250,000	1,250,000
Current assets	650,000	500,000	650,000
	1,700,000	1,750,000	1,900,000
Current liabilities	450,000	450,000	450,000
	1,250,000	1,300,000	1,450,000
Debentures	400,000	400,000	400,000
	850,000	900,000	1,050,000
Redundancy costs	—	250,000	—
Value of assets owned by ordinary shareholders	£850,000	£650,000	£1,050,000
Number of ordinary shares	500,000	500,000	500,000
Value per share	£1.70	£1.30	£2.10
B Earnings basis			
Maintainable annual profit after tax		£150,000	
Number of ordinary shares		500,000	
Earnings per share		30p	
Comparative price/earnings ratio		5	
Value per share		£1.50	

Conclusions Four different valuations have emerged ranging from £1.30 asset value on a liquidation to a £2.10 value of the assets as a going concern. Although the directors of EZ are willing sellers they cannot be expected to accept themselves, nor recommend to other shareholders, a price below liquidation value. This therefore sets a minimum value of £1.30 per share as this can be achieved should the company stop trading and sell its assets on a piecemeal basis.

Book value of assets is not very meaningful as it does not represent the value obtainable for the assets whether it keeps going or is wound up. The going concern value of assets would be more appropriate if the company was using these assets to full effect. A 20% pre-tax return on total assets of £1.9 million suggests EZ should be earning £380,000, which is well in excess of the £275,000 actually achieved. For this reason EZ directors cannot expect to receive £2.10 per share nor would any extra payment for goodwill be justified.

Shares in similar public quoted companies can be bought on a price/earnings ratio which value EZ at £1.50 per share. Stock market prices always relate to marginal purchases and a buyer of a controlling interest would expect to pay substantially more. However, EZ directors wish to sell out and with the 6% debentures repayable in a year's time they are not in a strong bargaining position.

All things considered, it might seem appropriate to value the shares in EZ around £1.50, being more than break-up value but valuing the assets on the basis of the earnings they produce. The eventual agreement will depend on the willingness of the public company directors to buy, and the EZ directors to sell out.

Further reading

The Blackstone Frank's Guide to Management Buy-Outs and Buy-Ins, D Franks and L Blackstone, Kogan Page.

Advanced Financial Accounting, R Lewis and D Pendrill, Pitman.

Self-check questions

1 What are the reasons for mergers and takeovers?

2 Whose clearance is required before large takeovers and mergers are allowed to proceed?

3 What are the three bases on which the value of ordinary shares can be calculated?

4 What is the difference between a management buy-out (MBO) and a management buy-in (MBI)?

18

Company taxation

The existence of a central government with the power to levy taxes means that it can influence firms' investment decisions through the tax system. There are two aspects to taxation, one being negative and the other positive. The negative side is the payment of tax on profits while the positive side is the receipt of tax allowances which reduce the tax payments.

Corporation tax is the system of taxation which applies to profits of all limited companies and nationalised industries, as opposed to income tax which applies to profits of the self-employed and partnerships. Differences between the two systems are confined mainly to the tax rates and the timing of the tax payments. If we examine the principles of corporation tax first then the differences of the income tax system can be contrasted later.

There are two rates of corporation tax, either of which can apply, depending on the size of the taxable profit for the year. The normal rate is 33% at the time of writing but a small companies rate of 25% exists for firms whose profits are relatively low. There is a gradual increase in the rate from 25% to 33%, which applies to companies whose profits fall within the band where the 25% rate ceases to apply, but the full 33% rate is not yet applicable. Usually the Chancellor increases these limits in the budget but the actual rates of corporation tax are rarely altered.

The accounting year for many companies will not cover the same twelve months as the tax year which runs from 1 April one year to the following 31 March. If the rate of tax did alter from one tax year to the next and the company accounting year straddled both tax years, then the year's profit is apportioned pro rata for the number of months which fall into each tax year. The two rates of tax can then be levied on the respective part of the profit which falls into each tax year as shown in Figure 18.1.

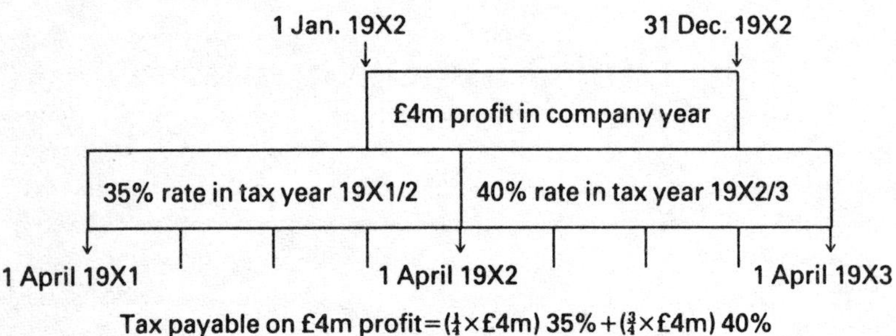

Figure 18.1 *Apportionment of year's profit over two tax years*

The profit on which corporation tax is levied (£4 million in the example) is not identical with the profit disclosed in the firm's profit and loss account, but is an adjusted profit figure after some costs have been disallowed and some other allowances received. The statement in Figure 18.2 shows the main adjustments that take place.

		£
Profit as per profit and loss account		4,040,000
Add back disallowed expenses	£	
Depreciation	200,000	
Entertainment	10,000	
Political contributions	5,000	
Provision for possible bad debts	1,000	216,000
		4,256,000
Deduct		
Capital allowances		256,000
Taxable profit		£4,000,000
Corporation tax payable is £4.0m × 33% = £1,320,000		

Figure 18.2 *Corporation tax assessment*

It can be seen from this statement that there are significant adjustments which affect the taxable profit. Depreciation charged by a company in its profit and loss account is added back to profit as though it had never been deducted. It is never possible, therefore, to reduce the size of the tax bill by charging extra depreciation in any one year that large profits happen to be made. Whatever figure a company charges for depreciation, the Inland Revenue will add back. The taxable profit each year comprises sales less all allowable operating costs excluding depreciation.

It would be unfair if companies were disallowed depreciation and given nothing in its place. Depreciation is the yearly charge for buildings, plant and machinery, vehicles, and office equipment. The only difference between these costs, as opposed to paying for wages and materials, is the time they last. Firms could not provide goods and services to customers without investing in these physical assets, unless they chose to lease them. In this case the lease or rent payments are included as expenses in the profit and loss account and tax relief is automatically obtained.

Capital allowances

The Inland Revenue have their own system of depreciation allowances which are called capital allowances or writing-down allowances. These are available to firms which buy new physical assets of the specified categories, although some allowances are restricted to specific industries only. Figure 18.3 is a list of the rates of capital allowances at the time of writing.

Industrial buildings	4% pa annual allowance on a straight-line basis for 25 years
Plant and machinery, equipment, furniture, and all vehicles	25% pa annual allowance on a reducing balance basis

Note See below for temporary changes made in the 1992 Autumn Statement.

Figure 18.3 *Rates of capital allowances as at March 1994*

The capital allowances on industrial buildings are restricted to firms operating in the specified industrial classifications. The other allowances apply to all industries. From this it can be deduced that no allowance is normally given for buildings used by service industries, although the equipment, furniture, and vehicles they use are eligible.

A deviation to this rule occurred in 1981 when new commercial buildings in 'enterprise zones' were also made eligible for capital allowances. Accelerated tax allowances may also be available here.

It may have struck you that some of these tax allowances on say plant and machinery are significantly higher than the equivalent depreciation rate used in a firm's profit and loss computations. This is because the Chancellor uses the size of tax allowances as an economic regulator and does not attempt to relate allowances to individual company needs.

An illustration of this arose with the Chancellor's 1992 Autumn Statement. In it, he brought in an initial allowance of 20% on industrial buildings, plus a 4% annual allowance (based on original cost) for twenty years.

The 25% allowance on plant and machinery (excluding cars) was increased to 40% for the first year and 25% pa thereafter based on the reducing balance. Both these accelerated allowances apply for a temporary period of one year ending 31 October 1993 and, in the case of industrial buildings, must be brought into use by 31 December 1994.

Tax allowances on motor cars are most likely to coincide with the firm's practice on depreciation. Most firms use the 25% writing-down allowance on reducing capital balance when calculating their car depreciation charge to include in the profit and loss account. Managers are no longer able to run a Rolls-Royce at the expense of other taxpayers because tax allowances are restricted to a maximum figure which effectively excludes all luxury vehicles. In the case of a car costing £12,000, the allowances shown in Figure 18.4 apply.

	£	
Purchase cost of car	12,000	
Year 1 – capital allowance	3,000	(25% of £12,000)
Written-down value – year 1	9,000	
Year 2 – capital allowance	2,250	(25% of £9,000)
Written-down value – year 2	6,750	
Year 3 – capital allowance	1,687	(25% of £6,750)
Written-down value – year 3	5,063	

Figure 18.4 *Capital allowances of 25% on reducing value of £12,000 car*

The annual allowance falls substantially each year but the written-down value never reaches zero. Whenever the asset is sold a balancing up with the Inland Revenue takes place. If we assume the above car was sold after three years' use, it is unlikely it would exactly realise its book value of £5,063. If it was sold for £3,000, the Inland

Revenue would give a 'balancing allowance' of the £2,063 difference. On the other hand, if the car realised £6,000, the tax collector would claim back excess allowances of £937 previously granted. This 'balancing charge' would result in the firm paying back £937 × 33% = £309 tax when it settled the tax bill for the year in which the sale took place.

When appraising new investment projects the availability of these tax allowances must be incorporated into the cash flows. Tax saved by claiming these allowances will occur in the year the payment would otherwise have taken place. We must now look to see when tax is due for payment.

Advance corporation tax (ACT)

One of the good things we can say about tax on limited company profits is that it is not payable immediately, but after a time lag. The present system of corporation tax goes back to 1972 and is called an 'imputation system'. When a limited company makes a dividend payment it pays a 'net' dividend to shareholders and a tax payment to the Inland Revenue. For example, on a net dividend of £800 the tax payment is £200 being equivalent to income tax at the 20% rate. Such tax is deemed to be an advance payment of the company's total corporation tax liability. The shareholder receives the net dividend of £800 together with a 'tax credit' of £200, so his or her total or gross dividend is £1,000. If the shareholder is not liable for tax he or she can claim this £200 back from the Inland Revenue except in the case of 'foreign income dividends' mentioned later. Conversely, if he or she is liable for higher rates of tax than the 20% already paid on their behalf, he or she will receive a further tax bill in due course.

Most companies make two dividend payments within any twelve months, namely, the interim and final dividend relating to their accounting year. This results in two payments of 'advance corporation tax' (ACT) being made. The interim dividend payment takes place after the first half-year profits are known, which may be about nine months after the start of the accounting year. The final dividend payment normally takes place after the annual general meeting has approved the directors' recommendation, which will be at least three months after the accounting year end. At this stage the total tax liability for the accounting year is computed along the lines of Figure 18.2 and agreed with the inspector of taxes. The previous payments of ACT are deducted from this total tax liability to arrive at the balance or 'mainstream' tax payable. This last payment will not be due until nine months after the company year end.

Some companies have problems with ACT when their UK corporation tax bill in total is too small to recover all the ACT paid. This can apply to companies earning a large proportion of their profit abroad and therefore paying tax abroad on it. When these overseas profits are passed on to shareholders as dividends, ACT must be paid in full to the Inland Revenue. The reduction of ACT to 20% in the 1994–95 tax year (announced in the March 1993 Budget) will reduce any unrecovered ACT for those companies with large foreign earnings. The introduction of foreign income dividends from July 1994, paid out of profits earned overseas, will help companies to recover surplus ACT.

Tax payments

The nature of the above three tax payments relating to the profits of any one year makes it very difficult to generalise about exactly when tax is paid. It depends on the proportion of profit paid out as dividends as well as when the company was formed. When appraising investments we need to incorporate tax payments into the yearly cash flows. A good rule of thumb is to assume an average delay of one year in the payment of all tax on profits.

As tax payments are made in arrears, the benefit of deducting capital allowances from profits to reduce these tax payments must also be delayed. Any capital allowances a firm can deduct from its year's profit will reduce the mainstream tax payment rather than ACT payments, which are solely dictated by the size of the dividends.

In an individual project appraisal where we need to include as a cash inflow the tax saved by claiming capital allowances, it is necessary to allow either a one- or two-year time lag. This is because the investment takes place at year 0, being the beginning of the project's first year. If this happened to be near the end of the company accounting year the delay could be only nine months. If the investment took place at the start of the company accounting year the tax saving could be twenty-one months away. Within our own company we may be able to make a more precise estimate of these delays in tax transactions. Similarly, if our company is loss-making at the present time, we would need to make an estimate of when the tax savings would be effective.

Public authorities

Corporation tax applies to any remaining nationalised industries and they should allow for payment of tax and the benefit of capital allowances in their project appraisals. In some cases nationalised industries have large losses or accumulated capital allowances they have not been able to offset against profits in previous years. It would be unrealistic to allow for tax payments and allowances in the normal way. If the level of future profits and the size of unused past allowances are such that it is envisaged the nationalised industry will never be liable for tax payments, then it is advisable to exclude tax completely from the cash flows. This will also be the case with local authorities and similar bodies, which are specifically excluded from corporation tax.

Income tax

Previous discussion has centred on limited companies which come under the auspices of the corporation tax system. Some business people trade in their own name, or as a partnership, without ever forming a limited company. Profits of these self-employed persons come under the income tax system which also applies to employees. Unlike limited companies, the self-employed do not pay dividends and any drawings or salary they pay themselves are not allowed when computing the taxable profit.

Profits from running a business are deemed to be the income of the individual or partner. Like limited companies, the various capital allowances on new investment all apply. The remaining profits are taxed in bands at rates presently varying from 20% to 40% after the personal allowances for the particular individual have been deducted.

Collection of income tax from employees takes place weekly or monthly under the PAYE system. The Inland Revenue cannot operate the same system with the self-employed because the income or profits are not known until the accounting year ends. In practice it takes a few months to prepare and audit accounts, so the delay is even longer. To overcome this problem the Inland Revenue charges income tax in the current year based on the level of profits earned in the previous tax year. More precisely the normal basis of assessment for ongoing self-employed firms is to take the profits of the accounting year ended in the previous tax year as the basis for assessing tax payable in the current tax year. This is known as the 'preceding year' basis. Because current profits can never be available, tax is based on out-of-date figures. This does not mean that there is a long delay in the payment of tax but simply that current tax is based on an outdated figure. The actual payment of tax is made 50% on 1 January in the current tax year and the remaining 50% on 1 July, which actually falls in the next tax year. (This long-standing preceding year basis is currently being reviewed by the Inland Revenue with a view to changing to a current year basis in 1997/98.)

Taking the example of a self-employed person whose accounting year ends 31 August, the profit for the accounting year ended 31 August 1992 falls in the tax year 1992/93. This profit will be used as the basis for assessing income tax for the tax year 1993/94, which tax will be payable equally on 1 January 1994 and 1 July 1994.

When incorporating tax payments and tax savings into investment appraisals the timing must be taken into account. In the case of self-employed persons there is no delay of one year in payment, but the size of the previous year's profits determines the size of the current year's tax payment. A time lag of one year should be assumed, however, when incorporating the benefit of capital allowances into the net cash flows for investment appraisal purposes.

A practical difficulty occurs here when the size of the profits is such that higher rates of tax are payable. The benefit of capital allowances shows up in reduced taxable profits, starting at the highest rate of tax which would have been payable if the investment had not taken place. If the size of the capital allowance is such that a number of bands of taxable income are eliminated then the tax saved should be calculated at the different marginal rates of tax applicable in that case.

Capital gains tax (CGT)

A capital gain takes place when a possession such as a building or asset is sold for more than was paid for it after its initial purchase cost is adjusted for subsequent inflation. This process is known as 'indexation'. There are various other exemptions and reliefs which reduce the amount of the gain and the tax payable on it.

Individuals and self-employed persons are taxed on any chargeable gains as if it was taxable income. They therefore pay CGT tax at the relevant rate depending on the size of their other taxable income.

A limited company includes any capital gains with its profits from trading activities each financial year. All the company's profit is then assessed for corporation tax. In practice, both companies and unincorporated businesses may not pay tax on certain gains. This is because 'roll-over relief' allows them to reinvest the proceeds from the sale of fixed assets in new qualifying assets. This defers the payment of capital gains tax until the disposal of the new assets. As this process can be repeated *ad infinitum*, capital gains tax may not be a problem for businesses able to take advantage of this relief.

Value added tax (VAT)

The standard rate of VAT is 17.5% as from 1 April 1991. This tax has little influence on business decisions although it may affect a company's cash flow. VAT is collected by the Customs and Excise in multi-stages and not just at the time of sale to the final consumer. When a firm buys goods and services it pays input tax to the suppliers as part of the invoice settlement. When the buying firm in turn sells goods or services it charges output tax to its customers, but pays only the difference between output VAT and input VAT to the tax collector. Some materials may go through a number of processing stages in different firms before eventually being bought by a final consumer, so some VAT is collected at each stage. The tax point occurs at the invoice date rather than the date cash is paid in settlement of credit transactions. However, small businesses have the option of accounting for VAT on a cash basis, ie when invoices are actually settled.

It is possible for the cash flow of a firm to be adversely affected by having to pay input tax to suppliers before tax has been received from customers. This will partly depend on the credit periods for purchases and sales. Where a much longer credit period is granted to customers than is received from suppliers, the balance of tax due to the tax collector may have to be paid before it is actually received.

Sales of some goods and services are zero rated, which means no VAT is levied on the final consumer. New house buildings are a case in point. Building firms will pay input tax on all building materials and services they buy in from other firms, which they then claim back from the tax collector. If they pay suppliers' invoices which include VAT before they get the refund from the tax collector, then their cash flow is adversely affected. It may be possible to arrange a monthly settlement in these cases in place of the more normal quarterly one.

The greatest criticism of VAT by business people is probably on the grounds of the extra administration required, particularly in very small businesses where office staff are minimal.

Further reading

Taxation, B Pritchard, Pitman.
Taxation, P Rowes, DPP.

Self-check questions

1 Do all companies pay the same rate of corporation tax irrespective of the size of profit made?
2 Does the capital allowance on an asset in any one year always have the same value as the company's own depreciation charge?
3 If a company pays corporation tax at 33% will the tax charge for the year exactly equal 33% of the net profit?
4 When is corporation tax paid to the Inland Revenue?
5 What is the written-down value of an asset costing £25,000 that has been depreciated at 20% pa for three years on the reducing balance method?
6 How does the Inland Revenue collect income tax from self-employed persons when it does not know how much profit they made in the same tax year?
7 Do firms actually bear the cost of the VAT they have to pay on the goods and services they buy in from other firms?

19
Overseas transactions

The UK is a prominent country in international trade, exporting approximately one fifth of its total output of goods and services and importing roughly the same amount in exchange. This means that many firms are directly involved with imports and exports or own subsidiary companies which operate in foreign countries. Knowledge of exchange rates, the financing of foreign trade, the minimising of risk, and the accounting treatment of profits arising abroad is essential.

Exchange rates

When a UK exporter quotes a price to a foreign customer it has to decide whether to quote in £ sterling, in the importer's currency, or in some other recognised currency such as the dollar. When quoting in sterling the exporter will know with certainty the value he or she will receive and be able to estimate the profit on the deal. If the exporter quotes a price in a foreign currency then the profit is subject to the uncertainty of fluctuations in the rate of exchange between sterling and that currency until the time payment is made.

Take for example a UK shoe manufacturer agreeing to sell a consignment of shoes to a French importer for 100,000 francs. At the time the contract was signed the rate of exchange between the two currencies was £1 = 10 francs. The importer suffers no exchange rate risk as it is paying in its own currency of francs. The exporter, however, could make a larger or smaller profit on the contract depending on what happens to the exchange rate up to the time payment takes place. Initially it expects to be able to convert the 100,000 francs into £10,000. If the rate of exchange for the £ went down to £1 = 9 francs the exporter would receive £11,111 on conversion of the francs. Conversely, if the £ had gone up to £1 = 11 francs it would receive only £9,091.

The UK abandoned the system of fixed exchange rates in favour of a floating rate in the early 1970s. Then in October 1990, we joined the Exchange Rate Mechanism (ERM) at a quasi-fixed rate of £1 = 2.95DM, but allowed to move 5% either side of that rate. In September 1992, the UK was forced to leave the ERM after an unprecedented attack by currency speculators anticipating a devaluation, or realignment, of the pound against other hard European currencies, such as the mark. The pound is now freely floating once more at the time of writing in September 1994.

Protection for importers and exporters is now more important than ever when exchange rates can fluctuate without end-stops. In a recent period of a few months, the pound has come down from £1 = $2.00 to £1 = $1.50, representing a fall of 25%. This fall has not been uniform, but composed of a series of sharp movements in small periods of time. Any contract that was settled during one of these periods of violent change could have resulted in a substantially altered profit to that originally envisaged.

Minimising risk

It appears that in foreign trade either the importer or the exporter is exposed to the risk of an adverse movement in the exchange rate. Which party it is depends on which currency is used to fix the contract price. Whether a UK firm is exporting or importing it will bear no exchange risk if the contract price is expressed in pounds sterling. However, the firm is exposed to exchange risk if the contract is priced in any other currency.

Pricing in a foreign currency makes the deal more attractive to the foreign importer who knows its commitment exactly because it is expressed in its own currency. This does not necessarily mean the UK firm has to bear the risk of an adverse movement in the exchange rate until payment is received. One of the simplest and most effective ways of eliminating this risk is to deal forward.

A forward exchange contract fixes the rate of exchange now between sterling and a foreign currency, for conversion of that currency into pounds at a later date, say three months or even a year hence.

Depending on the time interval and which way the currencies involved are expected to move, the forward rate can be either at a discount or a premium to the 'spot rate' of exchange obtainable now.

As an example let us suppose an exporter of goods priced in dollars can obtain a spot rate of £1 = $1.600 with the three-month forward rate quoted at 0.40 cents discount. By entering into a forward exchange contract with a bank it is guaranteed to be able to exchange the dollars it received in three months' time into sterling at a rate of £1 = $1.6040. Should the pound fall in value to only $1.50 during this time it would have been better off taking the risk itself as it would have received more pounds for the dollars it received. On the other hand if the pound rose to £1 = $1.70 it would have received less pounds for the dollars. The forward exchange contract guarantees receipt of a fixed value in pounds at very little extra cost. Such a contract cannot guarantee that the exporter would not have been better off taking the risk itself, but few would want to expose themselves to such risks in an increasingly volatile market quite outside their normal trading experience.

A variation on forward exchange contracts is possible where importers or exporters do not know the precise date of payment with certainty. They can enter into a forward exchange contract with an option to convert during part of this period. For example, a 'three months forward, option over third month' contract means that the trader can convert the foreign currency into pounds at the agreed rate at any time during the third month.

Another way to allow for exchange risk applies when an exporter expects to be paid in a foreign currency at a future date. If it borrows the same amount of foreign currency now and converts it into sterling at today's spot rate it can repay the foreign debt it incurred by the proceeds of the export contract. Provided it reinvests the loan any loss is limited to the difference between the rate of interest paid on the loan and that earned on the short-term deposit in this country. This method of exchange risk avoidance may be more appropriate to large contracts of lengthy duration.

Apart from the above risk associated with exchange rate movements, there is also the risk of non-payment for goods by a foreign buyer. The Export Credits Guarantee Department (ECGD) acts like an insurance company and covers such risks of non-payment, thereby removing a possible disincentive to export.

Risk of non-payment may also be avoided if an exporter receives orders through a 'confirming house' which acts as an agent for overseas buyers. Such institutions may arrange for the shipment of goods to their foreign importer as well as guarantee payment to the exporter so that it is little different from a sale on the home market. A relatively new source of cover for exchange risk is to use the services of a forfaiter, as discussed later.

Methods of payment

For internal trade in the UK it is quite usual for credit to be granted for a period of some weeks. Normal terms in many industries are for payment to be made by the end of the month following the month of delivery, which in effect means four to eight weeks' credit.

An increasing amount of foreign trade is being conducted on this same basis being known as an 'open account'. Payment never results in the physical movement of currency but by the adjustment of bank balances in the two countries concerned. This can be effected by a fax or telex message or use of the slower airmail communication.

'Documentary credits' are frequently used to settle payments in international trade. Such a document is a letter from a bank to the exporter guaranteeing payment for goods on receipt of certain documents which usually include a bill of lading, invoice, and insurance certificate. Payment may be immediate, or the bank may agree to 'accept' a bill of exchange, which is in effect a promise to pay at some future date, normally three months hence. The bank's acceptance of the bill guarantees its payment and it can be immediately discounted by the exporter for little more than the cost of interest for the period of waiting. In this way the exporter gets cash earlier than by waiting for the bill to mature.

When opening a credit, or accepting a bill of exchange, the bank is taking on the risk of the importer defaulting on the payment for the goods he or she imported. Banks will therefore approach such transactions as though they were lending money to the importer and may require guarantees or charges over company assets to secure their loan.

Financing foreign trade

In many cases exporters will view the financing of foreign trade in the same light as financing domestic trade. A mix of owners' capital and borrowed capital will provide the working capital required for both exports and domestic sales. A documentary credit or discounted bill of exchange may actually result in cash being received earlier on export trade than from sales at home.

Should further finance be required in the form of a bank loan or overdraft, the existence of ECGD insurance cover will greatly facilitate proceedings and possibly reduce the rate of interest. A variation on this theme occurs with 'buyer credit financing' where the buyer pays the exporter on delivery from a bank loan guaranteed by the ECGD. From time to time government tries to stimulate exports via special bank lending arrangements so investigation of this source is always worth while.

Invoice factoring is another way of financing export trade being somewhat similar to the factoring system used in the home market. Money is not advanced until the sale takes place when the factor buys the sales invoice and collects the debt from the foreign importer without recourse to the exporter. In this way working capital requirements are reduced, although not necessarily eliminated.

A similar new source of finance for exporters is now provided by forfaiting. When an export sale takes place, the forfaiter buys the bill of exchange, or promissory note, at a discount and takes over the risks of non-payment for both commercial and political reasons.

Exchange control

At the time of writing, exchange control no longer exists in the UK. This means that firms and individuals are free to invest abroad and firms can import goods without regard to foreign exchange availability or otherwise. This is not the case with many other countries whose balance of payments position demands that they ration out their scarce holdings of foreign currency by imposing exchange control. Such control specifies the amounts and purposes for which foreign exchange will be made available. A country may, for example, prohibit or impose limits on the amount of profits remittable as dividends by foreign subsidiaries to their parent company in the UK.

Separate from exchange control there may also exist a system of tariffs or quotas which prohibit or limit the importing and exporting of specified goods and services. There are international agreements specifying when, and how, such restrictions are to be used which may allow discrimination against unfair competition, the protection of developing industries, or restrictions on trade for political and security reasons.

Foreign subsidiaries' accounts

Subsidiary companies operating abroad will keep their accounting records in the currency of that country. From such records the trial balance and hence the profit and loss account and balance sheet will be produced. If a foreign subsidiary's accounts are consolidated with the parent and other subsidiaries into group accounts then they must be converted from the foreign currency to pounds sterling.

Assets and liabilities abroad are converted to sterling at the rate of exchange at the group year end. Due to a movement in exchange rates between the two currencies any exchange difference between yearly balance sheets is dealt with in reserves. Profits are also converted at the year end or average exchange rate, except for dividends actually remitted which should be included at the pound sterling equivalent on receipt.

The consolidation of foreign subsidiaries is something of a grey area in accounting where alternative treatment of items may be found. The precise policy adopted by a company is spelt out in the statement of accounting policies contained in its annual report.

Transfer pricing

The term 'transfer pricing' refers to the price at which goods and services are sold or transferred from one unit to another within a global undertaking. Take, for example, a holding company which owns two subsidiaries, one of which manufactures ventilation equipment while the other installs the same in addition to other makers' equipment. The performance of each unit, if measured in terms of return on capital, will have to take account of the transfer price of the equipment between the two units. Too low a price will result in a low return for the manufacturer and a high return for the installer, and vice versa for a price set too high. Prices should be set at normal commercial rates, that is at arm's length, but agreement on this could be a contentious point for the managers of the two units concerned.

Transfer pricing also has its relevance when holding companies trade with their foreign subsidiaries. In this case two further points will have to be considered. One relates to the level of taxation on company profits in the different countries and the tax treatment of distributed profits. It may seem advisable to let the bulk of the profit arise in the country where tax rates are low by transferring out at a high price or transferring in at a low price. But tax authorities around the world are aware of these practices and give them close attention. Some major trade countries, such as the USA, Germany, and Japan, issue detailed regulations on the criteria used to fix arm's length transfer prices.

The other point relates to exchange control regulations. If a UK company desires overseas subsidiaries to remit dividends, but these are blocked or restricted by foreign governments' exchange control regulations, then a solution might be to transfer out at a high price. This has the effect of artificially inflating the UK parent's profits and deflating the profit of the foreign subsidiary which would not have been allowed to remit the same funds as dividends.

Obviously both UK and foreign governments are aware of these possibilities and may try to regulate such practices. Trade unions too have been known to question transfer prices from the point of view that profits are a relevant factor in pay negotiations.

Further reading

Principles of Corporate Finance, R A Brealey and S C Myers, McGraw-Hill.

Advanced Financial Accounting, R Lewis and D Pendrill, Pitman.

Self-check questions

1 What risk does an exporter take when he or she prices in pounds sterling?
2 What risk does the importer take on the same deal?
3 How can an exporter eliminate some of the risks involved in such trade?
4 What special sources of finance are available to exporters?
5 Why are foreign subsidiaries not always able to remit dividends back to their UK parent?
6 What does the term 'transfer pricing' mean?
7 Why are national governments interested in transactions between arms of the same multinational company?

Appendix 1

Manufacturing, trading, and profit and loss account for the year ended 31 December 199X

		£000	£000
Sales:			1,000
Less Cost of sales			
Raw materials used		200	
Direct wages		400	
		600	
Add Opening work-in-progress		100	
		700	
Less Closing work-in-progress		200	
Prime cost		500	
Add Other factory expenses		100	
Gross cost of production		600	
Add Opening stock of finished goods		50	
		650	
Less Closing stock of finished goods		55	595
Gross profit			405
Less Administration expenses			
Salaries	30		
Printing, stationery, postages, telephone	10		
Rates, heat, light, and power	10		
Bank charges and sundries	10	60	
Selling and distribution expenses			
Salaries and commission	40		
Advertising	10		
Carriage and packing	20		
Motor expenses	20	90	150
Balance before charging			255
Depreciation		*20*	
Auditors' remuneration		*10*	
Debenture interest		*10*	
Directors' remuneration		80	120
Net profit before tax			135
Corporation tax			60
Net profit after tax			75
Dividends			20
Retained profit			55

Appendix 2

Balance sheet as at 31 December 199X

Fixed assets	*Cost* *£000*	*Depn* *£000*	*Net* *£000*
Freehold land and buildings	40	—	40
Plant and machinery	30	20	10
Fixtures and fittings	5	3	2
Motor vehicles	10	5	5
	85	28	57
Current assets			
Stocks: Raw materials	10		
Work-in-progress	20		
Finished goods	5	35	
Debtors *less* Provision for bad debts		30	
Cash at bank and in hand		8	
		73	
Creditors due within one year			
Finance debt	5		
Other creditors	25	30	
Net current assets (ie working capital)			43
Total assets less Current liabilities (capital employed)			100
Creditors due after one year			
Finance debt (ie loans, debentures)		12	
Other creditors		—	
Provisions for liabilities and charges		6	18
Total net assets (owned by shareholders)			82
Capital and reserves			
Called-up share capital			20
Share premium account			5
Profit and loss account			57
Shareholders' funds			82

Appendix 3
Glossary of terms

accrual Outstanding expenses for an accounting period which have not yet been paid or invoiced.

acid test ratio See *liquidity ratio.*

advance corporation tax A part of the total corporation tax liability which is paid to the Inland Revenue at the time a dividend is paid to shareholders.

asset Any possession or claim on others which is of value to a firm. See also *fixed assets* and *current assets*.

associated company A company in which another company owns a substantial shareholding exceeding 20% but not more than 50% of the total.

balance sheet A statement of the financial position of a firm at a point in time showing the assets owned and the sources of finance.

book value The original or historic cost of an asset less depreciation.

break-even point The level of output or sales value at which total costs equal total revenue.

budgetary control Financial plans to meet objectives in the accounting year against which actual results are compared.

capital allowance The Inland Revenue's equivalent of a company's depreciation charge. Allowances are granted on purchases of certain new assets and reduce taxable profits.

capital employed The permanent and longer-term capital used by a firm comprising share capital, reserves, and loan capital in the case of a limited company. It embraces all the sources of finance excluding current liabilities.

capital gains tax The tax payable by individuals or companies on the profit made from the sale of certain assets.

capital gearing See *gearing*.

capital reserves See *reserves.*

cash flow The definition depends on the context in which the term is used but is generally regarded as the profit plus the depreciation charge for the period, on the grounds that this latter is not a cash expense.

cash flow statement A financial statement showing the internal and external sources and uses of cash during a period of time.

consolidated accounts A combined profit and loss account and a combined balance sheet for a holding company and its subsidiaries.

contribution The difference between sales and the variable cost of goods sold, before charging fixed costs.

convertible loan Starts its life as a conventional loan but gives the holder the right to transfer into a specified number of ordinary shares at a later date.

corporation tax Tax levied on a limited company's profit. There is one standard rate (currently 33%) but a small companies rate applies to those companies with insufficient profit to be taxed at the higher level.

cost code A numbering system used to describe the type, source, and purpose of all costs and income.

cost – direct or indirect A direct cost is one which can be specifically allocated to a product, as in the case of materials used and labour expended. An indirect cost cannot be directly related to any particular product but is more general in nature. Indirect costs are alternatively called overheads and direct costs are sometimes referred to as prime costs.

cost – variable or fixed A variable cost varies in total pro rata to the volume of production. A fixed cost stays the same total sum over a range of output levels.

creditor Anyone to whom the business owes money.

current assets Cash and other short-term assets in the process of being turned back into cash. For example, stocks and debtors.

current cost accounting A procedure for adjusting items in a company profit and loss account and balance sheet for the effects of inflation.

current liabilities Short-term sources of finance from trade creditors, bank overdraft, dividend, and tax provisions awaiting payment within the next twelve months.

current ratio A measure of liquidity obtained by dividing current assets by current liabilities.

debenture A legal document acknowledging a debt by a company. It sets out details of the interest payment on the loan and the repayment of the capital. Also it will contain details of any company assets pledged as security in a fixed or floating charge.

debtor A credit customer or other party who owes money to the firm.

debt ratio The relationship of total debts to total assets.

deferred tax Tax which is not payable at one specific time but which may become payable at a future date.

depreciation A proportion of the original or current cost of a fixed asset which is charged as an expense in a company profit and loss account.

discounted cash flow yield A measure of the true rate of profitability expected on a project. It represents the maximum rate of interest which could be paid on the diminishing capital balance of an investment.

dividend A periodic profit distribution to shareholders in proportion to the amount of shares held.

dividend cover A measure of the security of the dividend payment obtained by dividing the profit after tax by the total dividend.

dividend yield The income obtained from the gross dividend as a percentage of the current market price of a share.

double entry bookkeeping The method of recording financial transactions whereby every item is entered as a debit in one account and a corresponding credit in another.

earnings yield The earnings per share expressed as a percentage of the current market price of an ordinary share.

equity See *shareholders' funds*.

factoring The acquisition of finance from a specialist company against the security of sales invoices which that company collects.

fixed assets Assets kept by the firm for the provision of goods or services to customers. They are not sold in the normal course of business and include buildings, plant and machinery, vehicles, furniture, and office equipment.

flexible budget A budget which is constructed to change in accordance with the actual level of activity achieved.

forfaiting A specialist form of finance for exporters.

gearing The relationship of prior charge capital to owners' capital.

goodwill The benefit accruing to a business due to its name and reputation. It is valued as the difference between the purchase price of a business and the value of the net assets acquired.

gross profit The difference between sales and the cost of goods sold before charging general overhead expenses.

gross profit margin Gross profit expressed as a percentage of sales.

group accounts See *consolidated accounts*.

historic cost accounting The recording of transactions at the actual cost incurred at the time of purchase irrespective of the item's current value.

holding company The parent company which owns a controlling interest in one or more subsidiaries.

income tax The tax levied on the income of employees and on the profits of self-employed persons.

inflation accounting See *current cost accounting*.

intangible assets Assets of a non-physical nature including goodwill, patents, trade marks, and royalty agreements.

internal rate of return (IRR) See *discounted cash flow yield*.

invoice discounting A form of factoring. See *factoring*.

liquidity ratio A measure of liquidity obtained by dividing debtors, cash, and short-term investments by current liabilities.

mainstream corporation tax The balance of the tax liability after the advance payments have been made.

marginal costing A system of costing used for decision-making which is based on the analysis of costs into fixed and variable categories.

minority interests The proportion of a subsidiary company which is owned by outside shareholders as opposed to the parent or holding company. Cannot apply to wholly owned subsidiaries.

net profit The profit after all deductions except tax and dividends.

net profit margin Net profit expressed as a percentage of sales.

ordinary shares The class of capital entitling the holders to all remaining profits after interest and preference dividends have been paid. They are also entitled to all residual assets once other claimants have been repaid on liquidation.

overtrading A liquidity problem caused by insufficient working capital to support the level of sales.

payback period The number of years taken to recover the original sum invested.

preference shares The class of capital entitling the holders to a fixed rate of dividend prior to any ordinary share dividend. On liquidation they are also entitled to the repayment of their capital before ordinary shareholders are repaid.

present value The equivalent value now of a sum of money receivable in a later year. The net present value is the sum of all negative and positive present values in an investment appraisal indicating that project's viability when positive.

price/earnings ratio A ratio used for comparing market prices of different companies' ordinary shares. It is calculated by dividing the market price of the share by the earnings per share.

profit and loss account Sometimes called the income statement. It summarises the income and expenditure of a company to arrive at the net profit or loss for the period.

ratio Two figures usually extracted from the profit and loss account and/or balance sheet and related together as a percentage, ratio, or function.

realisation An accounting concept which states that profit is earned when a sale takes place and not when cash from that sale is received.

related company A modern version of an associated company introduced by the Companies Act 1981. It refers to a non-group company in which voting shares are held long term with a view to exerting influence for the holding company's benefit. The holding can be any size up to 50% when it would assume subsidiary status.

reserves Revenue reserves are retained profits which can be distributed as dividends. Capital reserves are not available for distribution as they have not arisen from normal trading activities. They occur when fixed assets are revalued or sold at a profit and when a company sells new shares at a premium.

return on capital (ROC) Profit before tax and interest charges expressed as a percentage of capital employed.

rights issue An invitation to existing shareholders to subscribe for new shares when a company requires further capital.

scrip issue A free or bonus issue of new shares to existing shareholders in proportion to their existing holding. No new capital is received by the company which translates existing reserves into share capital.

share capital Money subscribed by shareholders in a limited company for ordinary or preference shares. Issued share capital is the amount of money actually received while authorised capital is the total amount the directors are empowered to issue at that time.

share premium account Is the excess money received by a company when it sells shares for more than their par value. It is a capital reserve and must be distinguished from the issued share capital in the balance sheet.

shareholders' funds The total amount of shareholders' investment in the company comprising both issued share capital, retained profits, and all other reserves. It equals the value of all the company's assets after deducting all debts owing to outside parties. (Sometimes called the net worth.)

standard costing A system of costing whereby predetermined product costs are compared with actual costs to highlight significant variances which are then investigated.

standard hour A measure of the volume of work achievable in one hour.

subsidiary A company which is controlled by another company which owns more than 50% of the voting shares.

transfer price The price at which one company sells to another in the same group.

trial balance The list of debit and credit balances on individual accounts from which a profit and loss account is prepared.

turnover An alternative word for sales.

turnover of capital The relationship of sales to capital employed, stating the number of times each £1 of capital has generated £1 of sales in one year.

value added statement A financial statement showing the wealth created by a company in a period of time and how it was distributed to the interested parties.

variance The difference between a budget or standard and the actual amount.

virement The ability to transfer from one budget heading to another.

working capital That part of a firm's total capital which is tied up in stocks, work-in-progress, and granting credit to customers. It is equal to current assets less current liabilities.

Z score A combination of certain accounting ratios used to predict business failure.

Appendix 4 Present value of £1

n Year	5%	6%	7%	8%	9%	10%	11%	12%	13%	14%	15%	16%	17%	18%	19%	20%	21%	22%	23%	24%	25%	26%	27%	28%	29%	30%	35%	40%
0	1.000	1.000	1.000	1.000	1.000	1.000	1.000	1.000	1.000	1.000	1.000	1.000	1.000	1.000	1.000	1.000	1.000	1.000	1.000	1.000	1.000	1.000	1.000	1.000	1.000	1.000	1.000	1.000
1	.952	.943	.935	.926	.917	.909	.901	.893	.885	.877	.870	.862	.855	.846	.840	.833	.826	.820	.813	.807	.800	.794	.787	.781	.775	.769	.741	.714
2	.907	.890	.873	.857	.842	.826	.812	.797	.783	.769	.756	.743	.731	.718	.706	.694	.683	.672	.661	.650	.640	.630	.620	.610	.601	.592	.549	.510
3	.864	.840	.816	.794	.772	.751	.731	.712	.693	.675	.658	.641	.624	.609	.593	.579	.564	.551	.537	.524	.512	.500	.488	.477	.466	.455	.406	.364
4	.823	.792	.763	.735	.708	.683	.659	.636	.613	.592	.572	.552	.534	.516	.499	.482	.467	.451	.437	.423	.410	.397	.384	.373	.361	.350	.301	.260
5	.784	.747	.713	.681	.650	.621	.593	.567	.543	.519	.497	.476	.456	.437	.419	.402	.386	.370	.355	.341	.328	.315	.303	.291	.280	.269	.223	.186
6	.746	.705	.666	.630	.596	.564	.535	.507	.480	.456	.432	.410	.390	.370	.352	.335	.319	.303	.289	.275	.262	.250	.238	.227	.217	.207	.165	.133
7	.711	.665	.623	.583	.547	.513	.482	.452	.425	.400	.376	.354	.333	.314	.296	.279	.263	.249	.235	.222	.210	.198	.188	.178	.168	.159	.122	.095
8	.677	.627	.582	.540	.502	.467	.434	.404	.376	.351	.327	.305	.285	.266	.249	.233	.218	.204	.191	.179	.168	.157	.148	.139	.130	.123	.091	.068
9	.645	.592	.544	.500	.460	.424	.391	.361	.333	.308	.284	.263	.243	.225	.209	.194	.180	.167	.155	.144	.134	.125	.116	.108	.101	.094	.067	.048
10	.614	.558	.508	.463	.422	.386	.352	.322	.295	.270	.247	.227	.208	.191	.176	.162	.149	.137	.126	.116	.107	.099	.092	.085	.078	.073	.050	.035
11	.585	.527	.475	.429	.388	.350	.317	.287	.261	.237	.215	.195	.178	.162	.148	.135	.123	.112	.103	.094	.086	.079	.072	.066	.061	.056	.037	.025
12	.557	.497	.444	.397	.356	.319	.286	.257	.231	.208	.187	.168	.152	.137	.124	.112	.102	.092	.083	.076	.069	.062	.057	.052	.047	.043	.027	.018
13	.530	.469	.415	.368	.326	.290	.258	.229	.204	.182	.163	.145	.130	.116	.104	.093	.084	.075	.068	.061	.055	.050	.045	.040	.037	.033	.020	.013
14	.505	.442	.388	.340	.299	.263	.232	.205	.181	.160	.141	.125	.111	.099	.088	.078	.069	.062	.055	.049	.044	.039	.035	.032	.028	.025	.015	.009
15	.481	.417	.362	.315	.275	.239	.209	.183	.160	.140	.123	.108	.095	.084	.074	.065	.057	.051	.045	.040	.035	.031	.028	.025	.022	.020	.011	.006
16	.458	.394	.339	.292	.252	.218	.188	.163	.141	.123	.107	.093	.081	.071	.062	.054	.047	.042	.036	.032	.028	.025	.022	.019	.017	.015	.008	.005
17	.436	.371	.317	.270	.231	.198	.170	.146	.125	.108	.093	.080	.069	.060	.052	.045	.039	.034	.030	.026	.023	.020	.017	.015	.013	.012	.006	.003
18	.416	.350	.296	.250	.212	.180	.153	.130	.111	.095	.081	.069	.059	.051	.044	.038	.032	.028	.024	.021	.018	.016	.014	.012	.010	.009	.005	.002
19	.396	.331	.277	.232	.194	.164	.138	.116	.098	.083	.070	.060	.051	.043	.037	.031	.027	.023	.020	.017	.014	.012	.011	.009	.008	.007	.003	.002
20	.377	.312	.258	.215	.178	.149	.124	.104	.087	.073	.061	.051	.043	.037	.031	.026	.022	.019	.016	.014	.012	.010	.008	.007	.006	.005	.002	001
25	.295	.233	.184	.146	.116	.092	.074	.059	.047	.038	.030	.025	.020	.016	.013	.011	.009	.007	.006	.005	.004	.003	.003	.002	.002	.001	.001	.000
30	.231	.174	.131	.099	.075	.057	.044	.033	.026	.020	.015	.012	.009	.007	.005	.004	.003	.003	.002	.002	.001	.001	.001	.001	.000	.000	.000	.000
35	.181	.130	.094	.068	.049	.036	.026	.019	.014	.010	.008	.006	.004	.003	.002	.002	.001	.001	.001	.001	.000	.000	.000	.000	.000	.000	.000	.000
40	.142	.097	.067	.046	.032	.022	.015	.011	.008	.005	.004	.003	.002	.001	.001	.001	.000	.000	.000	.000	.000	.000	.000	.000	.000	.000	.000	.000
45	.111	.073	.048	.031	.021	.014	.009	.006	.004	.003	.002	.001	.001	.001	.000	.000	.000	.000	.000	.000	.000	.000	.000	.000	.000	.000	.000	.000
50	.087	.054	.034	.021	.013	.009	.005	.003	.002	.001	.001	.001	.000	.000	.000	.000	.000	.000	.000	.000	.000	.000	.000	.000	.000	.000	.000	.000

Note The above present value factors are based on year-end interest calculations.

Appendix 5 Cumulative present value of £1 per annum

n Year	5%	6%	7%	8%	9%	10%	11%	12%	13%	14%	15%	16%	17%	18%	19%	20%	21%	22%	23%	24%	25%	26%	27%	28%	29%	30%	35%	40%
1	.952	.943	.935	.926	.917	.909	.901	.893	.885	.877	.870	.862	.855	.847	.840	.833	.826	.820	.813	.807	.800	.794	.787	.781	.775	.769	.741	.714
2	1.859	1.833	1.808	1.783	1.759	1.736	1.713	1.690	1.668	1.647	1.626	1.605	1.585	1.566	1.546	1.528	1.510	1.492	1.474	1.457	1.440	1.424	1.407	1.392	1.376	1.361	1.289	1.224
3	2.723	2.673	2.624	2.577	2.531	2.487	2.444	2.402	2.361	2.322	2.283	2.246	2.210	2.174	2.140	2.106	2.074	2.042	2.011	1.981	1.952	1.923	1.896	1.868	1.842	1.816	1.696	1.589
4	3.546	3.465	3.387	3.312	3.240	3.170	3.102	3.037	2.974	2.914	2.855	2.798	2.743	2.690	2.639	2.589	2.540	2.494	2.448	2.404	2.362	2.320	2.280	2.241	2.203	2.166	1.997	1.849
5	4.329	4.212	4.100	3.993	3.890	3.791	3.696	3.605	3.517	3.433	3.352	3.274	3.199	3.127	3.058	2.991	2.926	2.864	2.804	2.745	2.689	2.635	2.583	2.532	2.483	2.436	2.220	2.035
6	5.076	4.917	4.767	4.623	4.486	4.355	4.231	4.111	3.998	3.889	3.784	3.685	3.589	3.498	3.410	3.326	3.245	3.167	3.092	3.021	2.951	2.885	2.821	2.759	2.700	2.643	2.385	2.168
7	5.786	5.582	5.389	5.206	5.033	4.868	4.712	4.564	4.423	4.288	4.160	4.039	3.922	3.812	3.706	3.605	3.508	3.416	3.327	3.242	3.161	3.083	3.009	2.937	2.868	2.802	2.508	2.263
8	6.463	6.210	5.971	5.747	5.535	5.335	5.146	4.968	4.799	4.639	4.487	4.344	4.207	4.078	3.954	3.837	3.726	3.619	3.518	3.421	3.329	3.241	3.156	3.076	2.999	2.925	2.598	2.331
9	7.108	6.802	6.515	6.247	5.995	5.759	5.537	5.328	5.132	4.946	4.772	4.607	4.451	4.303	4.163	4.031	3.905	3.786	3.673	3.566	3.463	3.366	3.273	3.184	3.100	3.019	2.665	2.379
10	7.722	7.360	7.024	6.710	6.418	6.145	5.889	5.650	5.426	5.216	5.019	4.833	4.659	4.494	4.339	4.192	4.054	3.923	3.799	3.682	3.571	3.465	3.366	3.269	3.178	3.092	2.715	2.414
11	8.306	7.887	7.499	7.139	6.805	6.495	6.207	5.938	5.687	5.453	5.234	5.029	4.836	4.656	4.486	4.327	4.177	4.035	3.902	3.776	3.656	3.544	3.437	3.335	3.239	3.147	2.752	2.438
12	8.863	8.384	7.943	7.536	7.161	6.814	6.492	6.194	5.918	5.660	5.421	5.197	4.988	4.793	4.610	4.439	4.278	4.127	3.985	3.851	3.725	3.606	3.493	3.387	3.286	3.190	2.779	2.456
13	9.394	8.853	8.358	7.904	7.487	7.103	6.750	6.424	6.122	5.842	5.583	5.342	5.118	4.910	4.715	4.533	4.362	4.203	4.053	3.912	3.780	3.656	3.538	3.427	3.322	3.223	2.799	2.469
14	9.899	9.295	8.745	8.244	7.786	7.367	6.982	6.628	6.302	6.002	5.724	5.468	5.229	5.008	4.802	4.611	4.432	4.265	4.108	3.962	3.824	3.695	3.573	3.459	3.351	3.249	2.814	2.478
15	10.380	9.712	9.108	8.559	8.061	7.606	7.191	6.811	6.462	6.142	5.847	5.575	5.324	5.092	4.876	4.675	4.490	4.315	4.153	4.001	3.859	3.726	3.601	3.483	3.373	3.268	2.825	2.484
16	10.838	10.106	9.447	8.851	8.313	7.824	7.379	6.974	6.604	6.265	5.954	5.669	5.405	5.162	4.938	4.730	4.536	4.357	4.190	4.033	3.887	3.751	3.623	3.503	3.390	3.283	2.834	2.489
17	11.274	10.477	9.763	9.122	8.544	8.022	7.549	7.120	6.729	6.373	6.047	5.749	5.475	5.222	4.990	4.775	4.576	4.391	4.219	4.059	3.910	3.771	3.640	3.518	3.403	3.295	2.840	2.492
18	11.690	10.828	10.059	9.372	8.756	8.201	7.702	7.250	6.840	6.467	6.128	5.818	5.534	5.273	5.033	4.812	4.608	4.419	4.243	4.080	3.928	3.786	3.654	3.529	3.413	3.304	2.844	2.494
19	12.085	11.158	10.366	9.604	8.950	8.365	7.839	7.366	6.938	6.550	6.198	5.877	5.584	5.316	5.070	4.844	4.635	4.442	4.263	4.097	3.942	3.799	3.666	3.539	3.421	3.311	2.848	2.496
20	12.462	11.470	10.594	9.818	9.129	8.514	7.963	7.469	7.025	6.623	6.259	5.929	5.628	5.353	5.101	4.870	4.657	4.460	4.279	4.110	3.954	3.808	3.673	3.546	3.427	3.316	2.850	2.497
25	14.094	12.783	11.654	10.675	9.823	9.077	8.422	7.843	7.330	6.873	6.464	6.097	5.766	5.467	5.195	4.948	4.721	4.514	4.323	4.147	3.985	3.834	3.694	3.564	3.442	3.329	2.856	2.499
30	15.372	13.765	12.409	11.258	10.274	9.427	8.694	8.055	7.496	7.003	6.566	6.177	5.829	5.517	5.235	4.979	4.746	4.534	4.339	4.160	3.995	3.842	3.701	3.569	3.447	3.332	2.857	2.500
35	16.374	14.498	12.948	11.655	10.567	9.644	8.855	8.176	7.586	7.070	6.617	6.215	5.858	5.539	5.251	4.992	4.756	4.541	4.345	4.164	3.998	3.845	3.703	3.571	3.448	3.333	2.857	2.500
40	17.159	15.046	13.332	11.925	10.757	9.779	8.951	8.244	7.634	7.105	6.642	6.234	5.871	5.548	5.258	4.997	4.760	4.544	4.347	4.166	3.999	3.846	3.703	3.571	3.448	3.333	2.857	2.500
45	17.774	15.456	13.606	12.108	10.881	9.863	9.008	8.283	7.661	7.123	6.654	6.242	5.877	5.552	5.261	4.999	4.761	4.545	4.347	4.166	4.000	3.846	3.704	3.571	3.448	3.333	2.857	2.500
50	18.256	15.762	13.801	12.234	10.962	9.915	9.042	8.305	7.675	7.133	6.661	6.246	5.880	5.554	5.262	5.000	4.762	4.545	4.348	4.167	4.000	3.846	3.704	3.571	3.448	3.333	2.857	2.500

Note The above present value factors are based on year-end interest calculations.

Appendix 6
Financial Reporting Standards and Statements of Standard Accounting Practice as at August 1994

FRS no	*Topic*	*Issued*
1	*Cash Flow Statements* – requires companies to provide a primary financial statement analysing cash flows under specified headings.	1991
2	*Accounting for Subsidiary Undertakings* – aims to present financial information relating to a parent company and its subsidiary undertakings as a single entity.	1992
3	*Reporting Financial Performance* – requires the analysis of turnover, costs, and profit, separating continuing activities from discontinued activities. Also requires earnings per share (EPS) to include all profits and losses disclosed in the profit and loss account.	1992
4	*Accounting for Capital Instruments* – a crackdown on creative accounting with hybrid financial instruments so that debt and equity are more clearly defined.	1993
5	*Reporting the Substance of Transactions* – a further crackdown on creative accounting, this time relating to off-balance sheet financing, for example quasi-subsidiaries and sale and leaseback deals.	1994

SSAP no	*Topic*	*Issued*
1	*Accounting for Associated Companies* – deals with the accounting treatment of substantial (20%–50%) investments in other companies which are not subsidiaries.	1982

2	*Disclosure of Accounting Policies* – details the accounting concepts, bases, and policies which should be disclosed in the annual accounts.	1973
3	*Earnings per Share* – defines the method of calculation to be used with particular reference to corporation tax and the number of shares issued.	1974 Amended by FRS 3
4	*The Accounting Treatment of Government Grants* – states two methods of dealing with grants towards capital expenditure and how they are to be credited to revenue over the asset's life.	1990
5	*Accounting for Value Added Tax* – states that sales turnover shown in the profit and loss account should exclude VAT and that any fixed assets should include any related irrecoverable VAT.	1974
8	*The Treatment of Taxation* – under the imputation system of corporation tax – details to be shown in the profit and loss account and balance sheet.	1977
9	*Stocks and Work-in-Progress* – states the basis on which these items, including long-term contract work, are to be valued for balance sheet purposes together with disclosure of the policies followed.	1988
12	*Accounting for Depreciation* – details the basis on which depreciation is to be calculated and the information to be disclosed in the annual accounts.	1987
13	*Accounting for Research and Development* – states that fixed assets used for research and development facilities are to be depreciated over their expected life but other expenditure should normally be charged to the profit and loss account when incurred. Some development expenditure may be capitalised.	1989
15	*Accounting for Deferred Taxation* – specifies deferred taxation should be accounted for where profit in the profit and loss account differs from profit for taxation purposes.	1985
16	*Current Cost Accounting* – specifies how larger companies (as defined) should produce supplementary profit and loss account and balance sheet statements showing the effects of inflation on profit and asset values. Not mandatory after 1985.	1985 now defunct

17	*Accounting for Post-Balance Sheet Events* – states when subsequent events should be disclosed in prior period financial statements.	1980
18	*Accounting for Contingencies* – requires the disclosure of material contingent losses.	1980
19	*Accounting for Investment Properties* – states that such investments (excluding medium-term leaseholds) should not be depreciated but shown at open market value with changes in value incorporated in a special revaluation reserve.	1981
20	*Foreign Currency Translation* – specifies how transactions in a foreign currency are to be exchanged into pounds sterling.	1983
21	*Accounting for Leases and HP Contracts* – differentiates finance leases from operating leases and states the accounting treatment of assets and liabilities in the accounts of lessors and lessees.	1984
22	*Accounting for Goodwill* – states that any purchased goodwill should normally be written off against reserves immediately to be consistent with non-purchased goodwill which is not in the accounts. In certain circumstances purchased goodwill can be written off against ordinary profits over its useful economic life.	1989
23	*Accounting for Acquisitions and Mergers* – differentiates acquisition accounting from merger accounting and states the basis on which assets and liabilities are brought into group accounts in each case.	1985
24	*Accounting for Pension Costs* – details the disclosure required in the profit and loss account and balance sheet for both defined contribution and defined benefit schemes.	1988
25	*Segmental Reporting* – requires disclosure of turnover, profit, and assets for significant geographical or market segments where these exceed 10% of the whole.	1990

Appendix 7
Answers to self-check questions

Chapter 1

1 (a) Each business is regarded as a *separate entity*.
(b) Only transactions which have a *money measurement* can be recorded.
(c) Each transaction is entered twice under the system of *double entry* bookkeeping.
(d) *Realisation* means that a sale takes place on delivery not on receipt of the cash.
(e) *Accrual* means that expenditure incurred in the period is still accounted for when the cash payment has not yet occurred.
(f) *Matching* requires that sales are compared with the cost of sales for the same goods and services.
(g) *Depreciation* is the process of spreading the cost of a fixed asset over many accounting periods.
(h) *Continuity* means that it is assumed the business will continue as a going concern.
(i) *Stability* of money means transactions are recorded at their original cost to the firm.

2 Expenses and assets are debit balances. Liabilities are credit account balances.

3 *Gosforth Gardeners Association receipts and payments account*

	£		£
Cash at start of year	1,270	Bulk purchase of seeds, etc	2,510
Members annual subscriptions	560	Purchase of equipment	1,500
Sales of seeds, etc.	2,250	Cash at end of year	520
Hire fees received	450		
	£4,530		£4,530

4

Bank a/c

	£		£
Capital a/c	1,500	Equipment a/c	1,200
Sales a/c	28,000	A. Wholesaler a/c	16,000
Balance	2,700	Van hire a/c	3,600
		Drawings a/c	6,000

Capital a/c

			£
		Bank a/c	1,500

Equipment a/c

Bank a/c	1,200		

Purchases a/c

A. Wholesaler a/c	17,000		

A. Wholesaler a/c

Bank a/c	16,000	Purchases a/c	17,000
		Balance	1,000

Sales a/c

		Bank a/c	28,000

Van hire a/c

Bank a/c	3,600		

Drawings a/c

Bank a/c	6,000		

John Deel trial balance at year end

Bank a/c	2,700	A. Wholesaler a/c	1,000
Equipment a/c	1,200	Capital a/c	1,500
Van hire a/c	3,600	Sales a/c	28,000
Purchases a/c	17,000		
Drawings a/c	6,000		
	£30,500		£30,500

5

Baker's profit and loss account

	£		£
Purchases	47,200	Sales	86,500
Wages	22,700		
Rent, etc.	7,300		
Sundry exps.	2,700		
	79,900		
Profit	6,600		
	£86,500		£86,500

Baker's balance sheet

Fixtures, etc.	6,300	Capital	6,000
Bank balance	9,800	+ Profit	6,600
			12,600
		Creditors	3,500
	£16,100		£16,100

Chapter 2

1 Revenue account; income and expenditure account; profit and loss account.

2 False. Some monies received or paid out may relate to the previous year or the following year. Monies received during the year may be new loans while money paid out may be for additional assets, both of which go in the balance sheet and not the profit and loss account.

3 Depreciation has two aspects. First is the diminution in value of an asset through use and consequent wear and tear. Second is the charge of depreciation as an expense against income in a profit and loss account, reflecting the amount of asset value consumed in that period of time.

4 £8,192.

5

Profit and loss account

	£		£
Rent	500	Sales	3,600
Depreciation	100		
Cost of sales	1,500		
Wages	600		
Sundry expenses	200		
Electricity	150		
	3,050		
Profit	550		
	£3,600		£3,600

Balance sheet

Shop fittings	4,700	Capital at start	9,000
Stock	1,500	+ Retained profit	550
Prepayment	1,000		9,550
Bank balance	3,500	Creditors	1,000
		Accrued expense	150
	£10,700		£10,700

Chapter 3

1 A balance sheet is like a coin – it has two faces but only one value, reflecting the dual aspects of double entry bookkeeping. The assets owned by a company must be financed with capital provided by somebody; both have the same total value. Modern balance sheets no longer show this equality of assets with liabilities in the way they used to with a side-by-side presentation.

2 Fixed assets and current assets.

3 Shareholders' funds, ie share capital plus retained profits, and borrowings.

4 Goodwill built up over the years is difficult to value because such value does not represent money spent on it in any identifiable way, nor may its value stay constant over time if things go wrong. For these reasons, it is not placed in the balance sheet as an asset although it may well have substantial value in a takeover situation.

5 Operating leases relate to short-term hire where ownership of the hired asset remains with the lessor. Finance leases on the other hand are more long term and confer most of the benefits of ownership except the legal title. Finance leases are very similar to hire purchase.

6 Raw materials, work-in-progress, and finished goods.

7 Some outstanding customer invoices will never be paid in full due to dispute or business failure. For this reason, companies provide for an amount of bad debts, based on recent experience. The balance sheet value of debtors, reduced by this bad debt provision, will always be less than the total value of all customer invoices outstanding on the balance sheet date.

8 Preference shares are paid a fixed rate of dividend before ordinary shares and receive their capital back in full on a liquidation (funds allowing!) before ordinary shareholders are paid the balance of funds remaining.

Chapter 4

1 Because the Inland Revenue tax the whole profit (before any drawings are deducted) as income.

2 They may allow interest on capital and/or pay partners' salaries before dividing the residual profit in the agreed proportions.

3 Retained profit is the profit *after* the tax and dividend provisions have been deducted.

4 Consolidated accounts are prepared for a parent company and its subsidiaries to give a view of the group's profit or loss, assets, and liabilities, as if it was one entity.

5 Minority interests are the value of shareholders' funds in subsidiary companies owned by outside shareholders as opposed to the parent company.

Chapter 5

1 A historic cost profit is calculated by deducting from income the original cost of expenses consumed in a period. A current cost profit is calculated by deducting from income the current cost of expenses consumed at the time of sale. This is usually achieved by recording all transactions at their historic cost and adjusting the resultant historic cost profit at a later stage.

2 The firm will retain insufficient cash to replenish the stocks and replace fixed assets at their inflated cost.
3 Cost of sales adjustment, depreciation adjustment, monetary working capital adjustment, and the gearing adjustment.
4 Any increase or decrease in the value of an asset is matched by a corresponding change in the reserves.

Chapter 6

1 A ratio is a pair of figures extracted from the annual accounts and expressed as a ratio, a percentage, or a number of times. Ratios are used to measure the profitability, performance, or liquidity of a company.
2 Return on capital = Profit margin × Rate of capital turnover.
3 Very few ratios have an ideal value with the possible exception of the 1:1 liquidity ratio. Their use lies in comparison with previous years' ratios, with target ratios, or with competitors' ratios.
4 The liquidity ratio of liquid assets/current liabilities.
5 Interest cover for company A is 2 times and for company B 3⅓ times. Company A is therefore more vulnerable should profits fall.
6 Economy, efficiency, and effectiveness ratios.

Chapter 7

1 Only a trained analyst or accountant could interpret the cash movements from a profit and loss account and balance sheet.
2 Value added is the wealth created by a company in a period of time. It is measured by deducting from sales the cost of all bought-in goods and services consumed.
3 A profit and loss account.
4 It could calculate ratios and compare them with previous periods, for example, added value per employee or added value/sales %.
5 The four parties to whom the value added is distributed are: employees, government, providers of capital, and the company itself.
6 Employees.

Chapter 8

1 Costing is concerned with the detailed breakdown of revenue expenditure.
2 Invoices, timesheets, and stores issue notes.
3 A cost unit is a product or service provided to either internal or external customers. A cost centre is a location within an organisation, typically a department or section of a department.
4 Indirect costs have no specific link to the product or service being

provided to customers. They include support services and general administrative functions.

5 (a) Lighting of courts will vary with amount of usage.
(b) Raw materials going into the final products.
(c) Coal, oil, gas, etc., from which the electricity is generated is a variable cost to the generator. The sale of units generated to regional distributors becomes a variable cost to them.

6 On the basis of time or output or some combination of both. Typical payment systems are hourly rates, measured day work, incentive schemes, or premium bonus systems.

7 FIFO, LIFO, standard price, or weighted average price.

8 ABC crosses departmental boundaries to identify the activities incurring overhead costs and subsequently charging products for the activities they have consumed. A departmental overhead recovery system charges overheads to products benefiting from each department's services, using time or cost as its basis.

Chapter 9

1

Direct materials	180.00
Machine time – 3 × £50	150.00
Selling, dist., etc. – 3 × £40	120.00
	450.00
Profit oncost	50.00
Selling price to quote	£500.00

2 A profit margin of 15% is needed to give a 30% return on capital when the turnover of capital rate is two times.

3 Process costing.

4 By comparison with published data from other authorities or with its own past/target unit costs.

Chapter 10

1 Firm B is cheaper for mileage under 117 per day while firm A is cheaper for mileage in excess of that figure.

2 £15,000 profit.

3 Yes – the contribution of £15,000 on product C would be more than offset by the additional contribution of £24,000 on product A.

4 Yes – it is still worth tendering an even lower price which covers the direct materials cost and makes some contribution to the wages which have to be paid anyway. (Obviously firms cannot continue making such losses for long periods of time.)

5 Contribution per unit of product = £25 – £14 = £11.

Total contribution required = (20% × £1.5m) + £0.8m = £1.1m.

Number of sales required $\frac{£1.1m}{£11}$ = 100,000

6 Ranking order is ZYX on a contribution per hour basis. Only products Z and Y should be produced, using up all available labour.

Chapter 11

1 A standard hour is a measure of the amount of work which can be done in one hour under standard conditions.

2 The activity ratio relates the actual work produced to the budgeted work for that period calculated by:

$$\text{Activity ratio} = \frac{\text{Actual standard hours}}{\text{Budgeted standard hours}}\ \%$$

3 Plant layout, method study, work measurement, value engineering, value analysis, etc.

4 Adverse.

5 The labour efficiency variance compares the standard hours allowed with the actual hours taken for the work done evaluated at the standard rate per hour.

Formula: (Actual hours – Standard hours) Standard rate.

Note The expression within the bracket is to arrive at the difference which is then interpreted as favourable or adverse. It does not matter therefore whether standard or actual hours is placed first.

6

Budgeted profit for the week 1,100 × £6			£6,600
Variances:	*(F)*	*(A)*	
Sales price (£32–£31) 900	900		
Sales volume (1,100–900) £6		1,200	
Material price (50p–55p) 12,600		630	
Material usage (12,600–10,800) 50p		900	
Labour rate (£3–£3) 4,000	—	—	
Labour efficiency (3,200–3,600) £3	1,200		
Variable O/H expenditure £2,100–£1,800		300	
Fixed O/H expenditure £5,700–£5,500		200	
Fixed O/H volume (1,100–900) £5		1,000	
	2,100	4,230	£2,130(A)
Actual profit for the week			£4,470

7 Material cost variance = £20 (F)
(SC £4,500 – AC £4,480)
Material price variance = £320 (F)
3,200 × (£1.50 – £1.40)

Material usage variance = £300 (A)
(3,300m – 3,200m) £1.50

Chapter 12

1 The factor which limits or sets the level of activity for the budget period around which all budgets must be based.

2 Current level of sales; market research; sales representatives' reports; order book; seasonal trends; economic outlook.

3 A cash budget literally budgets the cash flowing into and out of a company on a monthly basis for the budget period.

4 A flexible budget calculates the costs that should have been incurred for the level of activity actually achieved and compares these costs with the actual costs to calculate variances. If therefore excludes the variances caused when actual costs are compared with fixed budgeted costs for a dissimilar level of activity.

5 Budgetary control and standard costing are both planning and control techniques setting standards of performance against which actual results are compared. This throws out variances for investigation where significant, and allows top management to practise management by exception. Their difference lies in the unit of comparison. Standard costs transcend departments and are product based. Budgets are department based and more global.

6

Closing stock	750
Production requirements	10,000
	10,750
Opening stock	350
Purchases required	10,400 kg

7 PPBS transcends departments and plans for programmes lasting a number of years, while budgets focus on functional departmental expenditure for one year only.

Chapter 13

1 High gearing is a large production of fixed return capital out of the total capital employed or in relation to shareholders' funds.

2 17%.

3 20% approx. (solved by calculating the DCF yield as in Figure 13.3).

4 7.8%.

5 Cost of equity capital = $\left(\frac{8\text{p}}{£1.50}\%\right) + 10\% = 15.3\%$

6 The excess of the yield on long-dated government stocks over the average dividend on ordinary shares of companies.

7 14.6%.

Chapter 14

1 Expansion, new product, diversification, replacement, cost saving, alternative choice, and alternative financing of investments.
2 5.6 years.
3 £2,848.
4 NPV = + £5,095.
5 21% approx.
6 18.2%.
7 Conclusion: The investment is worth while as there is a surplus NPV of £299 using the cumulative PV table at 14%.
8 When an investor receives annual interest of £100 on a £1,000 investment his or her nominal return is 10%. If inflation exists, the real return will be less as some of the interest is needed to maintain the purchasing power of the £1,000 investment. The real return is the nominal return less the rate of inflation.
9 The real DCF yield is 15%.

Chapter 15

1 Working capital is the amount of capital employed in the current assets after deducting the short-term sources of finance, ie the current liabilities. Therefore working capital is defined as current assets less current liabilities.
2 By calculating the current relationship of working capital to sales and applying that ratio to the increased sales expected.
3 N/A.
4 Bank and trade references; credit agency reports; analysis of latest annual accounts; informal grapevine through own sales representatives.
5 21% approx.
6 83 days.
7 Raw materials, work-in-progress, and finished goods.
8 Size of buffer stock; reorder level; reorder quantity.
9 Benefits from JIT include lower stock holding costs and reduced interest charges on capital employed.

Chapter 16

1 £1.22.
2 The advantages are that a preference dividend must be paid before any dividend is paid to other types of shareholder and in a liquidation preference shares are repaid before other shareholders. The disadvantages are that the rate of dividend does not in-

crease if profits increase and any surplus capital remaining on a liquidation goes to the ordinary shareholders.

3 Stock market value; asset value; comparative earnings value (via p/e ratio).

4 Goodwill is the name, reputation, and know-how of a firm which brings customers back and allows a firm to earn more profit than a new entrant to the industry. If one firm buys out another firm and pays more for the tangible assets than they are worth, the extra payment is for goodwill.

5 When share prices are high, price/earnings ratios will also be high. Takeovers can be financed by the issue of fewer new shares at high prices than is the case when share prices are low.

6 Market makers fix the prices at which they will buy and sell shares in a selected number of companies. Brokers act as intermediaries, or agents, between clients and the market makers, carrying out buying or selling instructions. Both market makers and brokers are members of the stock exchange.

7 Issue by prospectus; offer for sale at fixed price; offer by tender; introduction; placing.

8 Because the new shares are offered at a discount to the previous market price and this discount is now spread over all the old and new shares. Also because of the threat of new shares not being taken up by existing holders which will cause a temporary excess supply.

9 A scrip issue makes permanent the use of retained profits as extra share capital. It is sometimes required as a condition of a loan to safeguard the lender. Otherwise it is largely cosmetic, bringing down the market value of the shares pro rata to the size of the issue. Shareholders like more shares even though they are of the same total value. The dividend will now appear to be less per share after the issue which may help to prevent employee misunderstandings.

10 Dividend cover is the number of times the profit after tax covers the net dividend payment. The greater this figure then the more secure the dividend payment will be.

11 Gross dividend yield $= \dfrac{9\text{p} \times \frac{100}{70}}{£1.60} = 8\%$

Chapter 17

1 Economies of scale through integration of the activities of the combined firms. These may be technical, marketing, managerial, financial, or risk spreading.

2 Monopolies Commission.
3 Assets basis, earnings basis, and stock market price.
4 An MBO is where existing managers take over their company while an MBI is where outside managers take over a company. In both cases the management team will put up some of the capital, the remainder being provided by banks and venture capitalists.

Chapter 18

1 No – there is a small companies rate of corporation tax in addition to the standard rate.
2 No – in the case of, say, plant and machinery the capital allowance is 25% pa but no company will depreciate such items at that rate if they are expected to last, for example, ten years.
3 No – because of the answer in question **2**, the taxable profit will only equal the company's net profit as a coincidence.
4 At the same time as dividends are paid to shareholders with the balance paid nine months after the accounting year end.
5 £12,800.
6 By basing the tax payment for the current tax year on the level of profit made in the accounting year ended in the previous tax year. This is known as the preceding year basis.
7 No – firms are used to collect VAT which is borne by the final consumer of the goods and services. Any VAT which one firm pays is deducted from the VAT collected from its customers and only the balance forwarded to the Customs and Excise.

Chapter 19

1 No exchange risk is involved when exporters price in their own currency.
2 The importer faces the risk that his or her own currency will fall in value against the pound and he or she will have to pay more when settlement is made.
3 If the exporter prices in a foreign currency, he or she will be exposed to exchange risk which can be covered in the forward exchange market. The risk of nonpayment can be insured against with the ECGD.
4 Bills of exchange can be discounted immediately. Bank loans or overdrafts can be more easily obtained with ECGD cover. Buyer credit financing enables an importer to pay the exporter immediately from a loan guaranteed by the ECGD. Invoice factoring results in immediate payment.
5 Because of exchange control regulations in the foreign country or tax penalties on dividend remissions.

6 Transfer pricing means the price at which one company sells to another company within the same group. Prices can be fixed so as to reduce the overall level of taxation or help avoid foreign exchange control regulations on dividends.

7 Transfer pricing between different arms of a multinational company could be used to take profit in low-tax paying countries, at the expense of higher tax-rate countries. It can also be used as a means of avoiding dividend restrictions which are designed to conserve scarce foreign currency.

Appendix 8
Further questions

Part 1 The annual accounts

1 Claire Smith started her own business by renting a shop to hire out videos. Prepare T accounts, a trial balance, a profit and loss account, and a balance sheet from the following list of her first month's transactions:

	£
Opened business bank account with	4,000
Bought shop fittings for displaying video tapes	1,000
Paid first month's rent	300
Bought stock of video tapes to hire out	2,500
Paid first week's wages	200
Banked first week's sales	300
Paid second week's wages	250
Banked second week's sales	500
Paid third week's wages	250
Bought more video tapes to hire out	600
Banked third week's sales	800
Paid fourth week's wages	250
Banked fourth week's sales	1,100
Paid electricity bill for the month	100
Paid first month's rates to local authority	150

2 Explain the precise meaning of 'profit' by reference to any relevant accounting conventions. (*essay question*)

3 The following balance sheet items are in mixed-up order. Put them in groups under correct headings using the layout currently recommended.

	£
Stocks	92,825
Tangible fixed assets	116,612
Called-up share capital	44,985
Cash at bank and in hand	8,632
Finance debt (due within year)	7,543
Finance debt (due after a year)	28,303
Investments (in related company)	717
Share premium account	33,891
Other creditors (due within year)	73,617

Profit and loss account	88,279
Debtors	74,402
Other creditors (due after a year)	3,525
Provisions for liabilities and charges	13,045

4 A firm buys a piece of equipment for £40,000 and expects it to last for six years after which it will be worth about £2,000. Use the reducing balance method to calculate what the balance sheet value of the equipment will be in four years' time.

5 The following annual accounts relate to an advertising agency:

Balance sheet as at 30 April 19X7

	£000	*£000*	*£000*
Fixed assets (net of depreciation)			875
Current assets:			
Stocks and work-in-progress	310		
Debtors	770		
Bank balance	100	1,180	
Less Creditors due within year			
Trade creditors	620		
Proposed dividend	45	665	
Net current assets			515
Total assets *less* Current liabilities			1,390
Creditors due after one year			
12% Debentures			700
Total net assets			690
Share capital and reserves			
Issued share capital			450
Profit and loss account			240
			690

Profit and loss account for year ended 30 April 19X7

	£000
Sales	3,100
Cost of work done	1,375
Gross profit	1,725
Overhead expenses	1,055
Debenture interest	84
Net profit	£586

(a) Calculate the following ratios and compare them with the trade average shown in brackets:
(i) Gross profit margin (50%).
(ii) Net profit margin before interest (25%).
(iii) Return on capital employed (35%).

(iv) Turnover of capital (1.4 times).
(v) Current ratio (2.2:1).
(vi) Debtors' collection period (75 days).

(b)State whether the performance of this agency is better or worse than the trade average for each ratio and give one suggestion for improvement for each adverse ratio you find.

6 A colleague cannot understand why the firm you both work for needed a bank overdraft at the end of the year in which the firm made a record profit. You have at your disposal the following balance sheets for this year and the previous one:

	19X7	*19X8*
Tangible fixed assets at cost	700	868
Less Depreciation	120	148
	580	720
Investments in new subsidiary co.	—	120
Current assets:		
Stock	160	240
Debtors	100	120
Cash	4	—
	264	360
Creditors due within a year:		
Taxation	60	40
Other creditors	120	140
Proposed dividend	40	20
Bank overdraft	—	106
	220	306
Net current assets	44	54
Total assets *less* Current liabilities	624	894
Capital and reserves		
Called-up share capital	264	434
Share premium account	—	40
Profit and loss account	360	420
	624	894

Part 2 Management accounting

7 A firm plans to sell 3,000 units of its industrial suction cleaner in the coming year. Fixed overhead costs attributed to this product are budgeted to be £39,000 pa. Direct costs per unit are:
Direct labour 3 hours at £4.20 per hour;
Direct materials and components £16.26;
Direct expenses £3.19.

The capital employed on this production is £240,000 and the firm aims to make a 20% return on capital.
Calculate the selling price needed to achieve this objective.

8 Precision Ltd manufacture a metal fastener for the motor trade and its management want your advice. The following information is available:
(a) The product takes 12 minutes to make at £4 per hour.
(b) Raw materials cost 25p per unit.
(c) Variable overheads amount to £5 per hour.
(d) Fixed overheads amount to £90,000 pa.
(e) The proposed selling price is £2.50.
Management require you to produce the following information:
- A calculation of the break-even point.
- A chart to illustrate the break-even point.
- A calculation of the number of units needed to be sold to earn a 20% return on the £0.2 million capital employed in this area.

9 Explain why absorption costing is a dangerous tool to use when examining the effects of a change in the level of activity. (*essay question*)

10 JHL Ltd has budgeted the following figures for its three product lines for next year:

	A	*B*	*C*	*Total*
	£000	*£000*	*£000*	*£000*
Sales value	960	960	320	2,240
Variable costs	864	768	240	1,772
Fixed costs (allocated and apportioned)	48	72	100	220
Profit (loss)	48	120	(20)	148

The management of JHL Ltd are particularly concerned about product C and are considering various alternatives:

Alternative 1 To cut product C's selling price by 10% which is expected to increase demand for product C by about 40%.

Alternative 2 To substitute a new product D for product C. Estimated sales for product D are £280,000 in the first year and variable costs are estimated at 55% of sales value. In this case some £32,000 additional fixed costs directly attributable to D will be incurred but £18,000 of fixed costs directly attributable to C will be saved when it is dropped.

Alternative 3 To drop product C completely but not introduce any new product, nor increase sales of product A or B. In this case the £18,000 of fixed costs directly attributable to product C will be saved.

Calculate the effect on the total profit of the firm of each alternative course of action and state your preferred choice.

11 Your firm makes one-off equipment to customers' own specifications. You have just received an order which has been costed out at £20,000 on an absorption (total) costing basis and with a 20% mark-up gives a selling price of £24,000. The customer declines to place the order at this price and offers to pay £19,000. Explain the circumstances that might persuade you to accept this order at the customer's price. (*essay question*)

12 The standard material cost of fabric specified for a particular garment is £4.50 comprising 3 metres at £1.50 per metre. The standard time allowed for making up the garment is 15 minutes paid at the rate of £3 per hour.

Last week 1,000 garments were made using 3,200 metres of fabric which was purchased at £1.40 per metre. The total time taken to make up these garments was 230 hours which were paid at the standard rate.

(a) Calculate the material cost variance and the material price and usage variances.

(b) Calculate the labour cost variance and the labour rate and efficiency variances.

(c) Suggest any possible reasons why these variances may have occurred.

13 The following statement shows the actual profit for one month to be less than that originally budgeted. The firm in question makes a small standardised product in large volume for use in the engineering industry.

Profit and loss account for the month

			£
Budgeted profit			10,000
Variances:	*(F)*	*(A)*	
Sales price variance	1,900		
Sales quantity variance		4,000	
Material price variance		2,000	
Material usage variance	1,500		
Labour rate variance	—	—	
Labour efficiency variance		1,600	
Variable o/h expenditure variance	200		
Fixed o/h expenditure variance	500		
Fixed o/h volume variance		2,000	
	4,100	9,600	5,500
Actual profit for the month			£4,500

You are required to give possible reasons for each of the variances disclosed in the statement and to say how they resulted in the worse-than-expected profit.

Part 3 Financial management

14 (a) Explain the term 'capital gearing'.
(b) Discuss the advantages and disadvantages of a company increasing its level of capital gearing. (*essay question*)

15 (a) What is the cost of equity capital that is implied in the following information?

Market price per ordinary share	£3.00
Forecast dividend per share for current year	£0.30
Recent annual growth rate of profits	15% pa

(b) Calculate the weighted average cost of capital using the cost of equity above and assuming a debt: equity ratio of 25:75. All the debt has a fixed rate of interest of 14% and corporation tax is currently 35%.
(c) Explain why the weighted average cost of capital is less than the cost of equity alone.

16 A firm is considering buying a machine which costs £80,000 and is expected to last five years, when its scrap value will be about £2,000 only. Taxable savings are estimated to be £40,000 each year and the rate of corporation tax is 33%. Capital allowances of 25% on the reducing balance can be claimed but no allowances are available on the £30,000 working capital required for the duration of the project. The real cost of capital is 10% and this is regarded as the minimum requirement.
(a) Set out the yearly cash flows and find their net present value using the table provided.
(b) Find the DCF yield and state your conclusions as to the worthwhileness of this project.

17 A firm is considering whether or not to replace a machine which makes metal frames for umbrellas. The remaining life of the machine is put at four years. The product sells for £2 each at a volume of about 60,000 pa.

Three alternative courses of action have been suggested by the production engineer as follows:

A Keep the existing machine which originally cost £40,000 four years ago and is being depreciated at 12.5% pa on a straight-line basis. The total annual cost of this method (including depreciation) amounts to £85,000 and needs the existing working capital of £25,000.

B Buy a new machine costing £250,000 less a trade-in allowance of £10,000 on the old machine. The total annual running costs would amount to £95,000 including £60,000 depreciation. Further working capital of £5,000 would be required making £30,000 working capital in total.

C Cease the manufacture of frames and sell the existing machine to another firm for £20,000 who will also pay a royalty of 20p per unit sold. Sales volume would be identical with that expected from own manufacture. The existing working capital would be recovered in full.

Calculate which is the most attractive alternative on a net present value basis if the cost of capital is 16% and state your recommended course of action.

18 New Enterprise Ltd set up in business on 1 January 1993 as a supplier of specialised chemicals to a small number of other firms. Its management have made the following plans and estimates for the year 1993:

(a) On 1 January 1993 the company will purchase premises for £60,000 and furniture, fittings, and office equipment for £16,000. The latter will be depreciated over ten years on a straight-line basis but the premises will not be subject to depreciation.

(b) Sales will be only £5,000 in January but will hold steady at £20,000 every month except in July and August when they will reach £50,000 per month.

(c) The gross profit margin (ie sales less cost of sales), will be held at 40% of the selling price.

(d) On 1 January the company will purchase £8,000 of stock and maintain this level throughout 1993.

(e) Trade creditors demand payment on the last day of the month in which the purchase was made.

(f) All sales are on credit and it is expected that 80% will be received by the end of the month following the month of sale, and the remaining 20% received a month later.

(g) Overheads, wages, and salaries will amount to £6,000 each month except in July when it will be double that figure. Payment of these expenses will be at the end of the same month as incurred.

(h) There will be no tax or dividend payments during 1993.

Prepare a monthly cash budget for the year 1993 and use it to state the amount of share capital needed to be issued on 1 January if the company is never to borrow money during 1993.

Prepare a forecast profit and loss account for the year 1993 and a projected balance sheet as at 31 December 1993 based on the above assumptions

Suggest a scheme of financing (other than all equity) that may be more suitable, given the seasonal nature of the business.

19 Mr Smith is the Managing Director of Smiths Ltd, a medium-sized private company, all of whose shares are owned by himself and his wife. As he is nearing retirement age and as he has no family he has decided to sell out to a larger public company but is unsure of the value of his shares. The following information is available for Smiths Ltd:

Balance sheet as at 31 December 1992

	£000		£000
Issued £1 ordinary shares	800	Land and buildings	2,000
Profit and loss account	2,452	Plant and equipment	1,100
	3,252	Motor vehicles	220
10% loan	600		3,320
Other creditors	720	Stocks	582
		Debtors	590
		Cash	80
	4,572		4,572

The following values have been assessed by an independent valuer on a going concern basis:

	£000
Land and buildings	2,440
Plant and equipment	1,152
Motor vehicles	208
Stocks	400
Debtors	480

The profit after tax and interest was £340,000 in 1992 and is expected to be about £360,000 in the current year, rising by about 5% pa. The annual dividend for 1992 was £160,000.

The dividend yields and price/earnings ratios of three companies in the same field as Smiths Ltd are as follows:

		Divd yield %	*P/E ratio*
Company	A	6.0%	8.0
	B	4.8%	10.8
	C	5.3%	9.7

Advise Mr Smith.

20 Explain the procedures you would adopt for credit sales in order to limit the amount of working capital tied up in debtors and to minimise bad debts. (*essay question*)

Index

absorbtion costing 104
accrual 15
acid-test ratio 71
activity based costing (ABC) 100
activity ratio 124
advance corporation tax (ACT) 215
appropriation account 31
asset value 190
associated company 55
audit 46

balance sheet 20, 35
  consolidated 55
bookkeeping
  double entry 17
  single entry 16
break-even chart 113
budgetary control 133
buy-outs 203

Cadbury report 13, 47, 63
capacity ratio 125
capital allowance 213
capital budget 136
capital expenditure 89
capital gains tax 218
capital gearing 72, 147
cash budget 136, 178
cash flow statement 76
cash flows
  discounted 160
Companies Act (1985) 13
computers, use of 91, 172
consolidated accounts 53
contribution 115
control cycle 123
conventions 14
convertible preference share 190
corporation tax 211
cost centre 92
cost code 90
cost of capital 147
  borrowed 149
  equity 151
  weighted average 153
cost unit 92
costs 89
  controllable 138
  direct 93
  fixed 93
  indirect 93

variable 93
creditors 44
management of 184
credits and debits 17
current assets 40
current cost accounting 61
current liabilities 175
current ratio 71, 177

DCF yield 164
debits and credits 17
debt capacity 72
debt ratio 72
debtors 41
management of 180
depreciation 39, 214
discounted cash flow yield method 164
dividend cover 200
dividend policy 201
dividend yield 201
double entry bookkeeping 17

earnings per share 152, 193
earnings yield 152
economic order quantity 186
efficiency ratio 124
employee reports 84
exchange rates 221
risk 221
Export Credits Guarantee Dept 223

factoring 183
fixed assets 39
flexible budgeting 140
forfaiting 225
forward exchange contract 222

goodwill 40, 192
gearing 72, 147
gearing ratio 72, 148

historic cost accounting 59

income expenditure account 24
income cover 73
income gearing 73
income statement 24
income tax 217
inflation 59, 110, 140, 170
intangible assets 40
integration 204
horizontal 204
lateral 204
vertical 204
interim comparisons 74
internal rate of return *see* discounted cash flow yield method
investment appraisal 156
investments 40

just-in-time (JIT) 187

key factor 135

limited company accounts 31, 37, 51
limiting factor 135
liquidity 71
liquidity ratio 71, 177

management buy-in (MBI) 203
management buy-out (MBO) 203
manufacturing account 31, Appendix 1
marginal costing 111
material requirements planning 186
mergers 203
Monopolies Commission 207

net present value method 163

offer by tender 197
offer for sale 197
operating cycle 176
ordinary shares 43
  value of 190, 205
overhead recovery 98

partnership accounts 50
payback method 159
payment systems (wages) 95
placing 197
planning, programming and budgeting system (PPBS) 142
preference shares 43
  value of 189
present value 160
price earnings ratio 194, 205
price index numbers 61
pricing 103
  full cost 104
  marginal cost 119
product mix 118
profit and loss account 24
  consolidated 54
profit margin 67, 69
profitability 67
  of products 117
public authority accounts 52

quick ratio 71

ranking of investments 168
rate of return method 159
ratios 66, 124, 177, 183, 193
realisation 15
receipts and payments account 16
reducing balance method 27, 214
reserves 43
return on capital 67
revenue account 52
revenue expenditure 89
rights issue 198

scrip issue 199
self-employed accounts 49
share capital 43
source of funds 42
standard costing 123
  specification 125
standard hour 124
standard marginal costing 131
Stock Exchange 196
stocks 26, 40
  management of 185
stores pricing methods 97
straight line method 27
subsidiaries 53

takeovers 203
taxation 169, 211
trading account 31
transfer pricing 226
trial balance 19
turnover of capital 70

uncertainty 169

value added 80
  statement 74
  uses of 84
value added tax 219
variances 125, 139

wage payment systems 95
working capital 175

zero-based budgeting 135
Z score 73